TRADE, ENVIRONMENT & COMPETITIVENESS: *Sustaining Canada's Prosperity*

Editors

John Kirton and Sarah Richardson

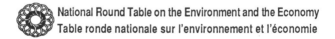

National Round Table on the Environment and the Economy
Table ronde nationale sur l'environnement et l'économie

Trade, Environment & Competitiveness

Canadian Catalogue Information in Publication Data
Trade, environment and competitiveness: sustaining Canada's prosperity
(National Round Table series on Sustainable Development)
Proceedings of a conference held in Toronto, November 4,1991
Includes bibliographical references
ISBN 1-895643-13-9
1. Canada - Commerce - Environmental aspects.
2. Environmental policy - Canada 3. International trade - Environmental aspects. 4. International economic relations. 5. Commercial policy - Environmental aspects
I. Kirton, John J. II. Richardson, Sarah, 1964- III. Series.
HF1479.T73 1992   363.7 C92-094951-7

Book Design, Typesetting and Graphic Consultants for Series:
sla Graphicus *Specialists in environmental graphic design*
Sims Latham Group, 109K Memorial Avenue, Suite 201, Orillia, Ontario, L3V 5X6 Tel: (705) 327-2191

Cover
Zebra Photo Design Studio

This book has been printed on Environmental Choice paper containing over 50% recycled content, including 5% post-consumer fibre, using vegetable inks. The cover board also has recycled content and is finished with a water based, wax free varnish.

National Round Table on the Environment and the Economy
Table ronde nationale sur l'environnement et l'économie
Series General Editor: Daniel Donovan
1 Nicholas Street, Suite 1500, Ottawa, Ontario, K1N 7B7
Telephone: (613)-992-7189 Fax: (613) 992-7385

1 Sustainable Development: A Manager's
  Handbook
2 The National WasteReduction Handbook
3 Decision Making Practices for
  SustainableDevelopment
4 Preserving Our World
5 On the Road to Brazil: The Earth Summit
6 Toward Sustainable Communities
7 Trade, Environment and Competiveness

Aussi disponible en français

Canadä

NRTEE MEMBERS

CONTENTS

Foreword

It's good to remind ourselves from time to time that Canada's large economy is somewhat out of proportion to its relatively small population. One of the main reasons for this is our success as a trading nation.

With more than a quarter of our Gross Domestic Product generated by exports, there's no question that Canada depends heavily on foreign trade. Without new markets beyond our borders, we would not be able to sustain our standard of living or pay for health and social programs that are envied around the world.

Free trade has allowed many companies like Du Pont Canada to offset a slump in domestic sales by increasing exports. It has allowed us to weather a protracted recession and maintain our workforce without any reductions in size. Obviously, we are looking forward to NAFTA, which will open up a market of 80 million people who can use Canadian goods and services.

But in this regard, companies like ours must have a dual commitment: not only to succeed in a more competitive – and international – marketplace, but also to continue to do what's right to help safeguard our environment on behalf of all our families. We believe this environmental commitment should remain constant no matter the community, or the country, where we are doing business.

Today, the success of any company depends on how it responds to the changing expectations of a wide array of stakeholders, including potential and current employees, shareholders, customers, governments and the public. In effect, they give us a "licence to operate".

More and more in the future, companies can expect their stakeholders to put absolutely everything they do under a microscope – their products, workplaces, financial performance, ethics and, not least, their environmental outlook and practices. Companies that wish to succeed must welcome this scrutiny, no matter what the competitive pressures.

And quite apart from the moral considerations, a cleaner environment makes good business sense. Innovative companies have the opportunity to develop products that are better for the environment than existing offerings – thereby gaining a competitive edge.

At Du Pont Canada, we believe in, and are committed to, sustainable development: growth today, without damaging the future. We also recognize the need for increased understanding and cooperation between all the diverse groups that are attempting to come to grips with many complex trade and environmental issues. This is why we are delighted to support this publication, which will shed important new light on such a crucial topic.

Arthur R. Sawchuk
President and Chief Executive Officer
Du Pont Canada Inc.

Preface
George E Connell

George E Connell is the Chair of the National Round Table on the Environment and the Economy. He is also the Vice-Chairman of the Ontario Environment Assessment Board. From 1977 to 1984 he was President of the University of Western Ontario, and from 1984 to 1990 President of the University of Toronto. Earlier, Dr Connell held a number of positions at the University of Toronto including Vice-President, Research and Planning; Associate Dean, Faculty of Medicine; Associate Professor of Biochemistry; and Assistant Professor of Biochemistry. He is the author of numerous scientific and administrative publications. A native of Saskatchewan, he holds a PhD in Biochemistry from the University of Toronto.

Our Common Future, the report of the World Commission on Environment and Development, (the "Brundtland Report") had a great deal to say about trade. It assumed throughout that the sustainable global economy is a trading economy. While it did not explicitly argue that sustainability can only be achieved with free-flowing global trade, that conclusion was implicit in much of the analysis and argument. Our ability to support the earth's population and to meet reasonable human aspirations depends on finding the most efficient and sustainable means of providing goods and services on a global scale.

Furthermore, sustainable development can be negated by trade practices that do not properly take account of environmental values. Trade in agricultural products provides the most egregious illustration. Reciprocally, inappropriate environmental laws and regulations can be very damaging to trade. There are already environmental trade barriers that are both self serving and irrational. No doubt there will be many more. Such barriers are likely to be extremely damaging to the interests of trade-dependent developed nations such as Canada, and potentially devastating to those of the less developed nations of the world.

The Brundtland Report asserts what may well be taken as the definition of the task of this volume; that

"two conditions must be satisfied before international economic exchanges can become beneficial for all involved. The sustainability of ecosystems on which the global economy depends must be guaranteed, and the economic partners must be satisfied that the basis of exchange is equitable."[1]

There was no better opportunity than the process surrounding the UNCED Conference in June 1992, to get these principles locked into the hearts and minds of world leaders and to secure commitments that could lead to action. Although the Conference is over, the work underlying the preparation of this volume could help to shape the contributions that Canada makes to that great cause, and to the equally important follow-up work in years to come.

The National Round Table on the Environment and the Economy (NRTEE) is part of Canada's response to the Brundtland Report. Its mission is to advance the understanding and implementation of sustainable development. In light of that, the Round Table is playing a major role in Canada's national dialogue on prosperity and competitiveness. It will make every effort to demonstrate that a commitment to sustainable development can enhance Canada's prosperity.

The NRTEE's first major initiative in this effort was the formation of a partnership with the Institute for Research on Public Policy (IRPP) and the appointment of a joint Senior Advisory Committee. The NRTEE and IRPP are fortunate to have on this Committee individuals with a great deal of experience in environmental matters, business, international relations and government. One of them, Jim MacNeill is a contributor to this volume, while two others, Yves Guérard and André Saumier, contributed to the conference on which this volume is based. The Chair of IRPP, the Honourable Donald S. MacDonald, and I serve as Co-Chairs of the Committee.

I congratulate the NRTEE's Foreign Policy Committee, its Co-Chairs, Pierre Marc Johnson and Geraldine Kenney-Wallace, and its staff and volunteers on the quality of the volume they have designed and the quality of the contributors they have recruited. I thank our co-sponsors of the preparatory conference: the International Institute for Sustainable Development, represented herein by Art Hanson, its President; Environment Canada, represented by Deputy Minister Len Good; and Industry, Science and Technology Canada represented by its Deputy Minister, Harry Rogers.

References

1. WORLD COMMISSION ON ENVIRONMENT AND DEVELOPMENT *Our Common Future* (Oxford: University Press, 1987).

Trade, Environment & Competitiveness

Preface
Arthur Hanson

Arthur J Hanson Chairs the International Institute for Sustainable Development, Winnipeg, Manitoba and is a Professor at the School for Resource and Environmental Studies at Dalhousie University, Halifax, Nova Scotia. He is an advisor to the Conservation Council of Ontario and to the W Alton Jones Foundation on Biodiversity Maintenance in SE Asia. He is also Advisor to the Executive Director of the Council on Biodiversity. Dr Hanson was a founding member of the Lester Pearson Institute for International Development at Dalhousie, where he has taught graduate courses since 1979. He holds a BSc and a MSc from the University of British Columbia, and a PhD in Fisheries Ecology from the University of Michigan.

The mandate of the International Institute for Sustainable Development (IISD) is to promote sustainable development in decision making at all levels. While it is an international institute, focused internationally, it is also concerned about events within Canada, particularly in reaching out to the business community, to individual decision makers in homes and communities, and to government.

Its work program is divided into two streams: policy research and communications. In the latter, particularly, it listens and learns what people are actually doing in the various fields of sustainable development. In examining trade and the environment, it is trying to look at the root causes of environment and development problems. The issue of trade and environment is central to its future research programs.

Trade-environment relationships are poorly understood. They are complex but they are fundamental for the future of sustainable development. The IISD's international perspective results in a strong concern that the voices and the views of developing countries are heard in this trade-environment debate, and that Canadians understand how their own future may be shaped by the needs of developing countries as well as their own.

The ultimate focus of the IISD is on how trade practices, worldwide and on the part of Canada, can support or enhance sustainable development. It is very pleased to see the wide range of interests represented in this volume. It is absolutely essential for sustainable development to have these links across different sectors, particularly in the area of trade. Sustainable development is the environment, the economy and the well-being of people. A wide range of interests thus needs to be represented in the debate.

Finally, the International Institute for Sustainable Development is happy to be partners with the National Round Table on the Environment and the Economy and hopes this will be a long lasting relationship. This is a unique model within Canada of how to bring together different interest groups. The IISD is particularly interested to see analogues appear, in other parts of the world, and perhaps in other forms.

Introduction
John Kirton & Sarah Richardson

On November 4, 1991, the Foreign Policy Committee of the National Round Table on the Environment and the Economy hosted a conference in Toronto on "Trade, Competitiveness, and the Environment." The purpose of the conference was to gather the major Canadian and international stakeholders from the government, business, environmental, and academic communities to exchange views on an issue of rapidly growing importance on the public policy agenda. Recognizing that this was the first such exercise of its kind in Canada, and that the multifaceted links between trade and the environment were still being charted, the conference sought a preliminary identification of the key issues at stake, the perspectives of major stakeholders, and their initial judgements about how such issues might best be addressed.

This volume is based on the edited version of the twenty-one major presentations made at the conference. It seeks to make information available to a much larger audience on an issue which is now a critical component of Canada's national initiatives to increase its competitiveness and promote sustainable development. In preparing this volume, the editors have sought to remain faithful to the authors' original presentations. So, apart from the changes necessary to convert orally delivered material into written form, and to remove direct repetition, no effort has been made to alter the text to impose a uniform, academic style or to take account of the many important developments in the trade-environment interface that have taken place in the months since the conference.

In order to provide the reader with a timely and comprehensive overview of such developments, however, two items have been added to the book. The first, included

1

as Appendix A, is an extensively revised version of the background paper Sarah Richardson prepared for the November conference. This paper was initially designed to provide a factual, historical background of how the issue has affected Canadian industry and has been dealt with internationally. It has been updated to take account of trade and environment-related developments over the past half year in Canadian industry, the European Community, and especially the North American Free Trade Area negotiations and in such major international forums as the organization for Economic Co-operation and Development and the GATT. It has also been extended to deal with the Trade Ministers Quadrilateral, the Seven Power Summit, the United Nations Conference on Trade and Development, and the United Nations Conference on Environment and Development, as the trade-environment issue has thrust itself onto their agenda.

The second addition is a concluding chapter by John Kirton, designed to consider the trade and environment issue in the context of Canada's effort to engender sustainable prosperity. It considers, and where appropriate offers some preliminary judgements on, what Canada's priorities in this area are, what policy stances it should adopt, how best to organize itself to deal with them, and where it should focus its efforts internationally to best secure the international regimes it prefers. Given the novelty and complexity of the links between trade and environment, these judgements are, at best, highly tentative. They do, however, point to areas where further thinking is required, and where opportunities for Canadian initiative might lie.

In preparing this volume and the conference upon which it is based, we are grateful in the first instance to those organizations that provided the funds required to mount the November conference: the National Round Table on the Environment and the Economy (NRTEE); the International Institute for Sustainable Development; Environment Canada; Industry, Science and Technology

2

Canada; Gowling, Strathy and Henderson; Ladner Downs; and Osler, Hoskin, Harcourt. We have also had more than the normal amount of assistance from a wide variety of individuals, especially those individuals who served as chairs, moderators, volunteers and staff at the conference: R C (Reg) Basken, Alan Dean, David Estrin, Cathy Heroux, Valerie Heskins, Patricia Larkin, Peter Manson, Marcel Massé, Hélène Massie, Agnes Pust, André Saumier, and Murray Smith. And we are grateful for the advice, assistance and information provided along the way by Richard Dearden, Pat Delbridge, Frank Frantizak, Julia Grossman, Charles Hayles, Gary Nash, François Rioux, Daniel Romanko, Patricia Wilson and the many officials in the Canadian and foreign governments and international organizations who spoke to us on a background basis.

We are further indebted to our colleagues on the Foreign Policy Committee of the NRTEE who nurtured this project from the initial concept through to the final conference stage. Timothy Egan provided essential conceptual, managerial and fundraising support. John MacDonald, the co-chair of the conference planning committee, brought a vital private sector perspective to the enterprise and served splendidly as the overall chair of the conference itself. Jim MacNeill drew upon his vast expertise, experience, and network of associates to ensure the requisite breadth and balance in the conference's agenda and speaker roster. From earlier conferences she organized for the NRTEE on Climate Change and on Canada-Japan Environmental Relations, Geraldine Kenney-Wallace provided an organizational model and intellectual stimulus. And Pierre Marc Johnson again displayed his extraordinary ability to sense the larger importance and dimensions of emerging issues, bring the appropriate individuals together, inspire a productive exchange, and identify a consensus amidst a diverse mix of strongly held views.

At the NRTEE secretariat, Ann Dale and Anne Fouillard worked with exceptional dedication and skill to organize and produce the conference itself and to assist us in the formidable task of converting raw conference speeches into finished prose. Ron Doering provided the encouragement, and found the resources to produce this volume, and to make this and other fruits of the NRTEE's labours available to Canadians as a whole. And George Connell, with his integrative mind and educator's instinct, identified the value of this work to the NRTEE's new initiative on Sustainable Prosperity, and the value of expanding the NRTEE-initiated dialogue on trade and environment to much larger forums.

Finally, we are most grateful to Du Pont Canada Inc for providing the funds required to support the publication of this volume and thus ensure that the results of the NRTEE's work in this field are shared with a large audience of Canadians. In all cases, the views expressed therein are those of the individual authors and editors, and not necessarily those of the National Round Table or any of the organizations that sponsored this work.

The Frog Pond
June 1992

A
Trade-Environment Links

1
Trade-Environment Links:The Global Dimension
Jim MacNeill

Jim MacNeill is President of MacNeill & Associates; a Senior Fellow at the Institute for Research on Public Policy (IRPP); a Senior Advisor to the Secretary General of the UN Conference on Environment and Development; a member of the National Round Table on the Environment and the Economy; and a member of several Boards, including the International Institute for Sustainable Development in Winnipeg; the Woods Hole Research Center, Massachusetts. As Secretary General and member of the World Commission on Environment and Development, he was principle architect and primary author of its report Our Common Future. *His other positions include Director of Environment for the Organization for Economic Cooperation and Development (OECD). The author of a number of books and articles, his most recent publication is* Beyond Interdependence *(Oxford University Press, 1991).*

Whoever said "the problem with the future is not what it used to be" must have anticipated the past five years. They have been amazing years.

Look at Eastern Europe. The Cold War is over and the massive shift in East-West relations suddenly opened doors of opportunity - making it possible, for the first time, for East and West to cooperate meaningfully on the critical issues of global change and human survival. Look at the shift in public values; the sea-change in public opinion. It has forced environmental issues to the top, or near the top, of political agendas in all the world's major capitals.

Who, in 1985, would have predicted that the concept of sustainable development would capture the imagination of people, politicians, industrialists and environmental leaders all over the world? Who would have predicted that leader after leader would undergo a public baptism as a born-again environmentalist? And who would have predicted that sustainable development would now be a regular feature of the debates of the UN system, the OECD, and the annual summits of the G7 group of major industrial democracies - or that it would have become a daily concern of many companies in the Fortune 500?

These have been breakthrough years and they have been marked by something else: a breakthrough in our understanding of the relationship between the environment and the economy. We used to believe that the world's economic and the earth's ecological systems were dual systems, with only a marginal impact on each other. We now know that, although they remain distinct in human-constructed institutions, they are totally and irreversibly interlocked in the real world.

Ever since World War II, nations have struggled to adapt their notions of sovereignty and governance to the realities of economic interdependence; that is, to the coupling of local and national economies with a global system. Now they must struggle with an even more complex imperative: economic interdependence has become meshed with ecological interdependence and the two systems are now one. Their impact on each other is enormous, growing rapidly, and could soon be decisive in defining our future.[1] This is the new reality of the late 20th century. It may well become the dominant reality of the new millennium. Notions of sovereignty and governance will have to be adapted to this reality, as will public and private institutions, where key economic and political decisions are made.

Nowhere, is this new reality more evident than in trade and the natural environment. The primary cities of the OECD and other industrial countries constitute the nodes of world trading networks. They draw on the ecological capital of all other nations to provide food for their populations, energy and raw materials for their economies, and even land, air and water to assimilate their waste by-products. This ecological capital, which may be found thousands of miles from the cities in which it is used, forms the "shadow ecology" of any economy. If cities like New York and Singapore, or nations like Japan, had to live without their shadow ecologies, even for a short period, their peoples and economies would suffocate.

This means that those nations heavily engaged in global sourcing have a growing stake in protecting their shadow ecologies wherever they exist. To this end, they need to ensure that the environment is fully considered in multilateral trade negotiations in the General Agreements on Tariffs and Trade (GATT), in regional negotiations like those for a North American Free Trade Agreement (NAFTA), and in negotiations within countries on national trade policy. They must not be considered as a process for an add-on environmental assessment (first negotiate the trade deal, then do a token environmental assessment against a 90-day fast track). Nor must they be considered as a parallel two-track process (trade on one track, environment on another, each with its own agenda and negotiators). These approaches simply reflect the current problem of institutional separation. They do not offer a solution. The only way to ensure that the environment is fully considered in trade negotiations is to create a single, integrated process, and require step-by-step assessment as an integral part of the negotiations.

Such assessment should include both the impact of environmental policies on trade and, conversely, the impact of trade policies on the environment. Until recently, talk about the environment-trade connection implied concern about one thing only: the potential negative impact of environmental policies on trade. In recent years, it has become clear that certain environmental policies can have a positive effect on trade and that trade policies can have negative, as well as positive effects, on the environment. The OECD and other bodies now recognize that trade liberalization can have both kinds of effects on the

9

environment and on the resource base of trading nations. A recent OECD paper declared:

"Trade and environmental policies should be seen as being mutually supportive rather than in terms of conflicting interests. Trade spurs economic growth and helps provide the technical and financial resources to protect the environment, while a healthy environment provides the ecological and natural resources needed to underpin long-run growth stimulated by trade... It is therefore important that trade policies are sensitive to environmental concerns and that environmental policies take account of effects on trade. Unlike sustainable development, free-trade is not an end in itself ..."[2]

The Impact of Environmental Policies on Trade

Few issues have caused as much conflict in trade talks as the steady proliferation of national health, safety and environmental standards and the wide divergence in these standards that exists between countries. These conflicts are bound to grow. The 1990s could see a greater increase in both the number and variety of these standards than occurred in the whole of the past five decades. The political climate is favourable and, given the increasing frequency, scale and impact of environmental catastrophes, it is likely to become even more favourable.

Green consumerism is growing rapidly: it is now entrenched in parts of Europe; it is sweeping Canada; it has a toe-hold in Japan and the United States; and it is emerging in other countries. In some, such as Canada, it is aided by government-sponsored labelling programs. As these gain momentum and spread throughout the world, they will clearly affect markets, both domestic and international. Indeed, that is their whole point.

Some industries are concerned that tighter standards will impose burdens on them, making it difficult, if not impossible, to compete with products from countries that cannot, or will not, impose similar standards. Industries in developing countries are concerned that bans and restrictions on the use of certain chemicals and food additives in industrialized nations will result in trade barriers against the products they export. These concerns are real but they address the symptoms, not the sources, of the problem.

Governments and industries in both industrialized and developing countries have been slow to learn the lessons of the 1970s and 1980s - lessons that Michael Porter highlights in his recent report on competitiveness.[3] Fortunately, an increasing number of leading German, Japanese, Korean, North American, Scandinavian and Swiss industries have learned these lessons. Pressed by high world oil prices and tight emission standards, they invented most of the industrial technologies of the 1980s and 1990s. Those technologies were not only energy and resource efficient; they were also environmentally efficient. And they were internationally competitive. They stole market share in almost every sector - from automobiles to pulp and paper, food processing, the service industries, and communications. They are still gaining market share.

Honda has now announced a 100 mpg automobile. How did North America's "Big Three" respond? None announced plans for a 110 mpg machine. Instead, at least one of them asked for more protection. This is a cop out. There has to be a better way.

It is in the context of these experiences that we should assess the commitments made by Japan and the nations of the European Community (EC) and the European Free Trade Area (EFTA) to stabilize fossil fuel emissions of CO_2 at 1990 levels by the year 2000, and to use pricing pressure, including energy taxes, to achieve them. Germany, in fact, has targeted a 25% reduction by the year 2005.

Staff in the European Commission have been quite frank about these policies and a recent Japanese government report is equally clear. It argues for a transition to a more efficient and sustainable economy based on high-technology and geared to meeting social and environmental needs worldwide as well as the growing demands for consumer durables. If Western Europe and Japan continue to pursue these goals in this way (they are currently engaged in a debate about them), their industries will invent the technologies of the first decade of the new millennium. In the process, their economies will become even leaner and more competitive.

The industries concerned are, in fact, leading the transformation to a new economy that is more efficient and potentially more sustainable: marked by people relying more heavily on information and intelligence; producing more goods, more jobs and more income while using less and cleaner energy, fewer materials and resources for every unit of production. This economy is the result of a complex combination of factors, including new technologies and changes in historic relationships between capital, labour, resources and, especially, energy. It is marked by less pollution and less resource depletion per unit of output. In fact, the link between the two has been broken and this will be most evident in those market economies open to change.

The industries leading this transformation will not wait upon the slowest member of any multilateral trade agreement. Nor should Canada, for it would then fall further and further behind. If sustainable development is about anything, it is about macroeconomic and macroenvironmental performance. When industry, agriculture and local communities achieve higher levels of resource and environmental productivity, the national economy in which they operate becomes more competitive. In fact, those countries that have achieved the most progress in this direction are at the top of the international list of economic performers.

Unfortunately, this is not where the environment-trade debate stands; the focus is on more trivial matters. Everyone is talking about inconsistent standards that can lead to unnecessary trade barriers and calling for international harmonization. There is nothing wrong with that, but it needs to be done with care.

My experience in directing one of the largest of such harmonization programs for seven years, the OECD Chemicals Program, suggests that the obstacles are formidable, even with maximum cooperation from government and industry. Health, food, safety and environmental standards are often inconsistent because governments want them that way. They want to use them as non-tariff barriers. I have looked into the cold, hard eyes of too many ministers protesting their innocence to be in any doubt. However, it is also true that standards are most often inconsistent because nations have different environmental endowments and because their electors have different levels of awareness.

When the countries concerned in an agreement are at similar stages of development, this situation need not pose an insuperable problem but when they are at widely different stages of development (like Canada and the United States in relation to Mexico), harmonization can raise enormous problems if safeguards are not provided for those countries that have already achieved a high level of health and environmental protection. If care is not taken, harmonization could weaken standards in those advanced industrial countries that have acted as pace setters. This would not protect health, safety and the environment, nor would it advance more sustainable forms of development.

Attempts to lower standards could have two effects:

• In the industrial field, governments and industries that understand the technology-forcing and market-leading impact of high standards will simply go it alone;

• In the health and safety field, governments could face untenable political pressures if, in response to harmonization agreements, they try to move standards in directions their voters, their media, and even some of their leading industries, refuse to support.

As the European Communities' proposal to GATT states:

13

"Countries which have achieved a high health status will find it difficult to systematically relinquish their national standards in favour of lower, albeit 'international' standards. It will therefore be necessary to provide for countries to continue to apply more stringent standards, where appropriate."

Until such time as these wide economic and cultural gaps have been narrowed, negotiators should treat the highest national standards not as falling ceilings but as rising floors. In any event, requiring the advanced nations to lower their standards in the name of harmonization may well be politically out of reach.

The Impact of Trade Policies on the Environment

The impact of trade and trade-related policies on the environment is already significant and growing rapidly. To quote the OECD:

"trade policies can contribute to environmentally adverse patterns of production, unsustainable exploitation of natural resources, and commerce in polluting or hazardous products."[4]

There are three major reasons for this:
• The *first* is that trade flows reflect market forces that usually have been distorted, sometimes grossly, by government intervention. Indeed, there may well be less to fear from the invisible hand of the market than from the visible hand of government.

The OECD countries that lead in rhetoric about the free market also lead in systems of production and export subsidies that are infamous:

a) in agriculture, subsidies in the OECD countries now cost taxpayers and consumers over $300 billion a year and encourage overproduction, market gluts, export subsidies and trade wars. They also underwrite a fast drawdown of

14

our most basic farm capital, our soils, wood and water, not only here in the North but also in the South, where we dump our surpluses and thereby undermine their agriculture;

b) subsidies also abound in energy: over $40 billion a year in the US alone; perhaps $4 billion in Canada. They tilt the playing field in favour of fossil fuels, result in more acid rain and global warming, and penalize efficiency and renewables;

c)in forestry tax concessions and sweetheart leases accelerate deforestation and species loss;

d) subsidies also exist in water development and other sectors.

These interventions in the market usually encourage the extraction and use of more resources per unit of output, not less. They are economically perverse, ecologically destructive and trade distorting, all at the same time: a "threefer" - an Australian hat-trick performed by governments standing on their heads.

The OECD has found repeatedly that these perverse and costly market interventions obstruct the sustainable use of environmental resources at the national and international level. Correcting them is something that free market liberals, fiscal conservatives, budget-balancers, and environmentalists can all agree on but find very difficult to accomplish.

It appears that no government or industrial sector really wants a level playing field. They all want to tilt it in ways that give them an edge. The percentage of imports subject to non-tariff barriers is increasing everywhere as interventions take on an almost infinite variety of forms. I have worked for governments of every political stripe in many countries and I have met very few politicians who are prepared to swear off promises of subsidies, tax abatements and other forms of intervention. The question is not *whether* governments will intervene in the market but, rather, *how* will they intervene? Subsidy systems and other interventions can be designed in ways that minimize their negative effects on trade while encouraging more sustainable forms of development. The Brundtland Commission's report, *Our Common Future*, is full of examples; my own recent book *Beyond Interdependence* provides more.

• There is a *second* reason why trade and trade-related policies can contribute to economically and environmentally adverse patterns of production and distribution. Trade does not, and cannot, take international externalities into account. It is blind to the different environment and resource endowment of nations. In the absence of a global regime, it will remain blind. The world needs an international "Polluter Pays" principle.

• The *third* reason why trade harms the economy and the environment relates to tariff and non-tariff barriers, which often distort global patterns of production in ways that cause very great economic damage resulting from accelerated environmental degradation.

The sugar tariffs levied by most OECD countries, including Canada, are a classic case in point. Japan's timber tariffs provide another example: for decades their tariffs have favoured raw logs and they virtually prohibit the importation of finished wood products; this is because they want to capture the value-added for their own economy. The impact on trade in tropical timbers has been dramatic: export revenues from tropical timber have been falling for years and are now worth about $8 billion.

A recent study for the International Tropical Timber Organization demonstrates that only a very small percentage of the world's tropical forests are managed in a sustainable manner. If current rates of deforestation continue, the 33 tropical countries that now export timber will be reduced to 10 by the turn of the century, and the value of their exports will decline to $2 billion per annum. One cannot sustain trade, employment, or profits, on a disappearing commodity.

Trade Liberalization

Phasing out tariff and non-tariff barriers and export and production subsidies of all kinds through trade liberalization would not only makes good economic sense; it would also make good environmental sense by leading to more sustainable patterns of energy, agricultural, forestry and industrial production. It could free resources that could be used to augment natural, as well as human-produced, capital assets.

Trade liberalization can broaden export opportunities for *developed* countries and, if OECD governments are serious, it can also broaden export opportunities for *developing* countries in areas in which they have a comparative ecological, as well as an economic, advantage. It could also broaden opportunities for the new democracies in Eastern Europe at a time when they need it desperately. Once again, however, we have to be careful to ensure that trade liberalization does not accelerate the net drawdown of forests, soils and other basic capital assets. It could easily do so. In fact, many believe that, without environmental safeguards, trade liberalization has had that effect.

Most of all, we have to ensure that trade liberalization agreements do not limit the range and choice of policy instruments that may be used to achieve environmental goals. That is a real concern, for three reasons:

• *First*, some have suggested that subsidies and other incentives to promote ecologically and economically sound farm practices could be considered trade distortions under GATT. If this is true, even though such incentives would reduce surpluses and the pressure for export subsidies, GATT's rules should be re-examined against the overriding global imperative to promote more sustainable forms of agriculture. This is also true for other sectors.

• *Second*, it has also been suggested that certain policies to internalize the external costs of production could be considered trade distortions under GATT. One example of

17

this type of policy is the imposition of a tax to ensure full cost pricing of chemicals, energy and other products that impact on the environment. This situation could seriously hamper measures to deal with a growing range of global issues. Reducing global warming will require an arsenal of policies to tilt the playing field against fossil fuels, including energy taxes and a range of regulatory policies to induce a steady annual increase in the efficiency of household appliances, electrical equipment, farm machinery, vehicles and buildings. Some countries are beginning to implement some of these measures unilaterally. They should be encouraged, not discouraged, by trade regimes.

• *Third*, there is concern about the use of trade instruments for environmental purposes. To date, trade restrictions have been used in a limited way to control flows of environmentally sensitive goods, such as hazardous chemicals and wastes and endangered species. The last major example was the Montreal Protocol on the ozone layer but many believe that it was just the tip of a rapidly growing iceberg. In the next two decades there could be a growing use of trade machinery to enforce environmental agreements.

Trade Policies and Global Issues

Several kinds of trade restrictions are currently being discussed, ranging from very minor restrictions up to, and including, boycotts. Countries that refuse to protect certain ocean species have been threatened, as have those who refuse to conserve vast forests and natural habitats. These resources are seen to be essential in upholding certain values, safeguarding the global climate or protecting essential life support systems.

This is an issue that needs a great deal of debate, on a case-by-case basis, and in which decisions should be guided by pragmatism, not dogma. In some instances, trade instruments may not be the most effective or efficient means of securing an environmental objective. In others, their use might simply provide a cover for governments to protect a home industry that cannot compete. However, in some cases where the use of other measures has been exhausted, trade sanctions, or the threat of trade sanctions, may be the only practical means of enforcing an international agreement to protect a resource that most agree is essential for survival.

Moral suasion is seldom sufficient to enforce environmental laws and can prove totally inadequate for international agreements which aim to reduce levels of CFCs and other greenhouse gases, to stop the dumping of hazardous wastes in developing countries, or to stop the trade in endangered species. In some cases, therefore, it may be that large countries - acting under an agreement, rather than unilaterally - will have to use the threat of trade sanctions to enforce environmental treaties.

A substantive global warming convention may prove to be a case in point. If and when a convention is negotiated that involves tradeable permits, energy taxes and other measures, the problem of free riders may have to be dealt with through restrictions on trade in regulated products with non-participating countries - and with participating countries who violate the agreement.

Governments should stop quarrelling over a failed paradigm based on the notion that the environment is the enemy of the economy and vice versa. Instead, they should begin to internalize the new paradigm of sustainable development and get on with the job of understanding how the environment, the economy, and trade can all be managed in ways that are mutually reinforcing. The time has come to build a trading system based on the realities of the 21st century.

References

1.   MACNEILL, JIM, WINSEMIUS, PIETER AND YAKUSHIJI, TAIZO (1991) *Beyond Interdependence: The Meshing of the World's*

Economy and the Earth's Ecology Oxford University Press, New York

2. ORGANIZATION FOR ECONOMIC COOPERATION AND DEVELOPMENT (1991) "Executive Summary, Trade and Environment" C/Min (91) 10, OECD, Paris

3. PORTER, MICHAEL (1992) *Canada at the Crossroads: The Reality of a New Competitive Environment* Gilmore Reproduction, Ottawa

4. OECD *op cit*

2

Trade-Environment Links: Issues for Canadian Industry
Thomas P d'Aquino

Thomas P d'Aquino is the President and Chief Executive of the Business Council on National Issues (BCNI), an organization composed of 150 chief executives of Canada's largest enterprises. He has been Special Counsel to the law firm of McCarthy & McCarthy, managed his own consulting firm acting as an advisor to clients in Canada and abroad on domestic and international policy and legal problems, and been associated with an international management consulting firm in London and Paris working on strategic business problems. From 1969-1972, he was Special Advisor to the Prime Minister of Canada.

The subject of trade-environment-competitiveness links is of great concern to the Business Council on National Issues (BCNI).[1] It is currently being studied by the BCNI's Task Force on Sustainable Development which is co-chaired by Jack MacLeod, President and CEO of Shell Canada Limited, and Adam Zimmerman, Chairman of the Board of Noranda Forest Inc. Sustainable development is currently one of the three highest priorities within the Council.

The trade and environment connection is fast becoming a major public policy issue of global proportions and will soon become a central issue of international economic relations and international trade. This issue has leapt into prominence quickly: a decade ago, the relationship between the environment and international trade was barely talked about, even in academic circles, but its leap to prominence is not without controversy. Some see it as the natural emanation of the sustainable development debate. Some see it as a promising weapon in the rapidly

21

changing arsenal of trade policy instruments. Some see it
as a catalyst for competitiveness, or as an impediment to
competitiveness, or the channel for North-South cooperation, or as the bedrock of fortified trading blocks.
Still others see it as the cornerstone of trade policy and
trade law reform.

To understand its various dimensions from a business
perspective, it is necessary to look in turn at the trade-
sustainable development link generally, the relevance of
this issue to Canadian industry, how environmental issues
are dealt with in some existing trade agreements, the
important issue of trade and the harmonization of
environmental standards, the issue of competitiveness
and sustainable development and, finally, how public
policy might respond to these new challenges.

The Trade-Environment Link

The Brundtland Commission demonstrated through the
concept of sustainable development that trade and
environmental protection are mutually reinforcing
objectives, *and* compatible with industrial competitiveness.
Similarly, trade liberalization is an indispensable tool to
promote more sustainable forms of development. Although
this point is the subject of some ideological conflict, the
case is clear - trade is a necessary pre-condition to world
economic development and to the progress of developing
countries. These countries rely increasingly on exports of
natural resources to earn foreign exchange. However,
current trade policies too often result in economic growth
in these countries that is achieved at the cost of
environmental degradation and long-term damage to the
country's future economic prospects. As is evident in the
current negotiations with respect to the Uruguay Round of
the GATT, developing countries are demanding better
trade access to the economies of the industrialized world.
They are likely to make new demands of the developed
world in return for agreeing to participate in many

international agreements on the environment (for example, on climate change, forests, and biodiversity).

The globalization of world trade, and the increasingly international dimension of environmental issues, means that the two policy agendas are rapidly moving towards each other. Indeed, there are three major developments affecting the nature of trade in the 1990s. The first is a rise in non-tariff barriers and other forms of protectionism in the developed countries of the North that have traditionally championed the cause of trade liberalization. At the same time, there is a growing openness and ability to trade in the South, and a significant lessening of their former protectionist orientation. The second is the growing importance of foreign direct investment as a closely related instrument of trade and, therefore, a more critical role for transnational corporations. The third is the potential for conflict between trade policy and environmental policy.

The growing relationship between trade and the environment has two important aspects. The first is that environmental protection measures, whether national regulations or international agreements, can have an impact on trade flows - indeed many measures are directly aimed at controlling exports and imports. The second is that trade policies and patterns can have significant implications for environmental protection, and for whether resource use is sustainable or not. For example, many current protectionist policies lead to mismanagement of resources in a way that harms the environment.

This issue is gaining increasing recognition because, as tariffs fall, attention switches to indirect means of protectionism, such as subsidies and technical standards. Distortions in trade are always possible when environmental standards differ between sovereign states. The concern is not so much with international agreements, which might contain trade restrictions as part of their implementation mechanisms, but rather with local regulations, which may have an environmental purpose but, explicitly or implicitly, also give an advantage to a

23

local product over an imported product. Developing countries rightly fear that developed countries will use strict environmental regulations as a non-tariff barrier to protect their higher cost producers. Added to this problem is the argument, often advanced by environmentalists, that countries whose industries have met the *full* costs of dealing with their own pollution should be free to take action, in the form of tariffs or countervailing duties, against those countries whose industries have not.

The Impact on Canadian Industry

This issue is gaining increasing attention from Canadian business for several reasons. The first is the importance of trade to Canada's economy, and its heavy dependence on exports of resource-based products. The second is the increasing costs of meeting environmental standards, particularly in resource sectors where Canada is a price taker, and the potential impact on the competitive position of these industries. The third is the threat of boycotts against certain industries (for example, forest products, Hydro Québec) and growing international pressure on Canadian standards from environmental lobbies outside this country. The fourth is the opportunities for exports of Canadian technology and environmental services.

The following recent examples of the interrelationship between trade and the environment in Canada demonstrate the complexities of this issue.

First, there are legitimate differences of view with respect to the necessity of certain regulations. For instance, the United States Environmental Protection Agency (EPA) has banned the use of asbestos in a number of applications. This is having considerable impact on the industry in Quebec, for which the United States was traditionally a major market. No similar regulations exist in Canada. In fact, the federal and Québec governments have taken the position that asbestos is safe when properly handled, and have supported the industry in its challenge of the regulations. This challenge was recently upheld by the United States Circuit Court of Appeals.

Second, regulations aimed at environmental protection, and which appear to accord national treatment, can nonetheless raise allegations of protectionism because of comparative advantages in different countries. For example, recent regulations in the United States requiring a particular level of recycled content in newsprint are affecting the ability of Canadian producers, compared to those in the United States, to sell in the US market because of their lack of access to large quantities of used newsprint (the "urban forest").

Third, states may attempt to compensate for what they perceive as lax environmental regulations, or inappropriate resource management in the country of export. Until challenged recently before a GATT panel, the United States Superfund legislation imposed higher tax rates on imported chemicals and petroleum products because foreign producers did not have to comply with strict US regulations. The softwood lumber dispute between Canada and the United States revolves around a perception that provincial government policy under-prices forest resources in Canada.

Fourth, even though states agree on common problems, differing approaches to the problem may cause trade distortions. Canada and many other countries have developed "eco-labelling" schemes for various consumer products. Because of the complexity of measuring environmental performance, it is entirely possible that different labelling programs will develop different criteria to deal with essentially the same environmental problem. This could lead to trade disputes if a competitor from outside the jurisdiction feels its product is equally deserving of being recognized as "environmentally friendly".

Fifth, whenever trade restrictions are used to further environmental objectives, there is a danger of casting the net too wide. The Basel Convention was primarily designed to prevent the export of hazardous wastes to countries which lacked adequate means to deal with them. However, the inclusion of recyclable material in the definition of "hazardous waste", and the onerous notification requirements, has had a significant impact on trade in recyclable minerals and metals for many Canadian companies.

Sixth, public perceptions of differing environmental standards can have a powerful impact on patterns of trade. Recent examples include the boycott in Europe of Canadian seal products, threatened consumer boycotts in Europe against the Canadian forest products industry, and domestic pressure applied to United States' utilities not to purchase power from Hydro Quebec because of the "Great Whale" project.

The Environment within Existing Trade Agreements

In order to understand the evolution of this issue, it is useful to review briefly how the environment is currently treated in existing and proposed international agreements with respect to trade.

The environment itself is not specifically mentioned in the General Agreement on Tariffs and Trade (GATT), since the GATT's creation pre-dates the more significant world attention now accorded to environmental issues. Thus, there is no specific mechanism in GATT to address environmental non-tariff barriers. Because it adheres to principles of consistency and national treatment, GATT cannot intervene where a country's laws apply equally to foreign and domestic producers. Under Article XX, other articles of GATT can be over-ridden where domestic legislation is designed to protect human, animal, or plant health, or to conserve natural resources. However, measures taken under Article XX must not arbitrarily discriminate against imports or constitute disguised restrictions on trade. In addition, the GATT Agreement on Technical Barriers to Trade (Standards Code) provides rules for recognition of national standards.

In 1972, GATT created a Working Group on the

Environment to respond to the recommendations of the Stockholm Conference (the United Nations Conference on the Human Environment) but this working group never met. However, in late 1990, a proposal was put forward to re-establish the working group, and it is expected that environmental issues will occupy a prominent place on the GATT agenda following the conclusion of the Uruguay Round.

One of the most significant developments is the recent GATT panel ruling on the United States-Mexico tuna trade dispute. The US had placed restrictions on tuna imports from Mexico because the nets used by many Mexican fishermen also kill dolphins. Mexico sought a ruling from GATT, arguing that the restrictions violated GATT rules. GATT's dispute resolution panel agreed that the tuna ban did not qualify as internal regulation, and the trade restriction was not "necessary" because the US failed to demonstrate it had exhausted all reasonable means of achieving its objective through GATT-legal means. This ruling has been widely interpreted to mean that a country does not have the right to restrict trade in the interests of protecting resources outside its territorial jurisdiction. It has been criticized in many circles for its perceived sacrifice of environmental protection to the interests of free trade. However, whether this one decision is a harbinger of future direction remains to be seen.

The Canada-United States Free Trade Agreement (FTA) allows each country to "maintain regulations to protect human, animal and plant life, the environment...". If such actions restrict trade, they will be permitted only if they can be demonstrated to "achieve a legitimate domestic objective". However, dispute resolution panels under the FTA are restricted to considering whether or not the laws of the importing country have been respected.

The North American Free Trade Agreement (NAFTA) is likely to be one of the first comprehensive trade agreements in which environmental issues are expressly addressed. Canada and the United States, responding to domestic criticisms, are putting pressure on Mexico to strengthen the enforcement of environmental standards. The United States and Mexico have also agreed to an in-depth review of United States-Mexico environmental issues as part of NAFTA. There is a strong possibility that there will be a comprehensive accord on these issues. It is less clear whether this might be a three-way accord. The Canadian government is conducting its own environmental assessment of NAFTA. But it cannot be completed until the terms of the trade agreement are known in more detail.

Member states of the European Community (EC) have agreed in principle to the development of common environmental standards. But progress has been slow. The Treaty of Rome allows member countries to impose stricter standards than those developed by the EC Commission if local environmental circumstances justify such action relative to its overall effect on trade. One recent case demonstrates how these rules may be interpreted. Danish regulations require returnable containers for beer and soft drinks, and also set up a licensing system for new types of containers. The EC Commission took Denmark to the EC Court of Justice, claiming this was unjustified discrimination against foreign producers. The Court recognized that these measures constituted a trade barrier but it decided they could be justified on the grounds of environmental protection and because the restriction on trade was *not* disproportionate to the final objective.

Trade and the Harmonization of Environmental Standards

To ensure that environmental protection measures do not amount to environmental protectionism in another guise, many would argue that it is necessary to pursue international harmonization of environmental standards. The so-called "level playing field" has long been an objective in international trading relations but the addition of the environmental dimension to international trade policy will not make it any easier to achieve. Harmonization appears to make the most sense as a long-term goal and is probably the best way to ensure harmonious trading relationships. However, it will not be easily attainable among sovereign countries with different priorities and resources, and at different stages of development. Although the ultimate objective may be to reach international agreement on environmental policies, it may be necessary to set different rates of progress to common standards in order to assist developing countries. This, in fact, is the approach adopted by the Montreal Protocol on Protection of the Ozone Layer.

There is also the important question of whether environmental standards *need* to be the same in various countries with different environmental conditions. While harmonization is the best approach to global issues and transboundary pollution problems, different environments have different absorptive capacities and local problems. If the carrying capacity of one country's environment is higher, should it have the same standards as others? There is also the possibility that different countries will have divergent views on the necessity and scientific justification for particular environmental measures (see below).

The Imperative to Integrate the Environment, Trade, and Competitiveness

The concept of sustainable development has brought with it a new view of competitiveness, both for individual enterprises and for national economies. There has also been a shift in many parts of world industry towards a new paradigm of development, fostered by companies producing more goods, services, jobs and income, while producing less pollution. There is also growing evidence that firms which have adopted company-wide policies on sustainable development are also on the leading edge technologically and competitively. The integration of resource and environmental considerations in investment decisions, in product and process design, and in marketing, has led to a steady reduction in the use of resources and the production of waste per unit of output. The result can be an increase in financial and natural capital, job creation, and in productivity and profitability.

The BCNI has attempted to capture this relationship between sustainable development and competitiveness in a major policy paper.[2] It has also recognized that business leaders in Canada have a responsibility to play a guiding role by adopting a series of principles to make sustainable development a reality within their companies.[3] The relationship between competitiveness and environmental protection is also a theme of the report on competitiveness prepared by Professor Michael Porter for the BCNI and the Government of Canada. Simply put, Professor Porter's thesis is that properly framed environmental regulations, which prescribe results and not methods, can spur companies to innovative new products and processes and actually enhance their competitive position. This issue, along with the overall theme of competitiveness, is the subject of ongoing work by the Business Council in the follow-up to the Porter report.

The Importance of Sound Public Policies

Some see more open trade as an anathema to environmental protection. They worry that competitive pressures will force states to opt for the lowest common denominator of environmental standards, and that developing countries will pursue unsustainable use of resources in a bid to earn more foreign exchange. Ultimately, however, trade and resource-sensitive competitiveness must be the means to further responsible growth in both developed and developing countries. This will provide the economic resources to move to higher environmental standards, to enforcement of those standards, and to more sustainable

30

forms of development. Clearly, this will also necessitate sound public policies to ensure that more open trade, a cleaner environment and enhanced competitiveness are the means to achieve this objective. Several important public policies contribute to this end.

One goal should be environmental standards which are scientifically sound, with appropriate allowances for a precautionary approach where full knowledge of all risks is not yet possible. There is also a need to design performance-based environmental standards, encouraging innovation by industry and allowing flexibility of response, rather than prescribing particular process requirements.

Greater use of market instruments is needed to motivate both producers and consumers to change their behaviour and to ensure the pursuit of environmental objectives in an efficient and effective manner. One of the most needed steps is the reform of current government interventions in the market that inhibit progress towards sustainable development, for example, certain subsidies for agriculture, energy, transportation, and water resource development.

If trade is to be a motor of economic growth and social progress for the less developed regions of the world, further liberalization of trade policy is necessary. This includes successful completion of the Uruguay Round of GATT, reform of agricultural policies that promote protectionism in developed countries and encourage unsustainable land use in developing countries, and further progress in developing common rules on investment, intellectual property, and subsidies.

GATT's purpose should remain one of promoting more liberalized trade. GATT cannot become an agreement to protect the environment. Rather, the objective should be to minimize the interference with trade caused by regulations developed for other purposes. This can be done by encouraging harmonization of environmental objectives.

A GATT dispute resolution mechanism is needed to address conflicts between trade and environment policy. Measures should be assessed according to the following four principles. The first is transparency, to ensure the trade impact is clearly identified. The second is legitimacy, as environmental standards must be scientifically sound. The third is proportionality, as restrictions on trade should not go beyond what is absolutely necessary to accomplish the particular environmental objective. And, the fourth is subsidiarity, for where the environmental objective can be achieved without resorting to a trade restrictive measure, this should be done.

The preferred approach for dealing with global environmental issues is multilateral negotiation towards international conventions that provide a global framework for the development of national standards. This would include agreement on broad environmental objectives and common procedures for measuring conformity with the convention. National enforcement of standards should be non-discriminatory and accord with GATT principles of national treatment and transparency.

Complete harmonization of environmental standards is probably not possible and may not be necessary, since not all countries have the same environmental problems. Efforts at harmonization of standards should concentrate on global issues (for example, climate change and ozone layer depletion). It will be difficult to get broad agreement in the beginning, particularly between developed and developing countries. Therefore, one avenue is a "bottom up" approach by regions, starting with those countries at similar levels of development, that is the European Community, and the OECD. As in the Montreal Protocol on Substances that Deplete the Ozone Layer, the approach could be to set common standards, but allow more time for developing countries to reach those standards. In these situations, the best approach might be to establish essential requirements, with accompanying measures that would be subject to the principle of mutual recognition. This was recommended by the World Industry Conference on Environmental Management (WICEM II), which met in Rotterdam in 1991.

Regional problems of transboundary pollution will require close co-operation among affected countries, with the possibility of harmonization of requirements. In other cases, rather than harmonizing standards, the parties should harmonize the approach they take to environmental issues, particularly in the setting of broad objectives and common approaches, with necessary differences to take account of local conditions.

One of the most important common approaches should be a greater use of market forces to protect the environment. The objective should be to ensure that everyone pays for the emissions, effluents and wastes which result from economic activity. This would mean less emphasis on harmonizing standards in favour of adopting a common basis on which charges for use of the environment are established.

Both government and industry have an obligation to assist developing countries to develop the technologies, products, and markets that will lead to more sustainable forms of development. This will require a commitment to foster technology co-operation that is beneficial to both parties. Policies should be developed to encourage foreign direct investment, joint ventures and partnerships. Protection of intellectual property rights should be a priority, to encourage transfers of competitive technologies on commercial terms. Innovative means need to be developed for the sharing of non-competitive technology, know-how, equipment and personnel, as well as providing training.

Companies in the industrialized world can work with firms in less developed countries to develop skills and management techniques, as well as sounder operating procedures. Creative mechanisms, such as the fund developed under the Montreal Protocol and the World Bank's Global Environmental Facility, can also be seen as instructive examples of how to finance transfers of environmentally beneficial technologies.

Conclusion

The trade and environment issue is crucial for Canada. It is vital for business. Many of Canada's key industries are particularly sensitive and vulnerable. Those in industry, supported by governments, must exert enormous energies to be players in the debate and to help shape the rules. If they are successful, the issue can, in large measure, work for them. If they fail, it certainly will work against them.

References

1.   The views expressed in this chapter are those of the author and do not necessarily represent those of the BCNI.

2.   BUSINESS COUNCIL ON NATIONAL ISSUES (1992) "Towards a Sustainable and Competitive Future" (Ottawa).

3.   BUSINESS COUNCIL ON NATIONAL ISSUES (1992) "Business Principles for a Sustainable and Competitive Future" (Ottawa).

B
Stakeholders' Perspectives

3

The Resource Sector's Perspective
Adam H Zimmerman

Adam H Zimmerman FCA has been the Chairman and Chief Executive Officer of Noranda Forest Inc since 1987, and Chairman of the CD Howe Institute since 1990. He began his career at Noranda in 1958 as Assistant Comptroller and has held a number of positions there including President and Chief Operating Officer. He is director of a number of companies including Confederation Life Insurance Company, Maple Leaf Foods, Southam Inc and the Toronto-Dominion Bank. He attended Ridley College, the Royal Canadian Naval College and the University of Toronto and has been on the Board of Governors of Ridley College since 1987.

There are many positive elements in the resource industry's response to the environmental claims made on it. It is notable that in Canada, perhaps uniquely amongst the advanced countries, the resources of the country are still owned by the people. Primarily they are owned by the provinces who lease them to the operators. This is a profoundly different situation from that in many countries where resources are under private ownership. Canada's situation is certainly not always advantageous, but it does dictate a sharing of responsibility.

Resource operators - both because of the owner from whom they rent and for many other reasons - act only by public consent. Despite media portraits, operators are not out to exploit quickly and run. Historically, however, a great many resource operations have been controlled in a lax fashion. People thought that if one dumped something in a river, it went away; that if one cut down a bush, it would grow back automatically; that if mine tailings were dumped, nothing would happen. These attitudes were seen at the time as natural. Although some operators were less than responsible, on the whole this behaviour was what society allowed and what society demanded. Indeed, in an everlasting search for jobs, public policy has been very much in favour of promoting the resource industries in Canada, sometimes in an irresponsible manner.

That lax period is now over. Operators know they are in a very strict regime no matter where they operate. They are watched over not only by those who are legally responsible, but also by quasi "vigilante" groups who care about their operations.

One of the operators' major problems now is that, although they may know how to deal with problems, they may not have the financial resources that this requires. The market has not yet really adjusted to environmentally friendly resource operations. There is a saying in the resource business that there is no such thing as shortages, there are just high prices. Today, there may just be a shortage of resources to do all the things the world would like operators to do, but the prices have not yet responded accordingly. Yet, in spite of this, there are many instances where the Canadian resource industry's response to environmental concerns has been positive, constructive and, indeed, world-leading.

One industry initiative was to build major pulp mills on inland waters in the mid-1960s. These mills were built with what was world-leading technology at that time. Their standard of environmental performance exceeded anything anywhere else in the world and they have largely maintained that position. That happened through an instructive symbiotic relationship between the owners, the provincial governments and the federal government. Together, they assembled a reasonable objective, for which a workable set of rules would be successfully implemented. While the usual image of pulp mills is of disgusting operations that pour out poisons, many mills in Canada are at the leading edge of responsible stewardship of the environment.

A *second* instance is the 1980 Forest Congress, a creature of the Canadian Pulp and Paper Association and the International Woodworkers Union. It was a first for union-management cooperation of that kind. Every participant in the forest sector was invited. The purpose of the Congress was to examine the condition of the Canadian forest. The stakeholders recognized that they were at a dangerous level of exploitation of the natural forest. The age of the planted forest had arrived, and a response from industry was required. Much was done after the Congress and now, the Canadian forest is healthy and improving. Canadians plant double the amount they cut, and unsatisfactorily restocked (NSR) areas are diminishing. On average, although there are some problem pockets, the forest is in good shape. This is because of the initiative of the industry.

A *third* instance is acid rain. In this case, the public took the lead, governments responded and industry cooperated. Today, the actual SO_2 output has diminished considerably, even if a great deal of sulphuric acid remains.

A fourth instance is dioxins. The response of the Canadian forest industry to this issue was really outstanding. In the space of a year, the generation of dioxins was cut in half. The problem is now well in hand.

A *fourth* and final instance, the recycling issue, is a genuinely "good news" story. The Canadian metals industry has participated heavily in recycling for a long time and the forest industry is now beginning to be a player. This has proved to be an economic and ecological advantage. The use of the urban forest as a raw material not only provides certain economies, but also takes the pressure off the natural environment.

At the 1991 World Industry Conference on Environmental Management (WICEM II) in Rotterdam, many people were asking what ought to be done: what was important, what was less important, and what was potentially important? Representatives from various environmental organizations recommended certain actions by

39

corporations. The positive initiatives of Canadian industry enabled Canadians to stand up and say, without fear of contradiction and with some pride, that they were doing it all. Indeed, it appeared that Canada was very much in the lead.

A further positive development has been the greening of corporate governance. Today, corporate governance in a well run business, such as Noranda, has a senior environmental officer (for example, a senior vice-president) with overall responsibility for environmental control and assessment matters. Environmental audits are conducted throughout the operations. There is a Board of Directors' Environmental Committee and the company publishes an Environmental Report. In other words, its environmental performance is transparent to the world, it is proud of that performance and will accept all the constructive help that is offered.

Despite these positive developments, an international level playing field has not yet been created. This is due to several factors, probably the most important of which is the contrast of conditions in developing and developed countries.

For instance, at the first WICEM conference in Versailles, when participants were discussing acid rain and smelters, a man, who identified himself as being from Ethiopia, said it was interesting that those in the North were fixing up their smelters but *he* wanted to build more smelters. His people were dying and he figured that additional smelters would improve their opportunities. This stark contrast shows the difference between actions open to the developed world and those available to countries who are literally fighting off starvation.

The concept of a level playing field is certainly being worked on. It is hoped that some large strides will be made following the United Nations Conference on Environment and Development (UNCED) in Rio de Janeiro in June, 1992. What is currently absent is a standard database. There is no standard of measurement in many fields.

40

There is no sense of what is important. Furthermore, technology has changed the definition of zero. A few decades ago, pollutants were measured in parts per million; in 1965, it was parts per billion; now, it is parts per trillion.

The third major international issue, after the range of conditions and database requirements, is the use of the best available technology which is economically achievable. This is different in different places and it is not generally accepted that what is good in Canada is the same as in Spain, Brazil or Sweden.

The fourth issue in this matter of environmental control is financing. Currently, resource industries are in an extreme depression and the financial resources are really not there. Even though all available corporate finances are devoted to what is mandated by environmental purists, there is not enough money for even normal maintenance operations.

This leads back to the issue of product pricing. In current product pricing, one gets virtually nothing for recycled paper and chlorine-free pulp. The pricing mechanism has not responded to the point where responsible people in society will actually pay for environmentally superior products. Loblaws will confirm that their green products only sell well in their upscale stores. This suggests that many people are not yet ready to make a financial sacrifice for the environment.

Finally, there is the issue of competitive environmentalism. When countries choose to deal with their resource pricing and management in differing ways, economic disadvantage will happen and this provides a strong argument for the need for a level playing field. Canada is well out in a leadership position environmentally. It is a matter of some concern for Canadian competitiveness that Canada does get not too far out in front.

4

The Environmental Industries' Perspective
Guy Saint-Pierre

Guy Saint-Pierre has been the President and Chief Executive Officer of the SNC Group Inc, Montreal, since 1989. Prior to that he was the President and Chief Executive Officer of Ogilvie Mills Ltd. M. Saint-Pierre has also held political positions with the Government of Quebec, including Minister of Education and Minister of Industry and Commerce. He is a Director of a number of companies, including the Conference Board of Canada, Suncor Inc, ESSROC Corp, Group Commerce Insurance Co, Royal Bank of Canada, the SNC Group Inc, and GM Canada Ltd. He holds a BASc in Civil Engineering from Laval University and a DIC and an MSc from the University of London.

Sustainable development was the fundamental principle underlying the message of the Brundtland Commission Report. Essentially, sustainable development attempts to achieve a balance between economic development and environmental protection.

Environmental clean-up is not just a goal to be achieved: it is a challenge that offers great opportunities for Canada. The environmental industry is one of the fastest-growing in the Canadian economy. It will be called on to play an increasingly important role in enabling Canada to penetrate highly competitive international markets and to establish a strong position in them.

The Canadian environmental industry employs about 150,000 people directly and indirectly with revenues ranging from $7 to $10 billion per year. A recent study by Peat Marwick, Stevenson & Kellogg indicates that environmental protection and conservation in North America represent a total market of over $100 billion; an amount slightly greater than the entire North American

43

aerospace and aviation industry (one of the largest industries on this continent). Measured in constant dollars, the environmental industry is growing at a rate of 7.5% per year, compared with 2 to 3% for the aerospace and aviation industry.

Rising energy costs and technological improvements that increase the energy efficiency of industrial machinery have led many industries to meet very strict pollution-abatement criteria. Many companies have discovered that their efforts to achieve better environmental results have harmed neither their productivity nor their competitiveness. Changes in management systems and investments in modern plants and equipment have improved their economic performance while also providing benefits for the environment.

Sustainable development also has important implications for foreign trade and investment in Canada. Companies that use manufacturing processes with a low environmental impact often gain an advantage in the marketplace so Canadian firms are sure to experience pressures to improve their environmental performance if they want to maintain good trading relations with their foreign partners and a strong position in the international market.

The environmental industry promises to be one of the most active markets in the 1990s. According to the Brundtland Report:

"The process of change, itself, is a process of dynamic restructuring that requires a high level of economic activity. We will have to promote technology that consumes small amounts of energy. We will also have to invest in infrastructure to satisfy a new model of future activity. Consequently, the private sector, the unions, and governments should recognize that this need for change will provide major opportunities both for investment and for employment."

Canadian companies and Canadian entrepreneurs have

every opportunity to develop and market new environmental technologies. The main ingredients for profitability with good environmental results are sound technical design and high-quality management, for which Canada's consultant-engineering industry is recognized throughout the world. This represents a precious asset for achieving our environmental objectives.

The North American Environmental Market: An Overview

An exhaustive study of business opportunities for the environmental industry in North America was conducted in 1991 by Richard K. Miller and Associates.[1] According to this study, the pollution-control and waste-management industry has annual sales of over $100 billion. Moreover, this industry is expected to experience rapid growth in the coming decade because government and industry will be increasing their expenditures in these areas appreciably (see Appendix 1 at the end of this chapter).

Furthermore, many industrial areas have been affected by the integration of environmental concerns, for example, the grocery industry, the automotive industry, and the construction industry. Virtually, every industry sector is affected by the environment. For most, it presents potential business opportunities. Further integration of environmental concerns in business will be seen in the future as people begin to understand more fully the relationships between the environment and the economy. In the natural environment, there is a vital ongoing relationship between water, land, air, flora, and fauna. Well over half of the economic wealth in North America is produced from environmentally-based activities. Therefore, it should not be surprising that these relationships are repeated in the economic context.

The environmental industry will undoubtedly be the hottest market sector in the 1990s. It will create knowledge-based, high technology jobs. It will give rise to new opportunities for investment and international trade. It will generate new businesses and, most importantly, it will help protect the natural environment.

Just as the 1980s saw a proliferation of "lite" products designed to meet growing consumer health awareness, the 1990s will be the decade of "green" products designed, packaged and marketed with a strong environmental perspective. A survey of consumer attitudes on environmentalism completed by the Michael Peters Group found that 89% of 1,000 Americans interviewed were concerned about the environmental impact of the products they purchased, and that 78% were willing to pay as much as 5% more for a product packaged with recyclable or biodegradable materials.

The strength of the environmental industry is due to the fact that there are so many market drivers. The strongest of these are the numerous and ever-increasing laws relating to pollution control and waste management. Another major force is the "green movement" or the new emphasis on protecting the environment which is being felt throughout North America and the world. Decreasing landfill capacity and the recent dramatic costs associated with waste disposal are driving the waste management industry. As well, directors and executives of corporations are receiving prison sentences for violating environmental laws. Finally, corporations are concerned about their public image and are spending huge sums of money to avoid the embarrassment that may be caused by being publicly labelled as major polluters.

Current Trends and New Directions

North American manufacturers spend in excess of $100 billion annually on pollution control measures and equipment. Still, the question remains: Why is such a moderate return on investment being achieved and what can be done to improve the failing pollution control situation?

To understand more fully how this critical point was reached, it is necessary to examine the ways in which North America has traditionally approached waste management. Often referred to as the "end of pipe" method, this single-media approach focuses solely on treating waste at the point of release into the environment. While effective in many instances and still widely practised, this approach has two major limitations.

First, the "end of pipe" method often only succeeds in transferring pollutants from one medium (air, water, land) to another. Also, treatment may not always result in waste that is environmentally acceptable. Instead, it may only eliminate certain harmful characteristics.

Second, the "end of pipe" method is a non-integrated approach to waste management. By focusing only on treating waste that has already been generated, this philosophy often blinds companies to the full range of opportunities that exist for reduced waste generation during daily process/engineering operations. In addition to hazardous wastes, these opportunities exist for solid waste and "industrial trash" as well as wastewater and discharges to atmosphere, which are often overlooked or considered to be inevitable by-products of the manufacturing process.

The waste management dilemma cannot be ignored. Government, the industrial community, and trade associations (including the National Association of Manufacturers and the Chemical Manufacturers' Association) believe that it is time to change direction. Collectively, they are endorsing a revolutionary new approach to waste management called "waste minimization" or "pollution prevention".

Industrial growth has been so rapid that the very definition of the role of an environmental consulting firm is undergoing a major transformation. Today, environmental consultants must be able to focus on more than just feasibility studies. Two distinct sectors for environmental consulting will emerge in the 1990s: very

47

large firms (20 to 30 in number) and niche-oriented firms. Companies that have not been in environmental consulting but have been in other engineering areas, such as land development, are currently trying to establish themselves in the marketplace. To meet demand, major firms are offering a full range of services, from planning and design to construction management. In the hazardous waste field, experts feel that there is going to be a strong trend toward consulting firms moving into remediation, where they will be involved in construction as well as design. Increasingly, private-sector clients will look to firms to provide a full range of services.

The environmental consulting field is facing the challenge of globalization. European firms are an increasing presence and competitive threat in North America. At the same time, US firms are expanding their activities abroad, where the market in Taiwan is seen as particularly attractive. There are also spot opportunities in Europe.

The US is ahead of most other countries in terms of environmental controls. This provides the Americans with tremendous opportunities in the global market: Eastern Europe, alone, could provide enough opportunities to last into the next decade. The Pacific Rim will also grant clean-up contracts worth hundreds of million of dollars in the near future. Many firms may not survive in the world market because of the different ground rules involved. The companies that will survive in the world market are those with global awareness "skills": more global representation on boards of directors and an understanding of local politics, banking and taxation (See Appendix 2 at end of chapter). Moreover, the new emphasis on waste minimization and pollution prevention is creating a demand for consultants who understand the industrial process. Front-end processing skills are now in demand rather than the end-of-pipe approach.

The fully integrated firm is the trend for the future. Industrial firms prefer that as few companies as possible handle their waste streams and become intimate with the production processes, believing that costs and liabilities are more readily assignable if one firm performs a turnkey job. A pure equipment supplier, lab services company or environmental consultant, will probably not be a successful company in five years. Rather, a total systems approach, including treatment and disposal, could become a requirement for doing business in this market (See Appendix 3 at end of this chapter).

According to John Naisbitt[2], the recession has taken its toll on available jobs across the continent, yet a handful of industries continue to offer career opportunities for people with the right education and the 1990s, the "Decade of the Environment", will open up an extraordinary variety of career opportunities, both technical and non-technical. Three fields in particular offer sure-fire job opportunities for the 1990s: computers, health care and environmental services. Toxicologists, pharmacologists, biochemists, geologists, and civil and chemical engineers will be in demand, along with professionals in chemical waste management, hazardous waste management, industrial hygienists, health and safety managers, hydrologists, environmental lawyers and recycling specialists.

Recycling laws, for instance, will bring a flood of jobs. The US Environmental Protection Agency aims to reduce trash headed for landfills by 25% over the next two years. In California, which wants to go further, state regulations require cutting the amount of trash in landfills by a quarter in 1995 and by half by the year 2000. Meeting those goals will require a huge increase in technicians and manual labourers and, while recycling efforts escalate, companies are seeking specialists to design environmentally-acceptable packaging.

Mounting concern over indoor air pollution will create a host of career opportunities for professionals trained in chemistry, biology, microbiology, heating and air-conditioning systems, architecture and indoor environmental planning. As well, the need for professionals to cope with environmental catastrophes, toxic waste, and dirty air, water and soil, is growing by 25% annually. A single United States federal program, the Department of Energy's campaign to clean up nuclear power plants, will open up 20,000 to 25,000 jobs over the next 30 years.

Not all the work is limited to technicians: the environmental movement and industry will need personnel managers and accountants with environmental experience, skilled writers to turn out written reports, marketing professionals to sell environmental products and locate new clients, and truck drivers and forklift operators to work at landfills.

The Canadian Environmental Industry

The environmental-protection market comprises a great many different goods and services. These goods and services can be classified into four major categories (See Appendix 4 at end of this chapter), each of which presents its own challenges and opportunities. These categories are: technology, goods, and services used by industry to protect the environment; multipurpose technology, goods, and services that have a wide range of applications, one of which is protecting the environment;   non-polluting industrial processes, whose use helps to protect the environment; and consumer goods and services that are not harmful to the environment.

This market is determined almost entirely by regulatory requirements and its growth depends largely on the introduction of new standards and regulations. It is now increasing by about 5 to 7% per year in constant dollars, and this growth will be steady. Municipalities are the largest potential customers, spending approximately $2 to $2.5 billion per year for goods and services. The pulp and paper industry is another important market niche, especially for wastewater treatment. Technical capability and price are key purchasing criteria in this market.

In a 1991 report, prepared by Ernst Young on behalf of Industry, Science and Technology Canada, the Canadian market for goods and services related to environmental protection was estimated at $5 to $7 billion per year. These figures included only goods and services that were purchased on the open market; they did not include non-purchased services, such as analyses performed internally by government laboratories. In addition, about $3 billion or more was spent each year on non-polluting industrial processes. Investment projects, including funds committed for engineering and construction goods and services, represented about $3 to $4 billion, or 60% of this market (See Appendix 5 at end of this chapter).

Canada is currently implementing a $3 billion "Green Plan" to clean up and protect its air, land and water over the next five years. Goals of the plan include reducing air pollution by 40%, creation of five new national parks, stabilizing CO_2 and other greenhouse gas emissions by the year 2000, reducing solid waste by 50% over the next 10 years, and developing detailed plans for cleaning up the Great Lakes.

The "Green Plan" includes some 100 initiatives involving dozens of federal agencies and sundry business and environmental organizations. New federal programs will be established, including a Great Lakes Pollution Prevention Centre by 1992 and a five-year Ocean Dumping Control Program. An Office of Waste Management will be launched to help achieve a 50% waste reduction by the year 2000. As part of that effort, a National Waste Exchange Program will be formed to seek market opportunities for waste materials re-use. A system to monitor the US's contribution to Canada's ozone problem will also be established. Negotiations will be held with the US on how to reduce transboundary emissions.

Under the clean air initiative, the government plans to phase out CFCs by 1997 and methyl chloroform by the year 2000. The plan also hopes to reduce Canada's ground-level ozone emissions by 15% over the next 15 years. In an effort to control hazardous wastes, new regulations to restrict harmful pulp and paper mill effluent were introduced in

51

1991. Thirty hazardous waste sites are targeted for cleanup by 1995. A database of hazardous pollutants used and released by industry and transport sources will be established. The federal government's Green Plan will unquestionably stimulate demand for industrial goods and services related to environmental protection.

Opportunities for the Canadian Environmental Industry

The domestic market thus offers some promising possibilities because of its current size and its potential for growth. Canadian investment in pollution-control equipment (excluding services) represented a market of about $1.4 billion in 1990, or an increase of 43% over 1986. Expenditures by municipalities for water and sewage treatment and treatment of solid wastes, along with expenditures by private industry (particularly the pulp and paper, oil, and metallurgical industries) to comply with new regulations, should greatly stimulate the environmental industry in Canada.

There are considerable opportunities for Canadian suppliers in this industry to expand in the domestic marketplace because Canadian companies control less than half (only 44%) of the domestic market for pollution-control equipment. Most of the pollution-control equipment purchased in Canada is imported, and 90% of these imports come from the United States.

Canadian involvement in export markets has also been very limited to date. According to one study, only 20 manufacturers and 20 service companies in the Canadian environmental industry export their goods and services, despite the image of a world leader in this industry that Canada enjoys abroad. Export markets have a number of features that could offer attractive opportunities for Canadian suppliers. Many studies have concluded that the environmental markets will experience rapid growth.

An overview of growth projections for US environmental

markets, prepared by Industry, Science and Technology Canada, suggests promising opportunities in solid wastes, hazardous waste, sewage treatment, water supply and solid waste disposal. Solid wastes present a growth opportunity for suppliers of goods and services to the American market. Government expenditures for disposal of solid waste amount to $7 billion per year in the US, compared to $600 million in Canada. As disposing of solid wastes becomes more and more difficult, recycling will become an increasingly important alternative in both countries.

In the United States, the markets for recycling will grow at an annual pace of 13% through 1994. For recycling of plastic packaging, the longer-term growth opportunities are also of interest: by the year 2002, recycling will account for 43% of the entire plastic-packaging disposal industry, as compared to only 1% today. Whereas 96% of plastic packaging now ends up in landfills, only 36% will be landfilled by the year 2002. The markets for recovering waste and converting it to energy will grow at an annual rate of 11% from now through 1994. The costs of disposing of hazardous wastes could increase to over $200 billion. Of the 850 priority clean-up sites identified by the US Environmental Protection Agency (EPA), only 6 have been cleaned up so far.

Capital expenditures by municipalities for sewage-treatment facilities will reach $2.8 billion by 1995. Expenditures for operations and maintenance will be three times this figure. The main areas where this investment will go are: engineering ($240 million), equipment ($370 million), instrumentation ($65 million), construction ($1.7 billion), and materials ($490 million). Public power utilities and industrial institutions also plan sizable investments for treating their effluent ($1.2 billion and $4.5 billion, respectively). The US government estimates that between now and the year 2000, industry will spend $60 billion to meet the standards imposed by the 1987 amendments to the Clean Water Act.

The annual budget for supplying water in the United States is in the order of $100 to $150 billion. Associated General Contractors estimates that requirements for water-supply infrastructure will be $139 billion between now and the year 2000. Real expenditures on public sewage systems in the US are rising at an annual rate of about 3 to 4%; the current figure is $13 billion. Associated General Contractors also estimates that $508 billion will have to be spent between now and the year 2000 on waste water-treatment infrastructure in the United States.

Other foreign markets may also present opportunities for Canadian exporters. The environmental market in Western Europe has now reached 40 billion ECUs (European Currency Units; in 1987, one ECU equalled $1.30 Canadian). Of this total, 21% was spent on controlling atmospheric pollution, 50% on water pollution, and 27% on treatment of solid wastes. West Germany is the largest market in Europe, amounting to $11 to $13 billion (US) dollars according to one study, or 14 billion ECUs per year according to another report. On average, the various sectors of the West German market grew at an annual rate of 6% to 8% between 1980 and 1987.

In the Far East, Japan is increasing its environmental-protection activities to solve serious problems that have become apparent. For example, only 40% of the country's population is served by public sewage systems. Taiwan has become an extremely dynamic country in environmental matters. Laws passed recently have helped to establish a $35 billion (US) program to clean up pollution on the islands by the year 2000. South Korea will spend $750 million on pollution-control equipment over the next 5 years. After that, its expenditures are likely to increase by $100 million per year. The government of Hong Kong also recently announced a $3 billion (US) pollution control program.

In the developing countries, purification of water for human consumption represents a major challenge. Only 18% of the rural population of Indonesia and 30% of the rural population of China has access to potable water. In China, Indonesia, and Thailand, supplying potable water is one of the main socio-economic objectives. According to one study, to provide potable water to everyone on earth would require an annual expenditure of 20 to 30 billion dollars. It would also take 20 million hand pumps.

The opportunities in Eastern Europe also deserve attention. In Romania, for example, SNC has recently made some interesting inroads.

Closer to home, *US News & World Report* conducted a survey of current conditions in Mexico. It found that indiscriminate dumping or long-term storage of industrial garbage and hazardous wastes is trashing the landscape and poisoning the water and soil. A slumgullion of chemical-laced industrial waste water and raw sewage pumped into canals and rivers is causing widespread gastro-intestinal illness, hepatitis and other long-term health problems - including a suspected increase in mortality from certain cancers. Massive discharges of toxic fumes have occurred in chemical plants and other factories. In the Matamoros-Reynosa region alone, seven major accidents, since 1986, have sent more than 350 people to hospitals and forced thousands to flee their homes.

Employees of Maquiladora (a program that allows US companies to operate in Mexico) - most of them women, who sometimes start work at 13 years old - are exposed to toxic substances and other workplace health hazards without being given safety instructions or basic protection, such as masks and gloves. There is also evidence of severe birth defects suffered by infants born to workers.

Because of the scope and severity of Mexico's pollution problems, the Mexican environmental protection agency, SEDUE, is working to reduce hazardous waste: new laws require factories, including US and foreign owned assembly plants, to comply with the nation's expanding hazardous waste laws. Millions of tons of waste will require treatment, storage and disposal at factories that, for the most part, do not yet exist.

Mexican President Salinas de Gortari is making pollution control and waste management a political priority. He has announced a $2.5 billion program to cut pollution in Mexico. The plan includes new restrictions on industrial waste generators and small generators. The plan also calls for a ban against any new industrial facilities in the Mexico City basin. More than 40% of the plan's funding will come from foreign countries, including Japan, France, Germany, Britain and the United States. As a result of the environmental plan, Mexican-based factories can expect increasing pressure from enforcement agents to start complying with Mexico's hazardous waste laws.

SEDUE estimates that it will cost Mexico $25 billion to solve the pollution problems in Mexico City alone. The Mexican government plans to spend more than $100 million over the next three years to fight Mexico city's pollution problems. The total market for pollution-control equipment in Mexico amounts to approximately $250 million and was growing at a rate of 10% per year until 1990.

The Japanese government has offered $805 million in untied credits to Mexico for environmental projects. While current business opportunities under Japan's development assistance program targets air pollution from fuel oil, leaded gasoline and old railroad locomotives, future projects may include engineering, construction and equipment for water, solid and hazardous waste treatment.

The environmental, waste management, and pollution control programs of the United States, Canada, and Mexico present a market opportunity to businesses in all three countries. Mutual business opportunities are also evident between Mexico and their North American neighbours. The experience gained in the recently expanding national environmental efforts by several leading Mexican environmental firms could give them a competitive edge in some US and Canadian markets. At the same time, these expanding efforts offer opportunities to the environmental businesses of the United States and Canada.

Problems and Prospects

Canadian environmental businesses are not going to penetrate the international marketplace simply by magic. In the United States, for example, the Buy America Act of 1933 poses a major obstacle to the purchase of Canadian materials by the government. Under this law, US products enjoy a 6% advantage for most government contracts, and a 12% advantage for contracts reserved for American small businesses and in areas where there is a labour surplus. Services are not covered as part of the Canada-US Free Trade Agreement that deals with government contracts. Thus, the Buy America Act applies to services procured by the US federal government through a tendering process. All materials put out to tender under contracts for services are also subject to the Buy America Act; consequently, Canadian materials are placed at a 6 to 12% price disadvantage compared to American materials.

Moreover, purchases by state and local governments are not subject to the portions of the Canada-US Free Trade Agreement that deal with government contracts. Clauses giving preference to American suppliers can be found in the contracts awarded by at least 32 states and many local governments. Some of these clauses are intended to give preference to local suppliers, whereas others simply favour American products in general.

Though the international market may be growing vigorously, to achieve any significant penetration of this market, the Canadian environmental industry will have to make major efforts and meet certain conditions. Four efforts in particular will be critical.

The first is developing a strong domestic market that will enable the Canadian environmental industry to achieve a critical mass of expertise, with leading edge technologies and human resources. For this to happen, governments must carry out major environmental programs and influence the industrial, manufacturing, and trade sectors of the economy to do the same.

A *second* condition is tighter co-operation between governments and the environmental industry. This is essential in order to strengthen partnerships both within Canada and with foreign counterparts, to establish rules that are fair to all parties concerned, and to promote access to the most up-to-date information on technologies, business opportunities, financing programs, and changes in regulations. Companies that know what is going on in the international marketplace will be able to foresee Canadian legislative developments more accurately. They will be better prepared to take advantage of opportunities to transfer or acquire technology and to forge strategic links with various partners.

A *third* requirement consists of efforts to give the Canadian environmental industry a shot in the arm. Too often, there is a lack of communication between Canadian suppliers of environmentally-protective goods and services and their customers in Canada and elsewhere. Research has shown that many potential buyers are not familiar with Canadian suppliers or the technology they offer. Companies (especially those with new technologies or technologies under development) can benefit greatly by ensuring that increasing customer awareness is a key part of their marketing strategy. Government, for its part, should continue to implement policies to stimulate research on - and development and transfer of - environmental technologies, as well as marketing-assistance programs and measures to help train environmental specialists. It was recently announced that $100 million will be spent for such initiatives under the Green Plan. This is a step in the right direction.

Fourth and last, the Canadian environmental industry must organize itself, at both the national and regional levels, to express its views (a) on matters affecting its own development (technology, information, co-operation, and regulation); and (b) on international environmental matters (Canada's participation in the OECD, GATT, and North American Free Trade; relations with the United Nations

Environmental Program, the European Community, and countries of the Francophonie; international trade; and financial agencies).

In short, with a strong domestic market to support it, the Canadian environmental industry can carve out a place in the international market, if two conditions are met: Canada must improve its own structure and organization; and it must take a more coherent approach to co-operation with the public sector.

Appendix 1

Summary of 1990 Environmental Market in North America

Air Pollution Control	$ 2.4 billion
Water and Wastewater Management	$ 8.0 billion
Solid and Municipal Waste Management	$29.5 billion
Recycling	$13.0 billion
Environmental Consulting Services	$ 9.0 billion
Waste-to-Energy	$ 2.5 billion
Hazardous Waste Management	$ 6.0 billion
Pollution Prevention/Waste Minimization	$ 5.0 billion
Indoor Air Quality	$ 5.0 billion
Asbestos Abatement	$ 3.5 billion
Remediation	$ 3.0 billion
Spill Clean-up and Control	$ 2.0 billion
Environmental Instrumentation	$ 1.2 billion
Nuclear Waste Management	$ 1.0 billion
Environmental Test Laboratories	$ 1.0 billion
Medical Waste Management	$ 1.0 billion
Noise Abatement	$ 1.0 billion
Underground Storage Tanks	$ 0.8 billion
Environmental Software	$ 0.5 billion
Radon Abatement	$ 0.2 billion
Lead-Based Paint Abatement	$ 0.1 billion
Electric and Magnetic Field Exposure	$ 0.0 billion
TOTAL	$95.7 billion

The Largest Sectors of the Environmental Industry are:

- solid and municipal waste management ($29.5 billion)
- recycling ($13 billion)
- environmental consulting services ($9 billion)
- water and wastewater management ($8 billion)
- hazardous waste management ($6 billion)
- pollution prevention and waste minimization ($5 billion)

The sectors expected to experience the most growth are:

- pollution prevention and waste minimization (35%)
- soil and site restoration (25%)
- environmental consulting services (15%)
- recycling (11%)
- all categories of waste management* (10%) (*hazardous waste 42%; solid waste 7%; water 41%; air 10%)

Other sectors that may present opportunities:

- biomedical waste management
- indoor air quality
- management of underground storage facilities
- conversion of waste to energy

SOURCE:
Environmental Markets 1991-1993
R K Miller & Associates Inc

Appendix 2

Examples Of Leading Corporate Environmental Efforts

• DuPont is pulling out of a $750 million-a-year business because it may harm the earth's atmosphere.

• McDonald's, which uses hundreds of millions of pounds of paper and plastic waste annually, has become a crusading proponent of recycling, and aims to become one of America's leading educators about environmental issues.

• 3M is investing in myriad pollution controls for its manufacturing facilities beyond what the law requires.

• Procter & Gamble and other smart marketers are moving to cast their products in a environmentally friendly light.

• Pacific Gas & Electric teams up with environmental groups - some of which it used to fight - to do joint projects, such as a $10 million study of energy efficiency.

• Sun Co. will spend $126 million on its Atlantic subsidiary to improve the environmental integrity of that division's Philadelphia refinery and its products. The firm plans to build three new units and upgrade another one.

• Unocol announced a program which would pay owners $700 each for the first 7000 scrap pre-1971 cars turned in. Older cars cause up to 30 times the pollution of new models. In addition, the company's stations will offer free emission inspections and anti-pollution adjustments on pre-1975 automobiles.

SOURCE:
Environmental Markets 1991-1993
R K Miller & Associates Inc (Vol 1, p.48)

Appendix 3

The Environmental Business: What Scope?

Most assessments of the environmental market include:

• Capital expenditures for pollution control and waste management products and equipment
• Expenditures for the construction of pollution control and waste management facilities
• Operations and maintenance costs of pollution control facilities
• Expenditures for pollution control and waste management services

However, the entire scope of the environmental market should be viewed as much broader, including the following:

• Shifts in commercial expenditures attributable to environmental considerations
• Shifts in consumer expenditures attributable to environmental considerations
• Income to the support businesses: education and training, research and development, publications, insurance, financial services, etc.
• Investments in environmental businesses, financing and banking, and interest paid for loans on environmental projects
• Governmental and private sector expenditures which encourage or legislate environmental objectives
• Expenditures for the development and production of environmentally compatible substitutes
• Legal consultation, litigation costs, and penalties
• Expenditures for pollution prevention and waste minimization

SOURCE:
Environmental Markets 1991-1993
R K Miller & Associates Inc (Vol 1, p.31)

Appendix 4

Categories of Goods And Services
Related to Environmental Protection

Category 1
Technology, goods, and services used specifically to protect the environment
    Environmental impact studies
    Laboratory services
    Membrane technologies
    Aeration tanks
    Ultraviolet radiation equipment
    Air-quality monitoring equipment

Category 2
Technology, goods, and services with multiple applications, including protecting the environment
    General engineering services
    General construction services
    Water pumps
    Pipes and valves

Category 3
Non-polluting industrial processes
    Closed-loop water supply systems
    High-efficiency fuel burners
    High-efficiency motors
    Electrical arc furnaces

Category 4
Consumer goods and services that are not harmful to the environment
    Reusable plastic containers
    Reusable pallets and packaging
    Phosphate-free detergents
    Recycled paper
    Diaper services
    Environmentally friendly lawn-care services

SOURCE:
Report prepared by Ernst and Young
on behalf of Industry, Science and Technology Canada, 1991

Appendix 5

Amounts Spent on Goods And Services Related to Environmental Protection, By Market Segment

(in $m)

Market Segment	Air	Water	Solid waste	Hazardous waste	Conservation	Other*	Total
Municipalities	150-175	1,700-1,900	400-600				2,100-2,500
Pulp and paper		500-600	50-75				700-900
Forestry services					400-500		400-500
Chemicals & chemical products industry	100-130	100-130	10-20	90-120			300-400
Public utilities	230-250	25-30	10-15	**not determined	30-40		300-350
Mining	80-125	80-125	40-50				200-300
Oil and gas	50-100	50-100	5-10		45-90		150-300
Federal & provincial governments						150-240	150-240
Other industries & manufacturing	10-20	50-60	15-20				75-100
Iron and steel industry	10-20	30-60	10-20				50-100
Industrial minerals	5-10	5-10	5-10			**not determined	20-30
Other	50-150	50-150	500-600				500-900
TOTAL	685-980	2,590-3 165	1,045-1 420	95-125	475-630	155-245	4,945-6,620

* Includes noise control, laboratory equipment, and monitoring equipment
** Not determined; a limited market whose size has not yet been determined. The totals include these markets.

SOURCE: *The Canadian Market in Environmental Products and Services* (ISTC, 1991)

References

1.   MILLER, RICHARD K. & ASSOCIATES INC *Environmental Markets 1991 - 1993* (3 vols)

2.   NAISBITT, JOHN (1991) "Trend Letter"in *Inside Guide* Sept.

Bibliography

GOVERNMENT OF CANADA (1991) *Crossroads '91: Market Profiles - Environmental Equipment and Related Services* Department of External Affairs and International Trade.

GOVERNMENT OF CANADA (1991) *A $100 Million Initiative* Environment Canada, October.

GOVERNMENT OF CANADA (1991) *The Canadian Market for Environmental Protection Products and Services* Department of Industry, Science and Technology .

GOVERNMENT OF CANADA (1990) *Markets for the Canadian Environmental Industry* Department of Industry, Science and Technology, July.

GOVERNMENT OF CANADA (1991) *Investing in Canada* Investment Canada, Spring, Vol4/4.

5

The Environmental Community's Perspective
Michelle Swenarchuk

Michelle Swenarchuk is the acting director and counsel for the Canadian Environmental Law Association. She is lead counsel for the environmental coalition on Forests for Tomorrow at the Environmental Assessment of Forestry on Crown Lands in Ontario. She is also a member of the Forests Sectoral Task Force established under the Ontario Round Table on the Environment and the Economy. She has written extensively on the environmental effects of trade. In addition to practising environmental law, she has been a practitioner and policy analyst in the fields of labour, native rights, and aviation law.

In Canada today, a great deal is said about the economic crisis in which we are living and a great deal of attention and public policy debate centres on that crisis. No Canadian political leader has yet argued, however, that we live in an era of serious ecological crisis.

Environmentalists approach most questions, including trade, from that perspective. The global ecological crisis has become clear and examples abound:

a) global warming will have an enormous impact on our lifestyles, agriculture, forests, fisheries, sea levels, and on coastal regions around the world;

b) there is also the depletion of the ozone layer; there are catastrophic and worsening levels of poverty in the Third World, which are linked closely to environmental problems;

c) we have seen ever increasing rates of exploitation of natural resources by industrialized nations;

d) we are experiencing international problems of ecosystem pollution - air, surface and ground water, as well as soil pollution.

At the Canadian Environmental Law Association,

discussions about trade and environment matters and environmental protection always deal with the pollution aspect of environmental protection: environmental standards, health, human and animal standards, and industrial emissions. They also deal, increasingly, with questions of resource management and conservation. Examining environmental concerns from these two vantage points makes it clear that the question of resource use relates to the entire use of the planet.

Resource management and mismanagement, conservation and lack of conservation, are dichotomies grounded in our industrial philosophy, a philosophy which is incompatible with environmental protection. Limitless growth, which has been a characteristic of society, is now clearly and demonstrably incompatible with sustainable development. The use of resources - wherever they may be obtained - without provision for future generations is environmentally destructive.

Canadians are the most profligate users of energy in the world. The Brundtland Commission has advised Canadians to make massive reductions in energy use. At this time, however, and partly as a result of the Canada-US Free Trade Agreement, Canadians continue to expand energy use and extraction.

The idea that trade agreements (dealing as they do with both resource use trends and the establishment of standards) are intimately connected to the environment, may seem self-evident. However, as recently as 1988, during the Canada-US Free Trade debates, it was the position of the Canadian government that the US-Canada Agreement was a commercial agreement between trading partners that did not concern or affect the environment - and this about a deal that contained an entire chapter on energy (the underlying resource that drives every economy), as well as sections pertaining to agriculture, pesticides, forests, fisheries and that tradeable good, water.

Most environmentalists see the structure of GATT, the Canada-US Free Trade Agreement, and the projected directions for the proposed Canada-US-Mexico trade deal, as inherently environmentally destructive. These agreements entrench current practices of industrial exploitation of resources and interfere with the sovereign rights of countries to set and retain environmental standards. There are fundamental problems in treating environmental standards as non-tariff barriers to trade. Another problem is the failure of trade agreements to acknowledge that there are values, other than commercial ones, of importance to human and planetary systems. Even if an environmental standard has an impact on trade, unrestricted trade should not have such sacrosanct status that the environmental regulation would fall.

There are very real concerns about the use of the Free Trade Agreement to defeat Canadian (and American) environmental standards: one example is the requirement of the Canadian Fisheries Act for the landing of Pacific coast salmon and herring being found incompatible with the Agreement; in another, the Canadian government intervened in the asbestos case in the US, arguing that the EPA ban contravened the FTA provision regarding standards-related measures that created unnecessary obstacles to trade, and a US Environmental Protection Agency standard was struck down.

Many share these concerns. For instance, the GATT decision with regard to the tuna-dolphin case created enormous anxiety in some American legislators who wondered how it was that a trade panel, not on American soil, had the authority, essentially, to strike down the Marine Mammals Protection Act, a piece of legislation passed in accordance with the American Constitution.

Another concern to environmentalists is the process of negotiating international trade agreements. While environmental protection initiatives have often been achieved as a result of information becoming accessible to the public and a resultant rise of public concern and pressures for change, these initiatives are being thwarted by international trade agreements. The latter are

69

negotiated in secret by business and government representatives without any particular environmental knowledge or concern, and without consultation with the public. They are implemented by non-elected national and international bureaucracies that are not responsible to an electorate or even known to the public. These two elements make the process fundamentally anti-democratic. Yet the results of these negotiations - the trade deals - are being used to strike down laws established by democratically-elected governments.

No environmentalists were involved or consulted in the drafting of the Free Trade Agreement. Nor are they directly involved in the current negotiations of the Canada-US-Mexico deal. The Minister of the Environment, Jean Charest, appears to have only one environmentalist on a large advisory committee that is not directly involved in the negotiations and that person is sworn to secrecy and unable to communicate with the entire community. Clearly, one environmentalist cannot make much of a contribution to the process and these negotiations should be subject to public debate and information.

Environmentalists are looking for several elements in these trade agreements.

First, there is a need for environmental assessments of trade agreements. These could identify potential adverse effects of trade, and available alternatives. The implementation of a comprehensive environmental impact assessment, and action on the results, would be a true test of any nation's commitment to integrating environmental concerns and economic policy.

There are several important steps in the successful assessment of trade agreements. The first, which is essential to making the process credible, is timing:

a) the timing of environmental impact assessment should be directly related to the negotiating and decision-making schedule of the agreement to ensure that the environmental impacts of the agreement are known and addressed during negotiations;

b) it should be completed well before negotiations are concluded, in order to allow government agencies and the public adequate time to review the study and address the changes considered necessary before the negotiations are over;

c) there should be meaningful and timely public participation in the evaluation and review of the environmental impact assessment. The public must be able to comment fully on the study and its identified options and alternatives. Their comments and views must be seriously considered and reasons given when proposals by the public are rejected.

Second, is the inclusion of environmental protection and resource conservation measures. In order to reverse the tendency of trade agreements to facilitate unrestrained resource and environmental exploitation, they must codify environmental protection and resource conservation as legitimate goals. Agreements must not fetter the ability of nations to act decisively in the national or international interest of the environment, in areas such as national control over resource export and import flows, resource depletion and the environmental costs of commercial activities. In addition, the creation of an international trade and environment panel is warranted. This must be granted the jurisdiction, pursuant to any trade agreement, to identify, monitor and resolve environment and trade issues as they pertain to the agreement itself. Direction should be provided to national governments so that they may initiate domestic and/or coordinate international actions to promote environmentally sound practices. It would also facilitate the process of amending trade agreements, where necessary, to effect these changes.

Third, the environmental community recommends the establishment of an environmental fund and other incentives. This could include a financial mechanism whereby monies received from any levy placed on imports bearing environmental costs from developing countries would be transferred back to these countries for the purpose of improving their environmental and regulatory enforcement programs.

Fourth, trade agreements should provide for the enhancement of environmental programs. Instead, the potential exists within trade agreements for the harmonization of environmental standards to the lowest common denominator among nations. To prevent such weakening, trade agreements should observe the following environmental protection measures:

a) uniform minimum standards must not interfere with the regulatory power of any level of government within a given nation to apply higher domestic environmental protection and national resource conservation standards;

b) the negotiation of any harmonization measures must be undertaken by democratically accountable political institutions, and should take place in an open, transparent forum which offers full opportunities for public participation;

c) developing countries must be offered further technical and financial assistance so they may improve their environmental, health and safety standards.

Third World environmentalists from Mexico are very concerned about what they see as the proposed agenda for a Canada-US-Mexico deal. They propose an alternate approach to development in Mexico: starting from an analysis of political, economic, institutional, social, environmental and other factors. Over two hundred and forty million human beings in the region have been subjected to conditions of degradation without historical precedent. These conditions include the absence of democracy, states incapable of stable long range policies, economic strategies that are non-viable in the long-term, concentration of income, marginalization, and poverty.

These environmentalists suggest that it is necessary to accept the existence of an environmental debt contracted by industrialized countries, as well as the debt the Third World owes to us. The environmental debt is made up of three elements:

a) the environmental deterioration caused in the Third World by the exploitation and/or the export of natural resources and raw materials;

b) the loss of income brought about by the systematic deterioration in trade since the Third World's principal export products consist of renewable and non-renewable raw materials; and

c) the social and environmental damage caused by the introduction, production and/or marketing of, medicinal and agro-chemical products that have been banned in developed countries.

The payment of even a part of this debt should become a source of resources essential to the implementation of environmental recovery and protection programs in the Third World.

As economies and industries globalize, so do the environmentalists. International networks have been established in which environmentalists are discussing trade issues, just as they are being discussed in industry. It is undoubtedly possible to share the world and trade its resources equitably and sustainably. That must be our overall priority, and it should be included in the negotiation of international trade agreements. Given the global ecological crisis, our children's future requires it.

6

The Aboriginal Community's Perspective
Rosemarie Kuptana

Rosemarie Kuptana is the President of the Inuit Tapirisat of Canada, a position she has held since April 1991. From 1986 to 1989, she served as the Canadian Vice-Chairperson of the Inuit Circumpolar Conference (ICC). From 1983 to 1988 she was President of the Inuit Broadcasting Corporation (IBC). In 1988 she was awarded the Order of Canada. She has recently published No More Secrets, *a book about child sexual abuse in Inuit communities. She was born in Sachs Harbour on Banks Island in Canada's Northwest Territories and attended school in Inuvik.*

Economic development, and economic policies, are of great - and growing - importance to Inuit, just as they are for all Canadians. The Inuit Tapirisat of Canada is the national political voice of Canadian Inuit - those residing in our traditional homelands in the Northwest Territories, Labrador, and Northern Quebec, as well as those resident outside the traditional territory. Sustainable development, and the relationship between economic development and environmental protection, are vital issues to the Inuit of Canada.

It is important to understand the Inuit view of sustainable development. Over the thousands of years that Inuit have lived in the Canadian North, we have come to see ourselves as the custodians of these vast lands. Our relationship with the land, the creatures, and the environment has enabled us not only to survive, but to celebrate life in a land that often seems harsh and forbidding.

The Inuit approach to the environment arises, not out of some abstract philosophy but out of our history of struggling to survive day-to-day, season-to-season, year-to-year. It has provided a concrete guide to living that has served well

75

for many centuries and is still of crucial importance today. Country food (fish and wild game) is still the cheapest and most nutritious food in the Arctic. It is a staple for most Inuit.

In the area of "trade, environment, and competitiveness," there are two major areas of concern for Inuit: one focuses on tariff and non-tariff barriers to trade; the other on government subsidies and incentives.

The northern economy is a *mixed* economy. With the exception of government administrative centres, it is community based, combining hunting for the table with small enterprises and limited wage employment. It is also an open economy. Inuit have always been a trading people, often moving goods for thousands of miles.

The question for Inuit economic development today is: "What do we have that is unique?" We are asking: "Where do our comparative advantages lie? In what areas can we trade *and compete* effectively?" In addition to spectacular tourist destinations, we are finding, more and more, that our advantages lie in the unique renewable resources of the North and the unique skills and experience that Inuit have in utilizing those resources. The renewable resource base is finite. We have to be inventive and find ways to build employment and technical skills, and add more value to our products locally. New skills must grow out of the old. If there is no market for raw seal pelts, then we can move into tanning the skins and marketing fine leather products.

Our goal is to pursue economic development, self-sufficiency, and a higher standard of living but, at the same time, we must also maintain our great natural resources, traditional skills, culture and way of life if we are to retain our Inuit identity. Inuit have unique skills; the Arctic has unique resources. From this base, we can create and market unique products that will satisfy the consumer's demand for "environmentally friendly" goods, without compromising our Inuit heritage or the future availability of the resources.

There is very little real advantage in the giant resource extraction projects that have been promoted as government policy in the past. In fact, large-scale mineral or energy development is probably costlier in the Arctic than anywhere else in the world, except in Antarctica or at the bottom of the sea. Studies have shown (to no-one's surprise) that, once government incentives and subsidies are removed, many of these large projects are no longer profitable and capital investment moves on to greener pastures. Furthermore, these projects have a limited life-span and limited benefits for Inuit and they perpetuate a severe boom-bust cycle in the northern economy.

There are other considerations which challenge the long-term viability of megaproject development as a model for the north. Environmental costs must be included in any cost-benefit analysis. We are only now beginning to receive the environmental clean-up bills for past mining and drilling projects. By their very nature, these projects are often damaging to the environment, to public health, and to renewable resources such as wildlife. There is no sense in running up huge clean-up bills (whether on short, medium, or long term credit, and whether individual corporations, governments or society as a whole will have to pay) while simultaneously compromising our natural renewable resource base and our future ability to settle those bills.

These resources are crucial to our future. I am talking about the seals, the caribou, the whales, the fish, the musk-ox, and the polar bears. I am also talking about the skills of our entrepreneurs, our hunters, our seamstresses and our carvers. Looking around the Arctic, I see that the real success stories are mostly renewable resource based, adding more value to locally-produced goods, and creating more diverse and marketable products. Self-sufficiency and an integrated economy are the long term goals. Inuit wish to have both a secure country food supply and diverse cash crops.

There is no doubt that so-called environmental

regulations have effectively become non-tariff trade restrictions. I am sure that many people already have an idea of the damage that some non-tariff barriers have caused to the northern economy. Studies confirm the damage that anti-fur, anti-sealing, and anti-whaling sanctions have already done. Examples would be the *US Marine Mammals Protection Act* which forbids trade in seal skins, bone carvings, or other whale products, and the European Community's ban on seal products. I do not even accept those sanctions as environmental protection, when so little is done about the toxic contamination of these same animals, on which we depend for food.

There are other trade restrictions that cause us problems. The Free Trade Agreement opened Canada's north-south trade but it did not address circumpolar trade restrictions. For example, when the market for seal pelts was effectively destroyed by anti-sealing pressure groups, the hunters began to look for alternate markets. Sealskin makes a high quality leather, so people in Pangnirtung and Broughton Island tried to ship seal skins a mere 300 miles across the Davis Strait to Qeqertarsuaq, Greenland, for tanning on consignment. They found that they would have to pay import duties on the full value of the tanned hides, making the proposition completely uneconomic.

We have also run into domestic trade restrictions. Often, federal, provincial, and territorial regulations are not designed for the northern context. For example, in order to market wild meat, the carcasses must be federally inspected. Portable abattoirs, complete with meat inspectors, are brought by helicopter to wherever the hunters and game are. As a result of this inefficiency, prices are too high for anything other than a luxury market.

Inuit are not waiting to be rescued by big capital projects or government subsidies. We are trying to get government to recognize and encourage the viability and self-sufficiency of our economy. There is a perception that Inuit are unfairly favoured with government handouts but no economy in the world operates with a pure 'free market'. In Canada, federal, provincial, territorial and municipal governments all play a significant role in economic decision-making. Inuit reject the stereotype of passive recipients of handouts in a welfare economy. We want to assist all levels of government in defining the most rational and cost-effective ways of helping us strengthen our economy.

When grain farmers are in trouble, or a steel mill is on the rocks, governments will step in with bail-outs, refinancing, and retraining but when the fur market goes through the floor, the hunters and trappers do not get any assistance. In fact, since 1987, the federal government has vetoed attempts by aboriginal land claim organizations to get modest support programs included in their agreements - even though the hunter income support program is widely recognized as one of the most successful components of the 1976 James Bay and Northern Québec Agreement.

One example of innovation gives me real hope for economic development in the North. I have discussed the dead end of some initial efforts to find alternate products and markets for seal skins Fortunately that was not the end of the story. With the Inuit Tapirisat of Canada's support, an integrated and environmentally safe tannery has been established at Broughton Island. Considerable value is added to the product at the community level and this enables the hunters to continue earning money with their traditional, and finely developed, skills.

The tannery's only by-products are soapy water and sawdust. It is also integrated into many other aspects of the local economy: seal meat is sold in the community or in other northern communities; seal oil can be mixed with heating oil for local use in conventional furnaces; the leather is used by a local sewing group, in addition to being marketed outside the community.

Our traditional Inuit ways and values are often seen as archaic, outdated and useless in today's world. Yet more and more, we find that the world still has a place for our unique skills and resources. Whether for smoked Arctic char, or for fine leather from seal skins, markets are growing and our people are finding business opportunities and productive, marketable uses for their knowledge.

Finally, I would like to link trade, environment and competitiveness with another issue that is of crucial importance to us. The skills we have used to survive in our hostile environment are being developed into the skills required to survive in the global economy. The values which supported traditional Inuit self-government are the basis for the inherent right to self-government which we intend to have entrenched in the current constitutional reform process. Defining our emerging role in Canadian federalism will allow us to find our niches in the global market and exploit them as efficiently as possible.

C
Federal Government Roles

7

The Government of Canada
Frank Oberle

The Honourable Frank Oberle is the Minister of Forestry, a position he has held since 1989. Prior to that, he was Minister of State for Science and Technology. He was first elected to Parliament in 1972 and has served on numerous Standing and Special Committees, pursuing his special interests in Regional Economic Development, the Natural Resource sectors, Indian Affairs and Northern Development. He has published a number of major reports on national issues including The Green Ghetto, Equity and Fairness, Human Resources Paradox *and* Reviving the Canadian Dream.

Everywhere, the relationship between the economy and the environment is being constantly refined in an effort to strike an acceptable balance between economic and environmental well-being, and between economic and environmental health. This has created a dilemma, of recent vintage, that has started to crowd its way into the public conscience and consciousness. As with most public policy issues, there are two extremes but, on environmental issues, there seems to be a larger distance than usual between the poles of the environmental spectrum.

Education may be the most effective means of bridging this gap. Everyone must understand that the economy and the environment are forever linked and cannot be uncoupled. Canadians must continue to create wealth if they are to live in tolerable comfort in a country with a harsh climate and expansive geography. Only new wealth can create new growth and further improvements in social conditions - but progress cannot be measured only in terms of increased volumes or size. Canadians must better understand the implications of industrial activities and then devise intelligent action plans to balance economic opportunities with environmental responsibilities.

This process is well under way in Canada. Norms of acceptable environmental behaviour, both national and international, are being developed and respected.

Forestry provides a fascinating case study of the various elements at play in the environment and economy debate. At the local level, the "jobs versus trees" argument is strident, emotionally charged and, regrettably, one that sometimes ends in violent confrontation. Regionally and nationally, the importance of the forestry industry cannot be overstated. From coast to coast, 350 communities live or die by the forest. The economic well-being of Canada is reliant on the foreign trade earnings of the forestry sector. Internationally, broad political and social policy issues arise from the perception of other countries as to how Canadians manage their forests; thus, market and trade considerations intrude.

In trying to reconcile an array of competing interests, the Government has made the principle of sustainable development a cornerstone of its forestry policy. The new Forestry Act imposes a legislated obligation on the incumbent minister to promote sustainable development and to report annually to Parliament on the state of Canada's forests. Sustainable development is a phrase that has gained wide currency. It has also acquired differing definitions. For the sake of simplicity, however, it can be thought of as leaving the planet a better place than we found it.

The federal government possesses, and has effectively employed, some very useful tools to promote the sustainable development of our forests. Among the most important are the Forest Resource Development Agreements (FRDA) between individual provinces and the federal government. In the last round of these agreements, which spanned the period from 1984 to 1989, the Government spent $1.1 billion in pursuit of certain objectives which are part of its National Forest Sector Strategy. These include research, technology transfer, education, training and public information. More important, however, is the greater emphasis on longer term perspectives that has resulted in more integrated and intensive management regimes. These are the principle components of the agreements and, together, they represent a shift from sustained yield to sustainable development, and a corresponding shift from forest management to forest ecosystem management.

Funds spent on improving the health of Canadian forests through these agreements and other government programs, whether provincial or federal, provide incalculable long term benefits. As their knowledge and depth of understanding of environmental issues grows, more and more Canadians are reaching the middle ground of the debate. While there are still "tree spikers" and "develop at any cost" advocates, there is steady progress in the public debate toward an equilibrium.

Sustainable development not only imposes obligations on those in the public and private sector who would profit from Canadian forests, but it also confers rights. Among the obligations is the requirement to manage prudently not only the traditional commercial aspects of the resource, but also its less tangible, non-timber values. These latter values are important but it is only recently that they have begun to get the recognition they deserve and a start has been made in accounting for them.

In regard to acquired rights, providing a forest manager has complied with the obligations of sustainable development - of putting back more than was taken out - he or she should have right of tenure, the right to harvest, and the right to manufacture and market forest products from sustainably-managed stands, without risk of arbitrary barriers erected by unfair or uninformed prejudice within Canada or abroad.

When Marshall McLuhan spoke of the "global village" so many years ago, he was referring to the way modern communications have shrunk the world. That shrinkage means that what is done in Canada does not escape

85

international scrutiny for very long. Because Canada possesses 10% of the world's forest, and because it is the second largest country in the world, Canadian practices have an impact on the global environment, an impact far out of proportion to this country's population.

This imposes serious obligations for all Canadians. Forests are not only one of the main engines of the Canadian economy but they are also a principal element of the ecological structures that sustain life on the planet. They are a global heritage that has been entrusted to Canada to be nurtured and maintained for all humanity.

Canadians are conscious of these obligations. Their forests are a part of their psyche, their identity as a nation, their self image. The creation of the National Parks Service, one hundred years ago, is a manifestation of how deeply rooted is the concern for the natural environment in Canadian culture and history. Recently, the Government launched another far-reaching initiative - the Green Plan - in which forests and forestry play a prominent role. It is the most progressive, far-sighted environmental commitment any nation has undertaken thus far. It will provide benchmarks against which Canadians and the buyers of Canadian forest products can measure the quality of Canada's stewardship of this global asset.

To be sensitive to environmental concerns and be a good corporate citizen makes good business sense. Enlightened self-interest is one of the most potent forces in the business world to ensure its long-term security and growth. One can ignore customer demands and legitimate public concerns for only so long before the price becomes too steep. Thus, it is important to be proactive with regard to the environment and, as with quality control in industry, it is usually cheaper to do it right the first time. The supermarket shopping cart resembles the world market in a microcosm and the "green label" has become as important a marketing tool as quality and price in the battle for market share.

If there are concerns about Canadian forestry practices

in countries where Canada sells its wood and paper, Canadians should put them to rest. They should find ways to show the world that Canadians are using enlightened, modern management to harvest the forests. Canadians do not blithely dismiss public fears and anxieties about the environment, no matter how misplaced. Failure to respond openly and quickly to such fears can inspire consumer boycotts and the erection of trade barriers.

I travelled to Europe, in October 1991, to try to dispel some of the mistaken ideas about forestry practices in Canada. It is reassuring to Europeans that Canada will preserve a full 12% of its entire space in a natural state, an area which will amount to 1.2 million square kilometres. That is one of Canada's Green Plan commitments. Most Europeans were unaware that, some time ago, Canada imposed a ban on leaded motor fuels and much stricter automobile emission standards than those which are the norm in Europe. They were surprised to learn that their farmers are using six times the amount of chemical fertilizers than would be allowed in Canada.

It is tempting to use comparisons like these to evaluate and rationalize Canadian performance but, in the end, it is not very useful as a marketing tool. It is always easier to practise virtue from a distance.

The market place should be fair and, whether among provinces or among countries, the ground rules should be reasonably equal. This will take time because of the different stages of development among the various political units. In Canada and other industrialized nations, public opinion at the check-out counter imposes its own form of environmental discipline. At the international level, however, achieving compliance to higher standards will require a different approach. All agree on the need to avoid situations where investment decisions are based on taking advantage of lower environmental standards to achieve cost advantages. That is why there is a need for a new global order embracing a myriad of environmental issues and imperatives - such as cross-border pollution, ozone depletion, global warming and climate change - just as human rights, peace and security issues have become supra-national in scope.

Canadians are among the world leaders in partnerships and strategic alliances and are prepared to make the necessary initiatives to forge new rules and standards - and to enforce them.

Canada will always be a forestry nation. Over time, however, we will have to lessen our economic dependence on the forest products trade. But with every passing day, the intrinsic value of this precious resource increases. The forests Canadians are preserving in their natural state today, and those they are managing in accordance with enlightened forestry practices, will become shrines in a world that increases its human population by 100 million every year. The Network of Model Forests which will be established under the Green Plan will be targeted for the most intensive treatment possible. Using the latest in modern technology and science will yield new knowledge and a better understanding of how much human intervention nature can sustain without harm.

That knowledge can, and will, be used to address problems in other regions of the world - problems that are infinitely more serious than those Canadians are addressing at home. Forests in the tropical regions of the planet are being depleted at a rate of 17 million hectares a year. Only about 12% of the volume of the fibre from this area is converted to wood products, for the rest is used for fuel or is simply burned to make room for subsistence agriculture. The threats to the tropical forest are poverty and hunger. Europeans, who sleep well because they have banned the importation of hardwoods from such forests, may not be spared from the spectre of massive losses of forest cover.

Canada's commitment to and concern for the survival and preservation of forests in the world's tropical regions remains high on its international policy agenda. Even now, Canada is spending in excess of $100 million every year to support projects that assist developing countries with the management of their forests. It is a record of which Canadians can be proud.

In respecting the environment, Canada's trade interests are not damaged, nor is its competitiveness diminished. Indeed, the opposite may very well be true. The alert, astute marketer, who first recognizes changing trends in public attitudes, will gain by meeting new customer demands. There are exciting new prospects in the development of environmental technology and services. One should recall what happened to candle-makers when Edison came along.

The biggest threat to the health of Canadian business may well be of Canada's own making. The EEC is now a 12 nation free trade zone for all goods, services, capital and labour that may eventually grow to embrace between 24 and 30 countries. Yet, in Canada, current discussions focus on dismantling trade barriers so that, by 1995, one might be able to buy a bottle of New-Brunswick's Moosehead in an Ontario pub.

This narrow parochialism, forced on many Canadian businesses through well-meaning but misguided regionalism, works against Canadians in the international sphere. Too often Canadian industries are not able to develop the critical mass at home that is needed to be able to successfully compete in global markets.

That is why the proposal that provincial trade barriers be removed was a key part of the Government's constitutional reform package. Knocking down interprovincial barriers will not solve *all* Canada's competitiveness problems but it would be an important first step.

Canada is more dependent on foreign trade than almost any other major nation in the world. Canadians are liked and respected just about everywhere, but that does not obviate the need for Canadian industry to be competitive. That is why the Government has launched its new Prosperity Initiative. There is precious little charity in the word so, unless Canadians learn to combine all their energies - in industry, labour and government - they will fail in realizing Canadian potential in international markets. That is what the Initiative is about. To win the day, Canadian products must be competitive in price, quality and service as well as being made in accordance with acceptable environmental standards.

8

External Affairs and International Trade, Canada
Louise Frechette

Louise Frechette is Canada's Permanent Representative and Ambassador at the United Nations in New York, after serving as the Assistant Deputy Minister, Economic Policy and Trade Competitiveness, at the Department of External Affairs and International Trade, Canada. Prior to that, she held a number of positions at EAITC, including Assistant Deputy Minister, Latin American and Caribbean Branch; Canadian Ambassador to Argentina and Uruguay; Director, European Summit Countries Division; Deputy Director, Trade Policy Division; and Deputy Director, Western European Division. She holds degrees from the College of Europe, Bruges, Belgium, the Université de Montréal, and College Basile Moreau.

There are, internationally, several developments on the environmental agenda that will affect Canada's trade interests and its ability to compete abroad. Indeed, as far as governments are concerned, the environment is definitely a growth industry. Hardly a week goes by without at least one international meeting of experts to address some aspect of the environmental agenda. The environment has become a regular item on the agenda of major world gatherings, from the annual Economic Summits to meetings of Commonwealth and Francophonie leaders.

The pace is such that many smaller countries find it difficult to keep up with negotiations that have the potential to affect significantly their economic and trading prospects. In 1991 alone, Canada was host to several such meetings, including the Halifax meeting on land-based sources of marine pollution, the Montreal meeting on environmental information, the meeting of the Executive Committee of the Montreal Ozone Protocol and the Yellowknife meeting on Arctic environmental cooperation.

Increasingly, environmental negotiations are moving beyond rhetorical declarations to concentrate on concrete commitments and enforcement provisions. In the course of a decade, the United Nations Economic Commission for Europe negotiated the first framework agreement on the long range transport of air pollution - in effect the first "acid rain" convention - and binding protocols on the reduction of sulphur and nitrogen oxides emissions. It is currently developing new instruments to cover other types of air pollutants.

International negotiations on the ozone problem proceeded at an even more rapid pace. Two years after the Vienna convention took force, the Montreal Ozone protocol, signed in 1988, provided for the gradual elimination of CFCs. The protocol was reviewed in 1990 and agreement was reached on an accelerated phase-out of these substances. A multilateral fund was set up to help developing countries meet the objectives of the protocol.

Preparations are now under way for the United Nations Conference on Environment and Development (UNCED). It will be held in Rio de Janeiro in June 1992. UNCED will be a land-mark event marking not only the conclusion of a number of major negotiations but also the beginning of a new phase in international environmental cooperation.

It is anticipated that there will be three main results of UNCED:

• The *first* is the signing of the first international convention on climate change, which will deal with emissions of greenhouse gases.

• The *second* is the signing of a framework convention on biodiversity for the protection of, and access to, genetic resources.

• The *third* is the adoption of "Agenda 21", an action plan for international cooperation on the full range of environmental issues from desertification to hazardous wastes, deforestation to problems of the urban environment, and the full range of issues related to the oceans, including

92

land-based sources of marine pollution, coastal management and the protection of living marine resources. Agenda 21 will also address issues related to institutional and financial support as well as technology transfers. Developing countries attach very high priority to these issues. Satisfactory solutions will have to be found if we are to obtain the cooperation that is required to address successfully the global problems threatening our planet.

Clearly, the goals set for UNCED are very ambitious. It remains to be seen how far the international community is prepared to go at this stage. There will be difficult negotiations to resolve differences, not only between developed and developing countries, but also among industrialized nations themselves. Sooner or later, however, agreements will be found that will impose new disciplines on production processes and trade flows. Energy and energy-intensive sectors will be affected by negotiations on climate change. Some industrial sectors, like the pharmaceutical industry, have a stake in the biodiversity negotiations. Existing instruments, such as the Ozone Protocol and the Basel Convention on the Transport of Hazardous Wastes, already contain provisions that have a direct impact on trade.

The need to harmonize and reconcile environmental concerns and existing trade rules is well recognized. In both the OECD and in the GATT, work is under way to develop a conceptual framework to deal with the two essential facets of the trade/environment issue:

• on the one hand, the need to ensure that the trade rules accommodate legitimate restrictions to trade for environmental reasons and thus protect countries from "environmental dumping"; and

• on the other hand, the need to prevent "green protectionism" or unwarranted restrictions to trade under the guise of environmental protection.

Bringing greater clarity and understanding to these issues is urgently required. National and international environmental rules are evolving rapidly and will present the trading system with difficult dilemmas.

Consider the Montreal Ozone Protocol, which restricts trade among contracting Parties of goods containing CFCs and other specified substances: would a similar restriction imposed on a non-contracting Party stand up in the GATT if challenged by a GATT member? A US ban on imports of tuna from Mexico on the basis of an American law designed to protect dolphins has already been challenged in the GATT, where a panel ruled the measure inadmissible under the GATT. Such disputes are likely to multiply over the coming years. They will severely test the existing system.

In addition to the global agenda, there is intense activity taking place within North America. Canada and the US are busy dealing with a long list of transboundary issues. These include the implementation of the Acid Rain agreement, sewage treatment on the West Coast and water quality on the Great Lakes. Concerns about the environment in Mexico, raised in connection with the negotiations for a North American Free Trade Agreement, are being addressed with a view to ensuring enforcement of adequate environmental standards. More broadly, the strengthening of environmental consciousness in the US and many of our other trading partners also creates new pressures that can affect our economic and trading interests.

Against this background of fast-moving international negotiations and increased popular awareness of environmental challenges, four basic elements underlie the Canadian Government's strategy internationally:

• The *first* is to be at the table and to exercise leadership. Exercising leadership does not mean being the "greenest" - it means using our influence, and the considerable credibility we enjoy with the international community on environmental issues, to shape agreements in a way that will best serve our interests and meet our objectives. Many of the draft texts currently under consideration in the UNCED preparatory conference were "made-in-Canada".

94

This is all to our advantage.

• The *second* element is to involve, as much as possible, the full range of stakeholders in the discussion of Canadian positions. The business community, indigenous people and a variety of NGOs are consulted regularly and are represented on the Canadian delegation to the UNCED preparatory meetings. There are also extensive consultations going on regarding the climate change and biodiversity negotiations. The International Trade Advisory Committee (ITAC) is involved in the discussions of trade-related environmental issues. Environmental NGOs have been invited to join the group. The issues involved are so far reaching as to require a real "concertation" among the key players.

• The *third* element of the Canadian government's strategy is to pursue a multilateral codification of the trade-environment links. Canadians have been among the first to press the OECD and the GATT to address the issues. On this, as on other trade issues, Canada continues to believe that a well-functioning multilateral system better serves Canadian interests than a world ruled by "la loi du plus fort".

• The *fourth* and last element is to actively support the promotion abroad and the export of Canadian environmentally-friendly products and technologies. The transfer of such technology is an essential part of the solution to the globe's current environmental problems. It also presents tremendous opportunities for those countries and those companies that are able to anticipate the changes being brought about by the need to conserve the environment and develop the technologies that will be required world-wide.

The environment is, indeed, a growth industry for governments, as it is also bound to be for the private sector. Japan is developing a 100 year Plan with a view to establishing its domination over the world market for clean technologies. This is a clear signal that the environment can indeed mean good business.

9

The Department of the Environment
Leonard Good

Leonard Good has been Deputy Minister of the Environment since May 1989. Prior to that he held various government positions, including Deputy Secretary to the Cabinet (Plans), Privy Council Office; Associate Deputy Minister for Energy, Department of Energy, Mines and Resources; and Senior Assistant Deputy Minister for Energy. He has taught at the University of Prince Edward Island in Charlottetown. He holds a BA in Economics and Political Science and an MA in Economics from the University of Toronto, and a PhD in Economics from the University of Western Ontario.

Canadians are living in very complex times; a fact reinforced everyday with media images from around the world portraying dramatic changes in the Eastern bloc, the Middle East and, indeed, all parts of the globe. These changes hint at the emergence of a "new world order" where the old rules of international trade and diplomacy no longer apply. There is a growing interdependence among nations. The world is getting smaller. Marshall McLuhan's dictum of the "Global village" has long ceased to be an abstract theory and has become reality with an infinite number of new and complex issues which must be addressed.

One of the most critical and complex of these new issues is the link between trade and the environment. In the past, these terms were considered by business and government to be almost mutually exclusive. However, with people becoming more aware of the environmental problems facing the world, the inextricable link between trade and the environment is becoming more evident. This has led to increased interest in developing trade policies that do not adversely effect the environment, and vice-versa.

Governments around the world are gradually dismantling barriers to trade and negotiating bilateral and multilateral trade agreements. At the same time, people are demanding comprehensive legislation to ensure the integration of environmental issues with these agreements. However, developing this trade and environment link is proving to be a very difficult task and does not seem likely to become any easier in the future. The new competitiveness in global trade has made it extremely difficult to pursue policies which are seen to give one nation an unfair competitive advantage over another.

Most nations still view the environmental regulations of their trading partners as indirect means of protecting inefficient industries and, unfortunately, this is often the case. Increased global competition has led to a dramatic restructuring of the global economy. It has also resulted in an increase in corporate failures and subsequent job dislocation in many countries. In these difficult economic times, many nations are resorting to enacting any legislation that will indirectly protect their industries. As a result, despite the obvious link with the trade and environment issue, it is, and will remain, a politically explosive and economically important issue for a long time.

Environmental/Economic Integration: A Broader Perspective

It is imperative that the relationship between trade and the environment be considered within the broader context of the integration of the environment and the economy. One cannot afford to lose sight of this fundamental issue. Integration of the environment with all sectors of the economy, not just trade, is the key to developing a global society which embraces the principles of sustainable development as set out in the World Commission on Environment and Development's 1987 report, *Our Common Future.*

This report, commissioned by the United Nations, was an outgrowth of an environmental revolution which began in the 1980s. Almost simultaneously, in all parts of the world, people suddenly became conscious of the fact that serious environmental problems were jeopardizing the lives of children and future generations. This sudden awareness led to a revolution that called for fundamental changes in business practice and decision-making. The people led the way in demanding the integration of environmental and economic decision-making. Green consumerism was a manifestation of this environmental revolution. It became so popular in most western countries that many governments responded with government sponsored labelling programs. In light of the public's enhanced awareness of environmental issues, most governments and opposition political parties also developed comprehensive environmental platforms.

Government and Business Taking Action

The Canadian government responded to this grass roots environmental movement by producing the "Green Plan", in which the federal government identified three key areas in which it could contribute toward the integration of the environment and the economy: the development of better inputs, better processes, and better instruments and regulations.

• Developing better inputs means improving the information available on the environment. The Government intends to enhance its ability to gather and to disseminate information through better science and better knowledge of ecosystems. In its monitoring and measuring of progress, or lack thereof, the Government's annual State of the Environment report also serves to inform both the private and public sectors. Finally, the Government is actively engaged in the development of educational programs which promote conservation of the environment as well as the broader concept of sustainable development.

• Developing better processes involves developing more relevant means of assessing environmental impacts and initiating active dialogues with all sectors of the economy. The Government is developing more comprehensive environmental assessment processes to ensure environmental concerns are included in all large scale developments. It is also actively soliciting advice from other bodies such as round tables, NGOs, business organizations, academics, and the general public on how to improve existing processes and to determine what processes are needed to ensure the integration of environmental and economic decision making, both at home and abroad.

• In order to develop better instruments and regulation, the Government is reviewing current environmental legislation with a view toward developing an optimal mix of economic instruments or tools, as opposed to developing more stringent environmental regulations. This review has been initiated with the active support of business, environmental groups, and the academic community.

Business is also responding to the public's demand for further integration of environmental and economic decision making. The introduction of green products is the most visible effort corporations are making to improve the environment. However, many larger corporations have initiated less publicized, internal environmental programs to ensure that sensitivity to environmental issues is reflected in corporate philosophy.

The creation of environmental vice-president positions, and the production of environmental audits and progress reports, are two typical methods being used by corporations to ensure the development of environmentally sensitive management practices. Business is also making a concerted effort to become more active in working with governments to develop strategies for promoting environmental/

economic integration. Participation on round tables by business executives is an excellent example of business working to improve the environment.

These actions of government and business are orientated toward domestic environmental and economic integration. The issue of trade-environment links, on the other hand, is external in its orientation. This does not diminish the efforts of government and business programs to integrate environmental/economic decision-making. It does, however, point to the limitations currently faced by governments and business on linking environmental issues with international trade agreements.

The issue of trade-environment links is still not clearly defined. Developed and less developed countries view these links from radically different perspectives. Developing nations are just recognizing that freer trade is the key to their development. They see the trend toward integrating environment and economy as a means by which developed nations can continue to prosper at the expense of the developing nations. They view the trade-environment link as another barrier to trade which will effectively stifle the growth of smaller and less developed economies. As a result, bilateral and multilateral negotiations that have attempted to develop this linkage have been largely ineffectual. For the most part, governments have been left to enact domestic legislation in the hope that it will have some residual effects on the environmental practices of their trading partners, particularly those in the Third World.

NAFTA: A New Stage in the Trade-Environment Link

The North American Free Trade Agreement (NAFTA) negotiations could, however, prove to be a ground-breaking process in developing the trade and environment linkage. Negotiations are proceeding along three tracks:

- *First,* environmental issues are included as an integral

part of sectoral negotiations. This means that advisory groups representing specific industries are playing a key advisory role in the attempt to incorporate sector-specific environmental issues in the trade agreement.

• *Second,* broad environmental issues are being included at the macro level where the Canadian, US and Mexican governments are negotiating a broader trilateral agreement.

• *Third,* a trilateral environmental policy statement is being developed and will be released upon conclusion of the negotiations. These negotiations are unprecedented in their inclusion of all sectors of society in the process and the chances of negotiating an agreement that is acceptable to all parties are, therefore, greatly enhanced. The deal is more likely to have the approval of a majority of Canadian, American and Mexican citizens.

Despite the ground-breaking nature of these negotiations, there remain many stumbling blocks to successfully linking trade and the environment. In particular, broader issues, such as competitiveness versus abuse and national sovereignty, must be considered in the integration of environmental concerns and trade agreements. Many nations still view environmental regulation as a form of protectionism. Environmental legislation that is applied to product standards of imports is not a significant problem as most nations accept the premise that any government has the right to set product standards that apply to all goods being sold within its national borders.

Environmental legislation and the application of its process standards to imports, however, is a controversial issue. It brings to light a bigger and much more important issue: the sovereign rights of a nation. Does any nation have the right to question how an imported product was processed as long as it meets domestic product standards? Does any nation have the right to impose its environmental standards on another? Until recently, the answer was an unequivocal: "no". However, as understanding grows about the trans-border nature of environmental problems

- acid rain, and soil erosion are but two - it becomes clear that one cost of negotiating bilateral and multilateral trade agreements will be the requirement to relinquish some control over domestic environmental policy.

Another issue raised by the application of environmental regulations to the process standards of imports is the ensuing trade-off between competitiveness and abuse. In the past, unilateral environmental actions tended to protect inefficient industries from competition by foreign producers. In a dynamic, competitive, global society, the implementation of unilateral environmental legislation by developed nations could have negative effects on their competitive positions. This same legislation, however, would have disastrous effects on the ability of less developed countries to compete internationally.

In order to create a level playing field between developed and developing countries, it is clear that GATT rules related to trade and environmental issues need to be re-examined. There is an obvious need for international conventions which truly develop the trade-environment link. Finally, it is clear that harmonization of environmental standards is required. This can only be achieved through multilateral, as opposed to unilateral, action.

Conclusion

Canada's role in developing the trade-environment link at the project, institutional and conference level has been forceful. Despite this, Canadians recognize the need to develop the link further. The overall pattern of trade and the environment is not yet clear. One can only hope that the United Nations Conference on Environment and Development (UNCED) will provide an opportunity to develop the process and will create the framework which will allow all nations to pull together.

103

10
The Department of Industry, Science and Technology
Harry G Rogers

Harry G Rogers is Deputy Minister of the Department of Industry, Science and Technology. Prior to this he was Deputy Minister of Revenue Canada, Taxation and served as the first Comptroller General of Canada. He has held various senior executive positions with Xerox in Canada and the US, including Vice-President Operations (Canada). He was also general manager of the Ford Motor Company in Japan. He is a Director of the Niagara Institute and a member of the National Council on Education of the Conference Board of Canada, the Interim Board of Directors of the Sustainable Development Education Program, and the Federal Business Development Bank.

The reality of links must be clearly understood if one is to appreciate government's role in, and reaction to, the trade, competitiveness and environmental equation. Not many years ago, senior bureaucrats from different departments would have sung completely different tunes on this subject. That is because, in the old days, they tended to adhere pretty strictly to the narrow terms of their mandates and left a lot of the "big picture," the vision or overview, to their political masters in Cabinet and to certain central agencies.

That is certainly not the case today. The Department of Industry, Science and Technology Canada (ISTC) is proof of how things have changed. ISTC's mission statement reads, "Promoting International Competitiveness and Excellence in Canadian Industry, Science and Technology". As a mission, it is clear and straightforward but as a task it is not so easy. It is not simply a matter of encouraging our industrial, scientific and technological communities to unite and use their combined talents to help Canada gain a competitive edge in the world marketplace. ISTC must also fulfil its departmental mission within the context of the Government's overall agenda.

In this case, the word "links" looms very large. Not only is ISTC charged with playing a major role in the national prosperity initiative, but it must do so in a manner that is compatible with other Government goals. It must encourage prosperity through competitiveness while at the same time enhancing Canadian unity, individual human dignity, and environmental well-being. ISTC must also be mindful of regional sensitivities, aboriginal aspirations, cultural imperatives, social responsibilities and environmental integrity. Every policy initiative it proposes, every program it recommends, must be considered from dozens of perspectives.

ISTC fosters excellence, efficiency, productivity and international competitiveness while, at the same time, paying more than lip service to the environmental imperative. It colours its mandate green in several ways:

• *First*, it undertakes joint policy ventures with Environment Canada to develop integrated, consistent, rational and workable solutions and initiatives in the areas of sustainable development and industrial regulation. In this area, confusion is the enemy. The Government's many departmental voices must all be delivering the same environmental message.

• *Second*, it has taken a very pro-active role in helping to develop an environmental industry in Canada. It helped set up the Canadian Environmental Industries Association (CEIA). Its officers in that sector work hard to find North American and European markets for the products Association members develop and produce.

•*Third*, ISTC also funds specific environmental programs. One is the St. Lawrence River Environmental Technology Development Program, intended to help clean up that national treasure. It assists industries along the St. Lawrence to adopt or adapt new technologies that will reduce the emissions of harmful substances into the waterway.

Part of ISTC's mandate is to work with broad sectors of the economy to help them become more competitive. This is done through ISTC's Sector Campaigns. Typically, ISTC officials work with a defined group of industries (for example, automotive parts manufacturers or the forestry industry) to help them find ways to make themselves more productive and better able to hold market share. Nothing in the departmental mandate directs them to consider environmental concerns when structuring these campaigns but, increasingly, they are doing just that.

For example, ISTC has initiated a "sector campaign" in the Pulp and Paper industry. As part of this campaign, it has entered into a Memorandum of Understanding aimed directly at environmental problems. It did so by linking its mandate to develop new, more productive industrial technologies with the Government's stated commitment to help put an end to dirty industrial practices. Industries in the sector know that if they utilize new technologies to limit pollution, they will qualify for financial assistance to add to their own incremental technology investments.

In general terms, ISTC views it as its duty to convince industry that environmental integrity can be a competitive advantage. It is working hard to make its officials more sensitive to the green challenge, and to work even harder to bring the message to their corporate clients. The message is that green makes sense. While it may cost money - in the short run - to protect the environment, it saves money in the longer term. It opens up new markets and it makes one more competitive in a world where more and more consumers want to play their part in saving the planet. By directing their dollars to environmentally sensitive industries, consumers can perceive themselves and these industries as friends of the earth.

For example, Black's Camera has made a financial commitment and marketed "System Crystal", which cuts pollution by way of a "closed loop" recycling system: chemicals are filtered and not dumped; water is cleansed and re-cycled, not adulterated and flushed into the sewage system. Black's "use and dump" days are over.

There were costs in bringing "System Crystal" on stream but they have been more than offset by the good public relations and customer interest this has generated and, in the long term, many liabilities may have been limited. In ten, twenty or thirty years, Black's competitors may find themselves facing heavy clean-up charges for the damage they are doing today. So, investments such as this can be very good for the bottom line as well as for one's peace of mind.

ISTC tracks environmental success stories, and makes sure manufacturers hear about them:

• Other steel mills should know that Dofasco in Hamilton will save close to a $1.5 million dollars in energy costs each year because it spent $17 million on new fume collection hoods for its steel production furnaces. The hoods are primarily designed to cut carbon monoxide and sulphur dioxide emissions. On the positive side of the ledger is free steam, a by-product which is a wonderful source of heat.

• Chemical users should know that Galvantic Industries in Dartmouth, Nova Scotia, has remarkably cut the volume of waste in its galvanizing plants by 95%. Less waste means lower waste disposal costs. The new process will pay for itself in less than two years.

• All ISTC's industrial clients should know that the effluents they now spend so much to dispose of may very well be a potential source of revenue. For years, General Motors of St. Catharines has been spending millions on liquid waste disposal. Much of what they were having trucked away was spent coolants, oils and detergents. Now, these wastes are being refined and costs are recouped through sales of the reclaimed oil to the highest bidder.

ISTC takes no credit for these success stories. What credit is due belongs to the industries themselves. But ISTC, is making an all-out effort to ensure that the stories do not remain best kept Canadian secrets. It is also encouraging other industries to follow suit.

ISTC's mandate is to build prosperity through

competitiveness. Its responsibility is to fulfil that mandate in ways that are compatible with the broader environmental challenges confronting Canadians today. The two goals are not incompatible. It is to be hoped that industry will weave competitiveness and environmental sensitivity into a revolutionary new Canadian corporate culture. That culture would declare freedom from pollution to be an inalienable right and would recognize the following propositions as self-evident:

- Environmental sensitivity is a competitive advantage.
- Environmental protection is a marketplace commodity.
- Environmental integrity is everyone's business.
- Environmental solutions outperform environmental regulations.
- Environmental problems do not recognize intra or international boundaries.

There is much more to international competitiveness and the reality of global markets, than business opportunities. There is more to Canada's prosperity initiative than a quest for a healthier bottom line. Government is committed to helping industry respond to the challenges of internationalism but it expects industry, in turn, to respond to the challenge of sustainable development. Together, Government and industry can meet both challenges. When they do, all Canadians will be the richer for it.

D
Regional Experiences

11

The North American Free Trade Agreement (NAFTA): The View from Washington
Joseph Greenwald

Joseph Greenwald is an attorney in Washington DC. He is also a member of the Editorial Advisory Board of Europe 1992, The Report on the Single European Market, a consultant to the US Council of the Mexico-US Business Committee, an adjunct professor at the American University Law School and recently chaired a GATT dispute panel. He has practised international trade law with the firm of Weil, Gotshal and Manges, and has represented the Bendix Corporation in the Far East and in Europe. He has also held a number of government positions, including Assistant Secretary of State for Economic and Business Affairs, US Ambassador to the European Communities, and US Ambassador to the Organization for Economic Cooperation and Development (OECD). Ambassador Greenwald received a BA from the University of Chicago, an LLB from Georgetown University and an MBA from Michigan State University.

How might the link between the environment and trade be dealt with in a North American Free Trade Agreement? To answer this question it is necessary, in turn, to analyze the elements of the environment and trade nexus, summarize the initial position of the United States Government regarding environment and the NAFTA, examine the relevant GATT provisions, review the relevant provisions in the US-Canada FTA and the European Community (Treaty of Rome), and discuss ways in which the environment could be handled in a NAFTA (including dispute settlement).

Environmental Issues in the NAFTA Negotiations

In the United States, the trade and environment issue emerged in public debate as a result of President Bush's request, on March 1, 1991, for the renewal of his "fast track" authority from the Congress to enter into a free trade area negotiation with Mexico and Canada. Environmental groups, allied with labour interests, opposed the extension, particularly for negotiations with Mexico. The debate and the lobbying revealed a fairly broad spectrum of views in the US environmental community. They ranged from extreme, doctrinaire positions against the proposed negotiations to more reasonable suggestions that environmental concerns be taken into account. Some of the environmental groups ended up supporting NAFTA negotiations.

The US debate was also marked by a great deal of rhetoric, expressing general, unfocused concern about the environmental impact of such a trade agreement. Many advocates voiced concern and opposition without being specific about the issues.

There are at least three categories of environmental problems which could come up in connection with a NAFTA:

• *First,* environmentalists talked about cross-border pollution problems. These issues, along with what are called global commons issues, are already the subject of multilateral or bilateral negotiations and agreements, whether or not there is a NAFTA.

• A *second* category of concerns for environmentalists is that products could be traded which did not meet US standards, either for the product itself or the process by which it was produced. This situation could directly raise problems regarding the protection of human, animal, or plant life or health.

• The *third* category, related to the second, deals with competitiveness. It concerns the effect of a NAFTA on both trade and investment. If environmental standards (or enforcement) in Mexico are more lax than those in the

United States and Canada, there will be trade and investment distortions. Trade in goods that are produced without the need to follow costly environmental laws and regulations would be considered unfair trade. Similarly, there could be an inducement to invest in Mexico to escape the higher standards in other countries. If a solution to such distortions were sought in harmonization of standards, the result could be environmental degradation. For federal systems, like the United States and Canada, this issue is further complicated by the existence of higher standards in particular states or provinces.

Initial Position of the US Administration

Some members of Congress took up the environmentalist cause. As part of the process of securing renewal of the "fast track" authority, the Administration agreed to submit an action plan addressing the concerns which had been raised about the proposed NAFTA. These concerns were contained in letters to the President from Chairmen Bentsen and Rostenkowski and from Majority Leader Gephardt. The President's response was submitted on May 1, 1991. On the same day, Chairman Rostenkowski of the House Ways and Means Committee announced his endorsement of the fast track extension.

The May 1 document is the most comprehensive statement available of the US position on NAFTA. Environment was one of the major areas covered. Much of the May 1 action plan is devoted to a description of what Mexico now does in the environmental field, a review of current US-Mexican cooperation to protect the environment, proposed methods for increasing informed public participation, undertaking an environmental review to ensure informed policy-making, and proposed future cooperative efforts to protect the environment.

In the Executive Summary, the May 1 paper draws a distinction between "Environmental Issues in the NAFTA" and "Joint Environmental Initiatives". Under the latter heading, it outlines an "ambitious program of cooperation" to be pursued "in parallel to the FTA negotiations". This follows the US-Canadian pattern, where the acid rain agreement was separately negotiated and signed. It will probably apply to cross-border or "global commons" issues in the NAFTA.

Part IV of the detailed administration position on environmental matters is entitled *"Environmental Trade Issues in the Free Trade Agreement"*. Its first sentence states "We intend to include environmental issues related to trade in the FTA". It then outlines several principles which will be guidelines for the US negotiators (but it is not clear whether or how they will be included in the FTA):

• The *first* set of principles is oriented to reassure those who fear lowering of standards: the United States will not agree to weaken US laws, regulations or standards in the FTA and will maintain enforcement. It also pledges to maintain the right of each party to take the necessary verifying measures within its own territory and to maintain the integrity of the US regulatory regime. Mixed in with these reassuring words about what the United States intends to do are a few principles stated in unilateral terms. These principles are non-discrimination (meaning, perhaps, national treatment), public participation in the regulatory process and use of available scientific evidence in the regulatory process.

• The *second* set of elements of the US position for inclusion as an integral part of NAFTA is related to the maintenance of US rights, "consistent with other international obligations", to limit trade in items or products controlled by international treaties to which the United States is a party. This section also identifies the US right to prohibit the entry of goods that do not meet US regulations. The principles mentioned above come back in (again, perhaps, unilaterally) with the qualification that the regulations must be based on science, not arbitrarily discriminate against imports, nor constitute a "disguised" trade barrier. The US paper gives these principles more status by suggesting the parties work together to enhance product standards. These are to be based on sound scientific evidence by sharing technical information and developing "an improved common basis" for environmental standards and by assuring "public participation in the regulatory process".

• The *final* section is headed "working together to promote improved enforcement of standards". It envisages activities, like joint meetings, to discuss enhancement of enforcement capability, exchange of information on analytical methodologies and training programs to instill Good Laboratory Practices. At the end of this section in the May 1 paper, there is a heading - dispute consultation mechanism - under which the US states:

"We will discuss establishing a mechanism for consulting and seeking to resolve disagreements on technical aspects of environmental and conservation issues."

Environmental Provisions in the US-Canada FTA and in the European Community

The US-Canada FTA did not include environmental provisions directly in the Agreement. To the extent that products are involved, the provisions of Chapter Six on technical standards (non-agricultural goods) might be applicable. More directly applicable to environmental issues are the provisions of Chapter Seven on agriculture, in particular Article 708. Although Article 708 applies only to agriculture, it contains a number of principles which might have wider applicability. For example, it has guidelines for harmonization, or equivalence where harmonization is not feasible, and calls for mutual recognition of inspection and certification procedures. With respect to implementation, Article 708 establishes eight working groups and a joint monitoring committee which reports to the US and Canadian agriculture ministers, to other ministers as appropriate, and to the

117

Commission set up in Chapter Eighteen. This institutional framework might also be adapted to the environment.

A similarly useful model is found in Title VII - Environment - of the amended Treaty of Rome. Article 130r sets forth the objectives of the European Community relating to the environment. It also lists the following three principles on which actions should be based:

- that preventive action should be taken;
- that environmental damage should as a priority be rectified at the source; and
- that the polluter should pay.

Article 130r further states that in preparing its action relating to the environment, the Community shall take account of:

- available scientific and technical data;
- environmental conditions in the various regions of the Community;
- the potential benefits and costs of action or of lack of action; and
- the economic and social development of the Community as a whole and the balanced development of its regions.

Finally, Article 130t of Title VII states that

"The protective measures adopted in common pursuant to Article 130s shall not prevent any Member State from maintaining or introducing more stringent protective measures compatible with this Treaty."

GATT Considerations

Because the GATT figures prominently in the US-Canada FTA and will probably be similarly incorporated by reference in the NAFTA, it is useful to examine environmental issues in the GATT context. Also, the GATT panel decision in the Mexican tuna/dolphin case has focused attention on the environment issue in the GATT. For example, on September 17 in a Senate speech, Senator Max Baucus urged the creation of an Environmental Code in the GATT modelled on the current subsidies code. In his view, the proposed code would be in force until negotiation of an international agreement setting environmental standards, which the Senator acknowledged "is likely to be decades away". He cited the recent GATT panel finding on US restrictions against Mexican tuna imports as demonstrating the need for such a code in order to avoid putting trade law above environmental considerations.

Although environmental issues were not directly addressed when the GATT was negotiated in 1947, some provisions may be applicable. In the general exceptions (Article XX), measures are permitted if "necessary to protect human, animal or plant life or health" as long as they do not constitute arbitrary or unjustifiable discrimination or disguised restrictions on international trade. Other exceptions relate to conservation of natural resources and measures necessary to secure compliance with laws or regulations not inconsistent with GATT provisions. An alternative to the code approach, suggested by Senator Baucus, would be to interpret these exceptions in a creative and imaginative manner in order to apply them to present day environmental issues. Recognizing the need to update the GATT with respect to the environment, the Contracting Parties have activated a committee to consider environmental issues.

Possible Environmental Rules and Institutional Arrangements for NAFTA

One of the major questions for the NAFTA negotiations is whether they should include (in the main body, or in an annex, or in a separate code) a set of principles to guide action on environmental matters. As indicated above, the United States May 1 Action Plan included statements which could be turned into principles. Similar material, as outlined above, is contained in the US-Canada FTA and in the EC Treaty of Rome.

In preparation for the United Nations Conference on the

119

Environment and Development (UNCED) to be held in Rio de Janeiro in June 1992, the international business community has been working on a set of principles which includes many of the guidelines covered. Appendix 1 is a list of the policy principles on trade and environment developed for the Second World Conference on Environmental Management (WICEM II) by an International Chamber of Commerce group. This document was issued at WICEM II held in Rotterdam in April, 1991. It was also endorsed by the OECD Business and Industry Advisory Committee, which recommended it to OECD Ministers.

• The *first* fundamental principle, which is probably not an issue in the NAFTA context, is that open trade and sustainable economic growth are necessary to provide the resources to enhance environmental protection.

• The *second* is that environmental measures should be devised to minimize distortions of international trade and investment flows and to avoid the creation of barriers to trade and investment. There are subsidiary principles related to this point, including the "Polluter Pays Principle".

• The *third* is that standards and regulations should be based on sound science and adequate understanding of environmental conditions and a cost/risk analysis.

• The *fourth* is that states should practice non-discrimination in the formulation and enforcement of environmental measures and the avoidance of the use of trade sanctions.

• The *fifth* is transparency and consultation with business; while

• The *sixth* is harmonization of standards, the use of performance rather then process requirements, and reliance on market-oriented measures.

The US environmental community has also been taking positions in connection with the NAFTA negotiations. In commenting on the May 1 Administration Action Plan, a consensus position was published by a group of environmental organizations (see Appendix 2). Rather than developing principles, the environmentalists focused more on process or institutional issues such as environmental review, implementation and enforcement, and monitoring.

This raises the second major question regarding the environment and NAFTA. Can or should the NAFTA have the kind of minimal institutional structure found in the US-Canada FTA? The environmentalists will be seeking a more elaborate system, at least with respect to the environment.

A third issue is dispute settlement. For the European Community, the question of whether "more stringent" protective measures (Article 130t) are "compatible with this Treaty" will be decided by the European Court of Justice. In the Canada-US FTA, Chapter Eighteen has a general dispute resolution mechanism which could be used, if a set of rules or principles regarding the environment were included in NAFTA. In addition, a joint monitoring system along the lines of Article 708 might be adapted. As pointed out above, the United States May 1 paper envisions a mechanism for the resolution of scientific and technical disagreements. Presumably, there will be some kind of environmental dispute resolution mechanism in the NAFTA.

Conclusion

Although trade and environment issues arise on a broader basis within North America, the NAFTA negotiations may provide the first opportunity to deal with these issues. In light of the strong feeling generated by the fast track debate, US Congressional approval of a NAFTA is not likely without substantial provisions dealing with the environment.

Thus, an effort should be made to reach agreement on a set of rules, guidelines or principles relating to the environment. Many of these principles have already been put into other instruments or have been developed by the business community. But the rules or principles will be very difficult to negotiate. As in the case of other sensitive subjects, an important element in successful NAFTA negotiations will be to have a heavy institutional structure, including special arrangements relating to the environment. It is most likely that any set of rules will have to be fairly general and that institutional provisions will be necessary to give a sense of participation to various interests and a sense of fairness in resolving disputes.

Appendix 1

Policy Principles on Trade and Environment

As part of the Bergen Industry Agenda for Action and the WICEM II process, the following set of Policy Principles on Trade and Environment have been drawn up. They will be further considered and, when necessary, refined through ICC's ongoing consultative processes.

Fundamental Principles

I. NEED FOR SUSTAINABLE ECONOMIC GROWTH AND OPEN TRADE
Economic growth is necessary to improve general social welfare, and to provide the conditions and resources to enhance environmental protection. Trade ensures the most efficient use of resources, is indispensable to economic growth, and therefore, a necessary element in enhanced environmental protection. Economic growth, open trade, and environmental protection are complementary and compatible objectives.

II. GLOBAL APPROACH
Environmental issues affecting the global commons should be addressed on an international basis, taking into account their impact on trade and economic growth, in addition to environmental effectiveness.

III. POLICIES BASED ON SCIENTIFIC UNDERSTANDING
Standards and regulations for environmental protection should be based on sound science and adequate understanding of environmental conditions, while at the same time recognizing the non-attainability of certainty and its risks resulting from both premature and delayed actions. The key lies in finding the appropriate balance between risk, effectiveness, and social and economic costs.

Standards and regulations should also be reassessed periodically to incorporate advances in scientific knowledge and to monitor their effectiveness.

IV. PERFORMANCE STANDARDS

Policies should incorporate performance standards whenever possible rather than prescriptive process requirements (i.e. specification of technologies and materials) which reduce flexibility.

V. HARMONIZED APPROACH TO GLOBAL ISSUES

Harmonization of standards and environmental measures should be the goal in order to minimize trade and economic distortions and to promote trade across national borders. However, harmonization may not always be immediately attainable or practicable and in such circumstances, the objective should be to establish essential requirements with accompanying measures that would be subject to the principle of mutual recognition. Regional problems may, in certain circumstances, require further close cooperation (including harmonization of requirements), e.g., for avoiding transboundary pollution and for any other measures necessary for the protection of health and the environment.

VI. DIFFERENT TIME SCALES

Because of differing levels of development among countries, harmonization of policies may also require different time scales. As with the Montreal Protocol on substances that deplete the ozone layer, however, the same standards should apply in the end.

VII.MARKET APPROACHES

Environmental policies should rely on market-oriented measures that encourage innovation in private and public sectors to find better ways to achieve agreed environmental goals. Policies should be examined for their effectiveness over the entire cycle of product life and use.

Subsidiary Principles

1. AVOIDANCE OF TRADE DISTORTIONS
Environmental regulations, and measures that have as their justification environmental protection, should be devised to minimize distortions of international trade and investment flows and to avoid the creation of trade barriers.

2. CONSULTATION
Governments should undertake to inform and consult each other about measures which have as their justification environmental protection and which may cause distortions of international trade and investment flows.

3. DISPUTE RESOLUTION
Mechanisms should be developed to resolve international disputes arising from trade and investment flows.

4. INTERNATIONAL AGREEMENTS
International conventions that provide a global framework for the development of national standards are particularly important for global environmental issues.

5. COMPLIANCE MEASURES
Such agreements should include agreement on common procedures for measuring and checking conformity and for enforcement.

6. COST-BENEFIT BALANCE
In some circumstances, the reduction of pollution beyond a certain level will not be practical or even desirable in view of the costs involved.

7. ENFORCEMENT
National enforcement of standards and other instruments should be fair, equally administered among nations and non-discriminatory. It should accord with the

GATT principles of most-favoured-nation treatment, national treatment and transparency.

8. TRANSPARENCY

Policies and regulations should be transparent and should not become non-tariff trade barriers. Business should be given adequate notice and opportunity to comment on proposed changes.

9. SANCTIONS

Trade sanctions to enforce environmental objectives should be avoided, and should be used only when there are agreed international standards and multilateral conventions governing the use of sanctions.

10. ROLE OF INTERGOVERNMENTAL ORGANIZATIONS

The OECD Guiding Principles (1972) should be maintained and re-endorsed to preserve open markets and minimize uneven effects on corporations through the application of such concepts as the "Polluter Pays Principle". Governments should promote cooperation and coordination in trade and environmental issues among intergovernmental organizations such as GATT, OECD and UNEP.

11. PRIVATE SECTOR INITIATIVE

Governments should encourage private sector initiatives to achieve environmental objectives, and as a partial alternative to regulation. Often the private sector is already engaged in related activities on a voluntary basis.

Appendix 2

Consensus Position by
National Audubon Society,
Environmental Defense Fund,
National Wildlife Federation,
and Natural Resources Defense Council
regarding President Bush's Action Plan for
Addressing Environmental Issues Related to
The North American Free Trade Agreement
May 10, 1991

President Bush's Plan for addressing environmental issues related to the North American Free Trade Agreement (NAFTA) identifies the need to address environmental problems related to trade and investment liberalization. In order to meet its stated objectives and address some of the environmental concerns that have been raised by the proposed NAFTA, the Plan should be more specific and could be clarified in a number of areas. In addition, it is important that negotiation of parallel agreements referred to in the Plan be linked to the NAFTA negotiations, afford meaningful public participation, and be concluded in conjunction with a NAFTA. Our organizations would be able to support continued fast-track authority if the Administration provided the following clarifications and assurances, all of which we believe are consistent with and would strengthen the President's Plan.

ENVIRONMENTAL REVIEW: The environmental review of NAFTA should not only assess its possible environmental effects, but also contribute to solving environmental problems. Preparation of the review should comport with the NEPA process, ensure effective public participation in its drafting, consider alternative actions, address the relationship and linkage to other parallel processes and be completed in a timely fashion in order to guide the negotiations. It will be important that USTR

127

acquire adequate environmental expertise to prepare the review effectively.

IMPLEMENTATION AND ENFORCEMENT: The NAFTA and related environmental agreements should contain effective monitoring, implementation and enforcement mechanisms to ensure that they meet their stated environmental objectives. The concept of a North American Commission assigned with these responsibilities should be explored as part of this process. Effective public participation in monitoring, implementation and enforcement of the NAFTA should be ensured.

COMPENSATING INVESTMENTS FOR ENVIRONMENTAL PROTECTION: The NAFTA should include a mechanism to recapture some of the benefits of free trade for environmental protection. Economic growth from trade needs to pay for its environmental impacts and costs. Compensating investments for infrastructure, monitoring and enforcement are necessary if growth is to benefit the environment. The Administration should have as a negotiating position that it will seek an agreement containing such a mechanism.

WORKING GROUP ON THE ENVIRONMENT: To negotiate the details of the above issues and to ensure the environment is considered in all aspects of the agreement, a separate working group for the environment is needed. The NAFTA needs to address environmental issues related to all aspects of free trade. These include investment and not just "products in trade". To do this, the Administration should announce its support for an environmental working group within the NAFTA talks which would be equal in status to any other negotiating group.

THE PROTECTION OF NATIONAL, STATE AND LOCAL ENVIRONMENTAL STANDARDS: Provisions of the NAFTA itself, and the mechanisms it creates, such as on dispute settlement, should ensure that national, state and local environmental laws, regulations and standards will not be subject to weakening. The NAFTA should make explicit that this applies not only to national but also state and local laws, regulations and standards. In particular, the burden of proof should be on the signatory challenging such measures to prove that they are disguised barriers to trade. Procedures for resolving disputes on this issues should be open to participation by the public. Any mechanism for resolving disputes over environmental measures must not undermine the ability of national state or local authorities to maintain or strengthen such measures.

12

Critical Issues in NAFTA: A Mexican Perspective
Gustavo Vega-Cisneros

Gustavo Vega-Cisneros is a Professor at the Centre for International Studies and Director of the Mexican-US Studies Program at El Colegio de Mexico. He is also the Research Director for North American Economic Integration project being financed by the International Development Research Centre (IDRC) based in Ottawa. He completed his doctoral studies at Yale University and has been visiting professor at the University of California at San Diego, Georgetown and Duke Universities in the US and the Centre for International Studies and Training in Japan. He has written numerous articles on Mexican-US economic relations. His latest publication (in Spanish) is Mexico in a North American Free Trade Area *(Mexico: El Colegio de Mexico, 1991).*

On February 5 1991, the Mexican, United States and Canadian Governments announced their intentions to begin trilateral free trade negotiations. In the United States, the next step was for the President to seek congressional authorization for "fast track" procedures, under which he is required to consult closely with Congress throughout the negotiations. In return, Congress must approve or disapprove the completed agreement promptly, without adding substantive amendments. This authorization was granted in mid-October, 1991, opening the way for the negotiations.

Incentives for Mexico-United States-Canada Free Trade Negotiations

The planned negotiations have met with a mixed reaction in all three countries. Mexico's decision to seek free trade with the United States, and eventually with Canada, was

131

a result of a number of internal and external factors. The most important was the opening of the Mexican economy. For over 40 years, Mexico's development strategy had emphasized growth based on the internal market. However, the weakness of the world oil market, and the scarcity of external funds following Mexico's debt crisis, caused the Mexican government to break with tradition in its import substitution policies and seek more revenues through exports.

In the last five years, Mexico has adopted liberalization policies that have made its economy one of the most open in the developing world:

• Mexico became a member of the General Agreement on Tariffs and Trade (GATT) in 1986.

• The maximum Mexican tariff fell from a level of 100% to 20% between 1985 and 1990.

• The country also liberalized its policies in such areas as foreign investment and intellectual property rights. In May 1989, Mexico made sweeping reforms of its rules governing foreign investment, which now allow it to accept 100% foreign investments in companies in unclassified activities.[1]

Similarly, Mexican law and enforcement of intellectual property protection underwent significant change. For instance, Mexico announced plans to strengthen process and product patent protection and improve the enforcement of trademarks and trade secrets.

Mexico is therefore serious about looking for new ways to integrate more efficiently into the global economy. Its active participation in the Uruguay Round of GATT and its interest in a free trade agreement (FTA) with the United States and Canada form part of that strategy. Since the Mexican government has already instituted a considerable amount of liberalization, the measures required to decrease protectionism in an FTA would have a less traumatic effect on the Mexican economy than they would otherwise.

Mexico's decision to seek free trade also stems from a realization that there is already a great deal of integration in the North American economy. About 70% of Mexico's trade is with the United States, and 30% of American trade is with Canada and Mexico. Canada is the largest trading partner of the United States, while Mexico is the third largest.

There are also substantial United States-Mexican and United States-Canadian foreign investment flows. While Mexico and Canada are not major trading partners, the effects of their trade are significant, especially for Mexico. In 1990, Mexico's total trade with Canada (almost $2.5 billion) was greater than its trade with all of Latin America. In seeking an FTA, Mexico was, therefore, recognizing the large degree of integration which already exists.

Mexico has also been disturbed by the rise of protectionism in industrial states, and its interest in an FTA has been partly defensive in nature. For instance, the consolidation of the European Community (EC) in 1992 could contribute to a considerable amount of trade diversion, particularly if the Uruguay Round is unsuccessful. Mexico, like Canada, also sees an FTA as an "insurance policy" against United States' protectionism and as a means of gaining more assured access to its largest export market. Mexico and Canada compete in exporting various automotive, textile and apparel, furniture, petrochemical and other products. To prevent Canada from gaining a margin of preference through its free trade agreement with the United States, Mexico feels that it, too, must pursue the free trade option.

Despite the Mexican government's interest in an FTA, such an agreement could create difficulties. For example, some Mexicans fear that an FTA would hinder their country's trade diversification efforts and increase their vulnerability to unilateral United States' trade policies. Nevertheless, another view is that participation in an FTA would induce Mexican companies to become more competitive as they gain economies of scale and rationalize production in North America. This, in turn, would enhance Mexico's competitiveness with countries outside the region and permit it to develop a more diversified trade profile in the medium term.

One of the main reasons for Mexico and Canada to pursue a trilateral arrangement with the United States is to set an appropriate precedent for extending free trade throughout the Americas. Some other Latin American countries (Chile, for instance) have already expressed interest in negotiating free trade with the United States. A single expanding agreement is preferable to a "hub and spoke" system in which the United States signs bilateral agreements sequentially with a host of countries.

Under the latter arrangement, each country would benefit from a bilateral agreement with the United States, but when the United States signed other bilateral agreements, the initial "spokes" would lose. The more "spokes" the United States has, the worse the problem becomes. Without a single expanding agreement, Mexico will eventually be in the same position as Canada. A Mexico-United States-Canada arrangement would, by contrast, provide better rather than worse access conditions in the US for Mexico and Canada.

However, the question arises as to why the United States would be inclined to accept one expanding agreement with Mexico and Canada rather than a series of bilateral agreements. The latter option has advantages in one respect: the United States could negotiate a variety of preferences with each country that would not be available to its other free trade partners.

Despite the benefits the United States derives from preferences in separate agreements, however, it would not benefit overall. The signing of many agreements would be less efficient and create numerous technical problems, thereby complicating the process of regularizing trade procedures. Furthermore, as the dominant power in the western hemisphere, it is not in the United States' interests to be seen as increasing this dominance at the expense of its partners. Thus, there are important advantages to the three countries to seek a trilateral agreement rather than separate deals. Nevertheless, the questions arises as to the appropriate agenda for the trilateral negotiations.

Options for Mexico-United States-Canada Free Trade Negotiations

From a trilateral perspective, there are two basic options for Mexico-US-Canada negotiations:
• On the one hand, Mexico could join the existing Canada-United States FTA to form a North American Free Trade Agreement (NAFTA).[2]
• On the other hand, a core or umbrella agreement encompassing Mexico, the United States and Canada could be negotiated with the addition of two or possibly three separate bilateral agreements.[3]

Pursuing the first course could pose various problems. For example, some provisions in the Canada-US FTA are a response to very specific bilateral needs of the two countries: notably, the clauses relating to energy, the automotive trade, services and the cultural industries. Difficulties could arise in adapting these provisions to the Mexican situation.

In contrast, the essential feature of the common core or umbrella option would be that there is "a common free trade area with common rules of origin for trade in goods among the three economies...(and) a common institutional framework for the North American FTAs."[4]

Possible Provisions of a Core or Umbrella NAFTA

The substantive provisions that a common core or umbrella agreement could have are as follows.

Article XXIV of the GATT directs that the parties to a general agreement eliminate substantially all trade barriers in goods as a prerequisite to the creation of a valid free-trade area. A Mexico-US-Canada Free Trade Agreement should regulate the three general types of barriers that currently restrict trade between the three

135

nations:
- tariffs;
- contingent protection measures; and
- other non-tariff barriers (NTBs).

Tariffs are the fundamental core of the free trade agreement. The Canada-US FTA calls for the elimination of tariffs on bilateral trade by the end of 1998. This is consistent with GATT rules because the cuts are part of a broader FTA that encompasses substabtially all of the trade between the two countries. Mexico would need to negotiate a similar arrangement with the United States and Canada.

The main tariff question is the speed with which the tariff will be eliminated for free trade between Mexico, the United States and Canada. In the Canada-US FTA, both governments agreed to eliminate tariffs on the basis of three formulae:
- immediate elimination;
- elimination in five annual steps; and
- elimination in ten annual steps.

Although the agreement does consider safeguards to protect domestic industry during the transition period (1989-1998) - in case imports from the other country grow enormously, endanger and thereby threaten local producers - no special treatment is given to newborn industry.

In contrast, Israel, in its agreement with the US, enjoys special consideration for its "infant industry," provisions which are applicable for new industries not previously existing in the country. Israel may, after the signature of the agreement, introduce and reintroduce ad-valorem customs duties not exceeding 20 percentage points above the level that would have otherwise existed. The total value of the products for which these measures are undertaken may not exceed 10% of the total volume of US imports from Israel. The newly introduced duties, once imposed, must decrease until they disappear, not later than 1995.[5]

It has been suggested that as a result of the rapid

unilateral tariff liberalization undertaken by Mexico in the last five years, the larger obstacle in terms of adjustment is already out of the way. Mexico's average weighted tariffs are now just higher than 20%. Therefore, Mexico could easily undertake a similar approach to tariff elimination as Canada, rather than that taken by Israel.[6]

This view, however, forgets that from 1985 to 1988, massive real exchange rate devaluation and real wage reduction in Mexico eased the blow, for import-competing industries, from severe adjustment difficulties that might have been expected from such pervasive liberalization. Since the Solidarity Plan was imposed in December 1987, which implied a return to a more fixed exchange rate, import-competing industries have begun to bear the brunt of liberalization. As a consequence, the Mexican government is being pressured not to agree to eliminate the remaining tariffs too quickly. Indeed, it is being pressed to ask for a slower phase-out of the remainder of Mexican tariffs over a period of fifteen years while the United States and Canada are asked to eliminate their tariffs in seven to ten years. This arrangement would provide Mexican producers with better access to the US and Canadian markets while they still retained some temporary protection in the Mexican market.[7]

Similarly, given the lowest cost structure of some Mexican industries, there are likely to be many more requests for extended rather than accelerated tariff elimination from US and Canadian producers. A realistic negotiating scenario, therefore, might involve the elimination of most tariffs over a period of ten, twelve or even fifteen years, with provisions for faster elimination for those industries that believe they are ready. In any case, the choice of a time period for tariff removal will probably hinge on an evaluation of the ensuing adjustment process. Thus, a decision as to the proper time to phase out a particular tariff will have to follow intense industry consultations. Whatever time frame is chosen, an extensive program of adjustment assistance and global safeguards will be desirable to achieve the benefits of free trade with the least cost.

In addition to a phased withdrawal of tariffs, the Mexico-US-Canada Free Trade Agreement would also have to deal with a range of Non-Tariff Barriers (NTBs). This subject is of particular interest to Mexico in its relations with the United States. As events of recent years have demonstrated, Mexico's exports of goods to US market are vulnerable to several types of barriers. The policy rationales and procedures governing these NTBs must be taken into account in designing a free trade agreement. US non-tariff barriers can be separated into two basic categories:

• measures of contingent protection, principally anti-dumping duties, countervailing duties and safeguard or "escape-clause" actions;

• laws and regulations which, either explicitly or through administrative practice, impose discriminatory burdens on goods of foreign origin through government-procurement practices, product-quality and safety standards, quantitative restrictions on agricultural products, and similar measures.

In the case of contingent protection, the first, and most important concern is for Mexican producers to obtain barrier-free market access under a negotiated arrangement that ensures access is dependable and secure from future political and legal challenges. Only if entrepreneurs and investors are confident of the permanence and effectiveness of the arrangements will Mexican industry make the necessary adjustments and long-term commitments required to maximize the economic benefits of free trade.

US trade policy is created and applied through political and legal processes which decentralize decision-making power and enhance the political influence of relatively small and narrowly-based interest groups, such as unions and trade associations. The most notable examples of this fragmentation of power within the US system are the legal mechanisms that produce contingent protection from import competition. These mechanisms usually involve countervailing duties, anti-dumping duties and emergency protection for US producers suffering serious competitive injury from imports. US legislation gives domestic producers the right to launch lawsuits against foreign rivals with little risk of loss if its claims of unfair and injurious import competition are proved groundless. Since these US lawsuits are initiated by private firms, it is seldom possible to predict when they will be launched. Thus, the threat of harassment they pose may deter Mexican investment in new plants and equipment when the future profitability of such facilities depends on uninterrupted access to the North American market. Since free trade will be of primary importance in Mexican industrial development, the Mexican government would need to anticipate potential problems and to spell out, as fully and precisely as possible, the rules and procedures governing any bilateral arrangement.

In achieving this purpose, the Mexican government would be well advised to take into account the precedent set by the Canada-US FTA. For instance, Mexico might, like Canada, obtain protection against "sideswiping" in US global safeguard (article XIX) actions. Only when the other party to the FTA is a substantial source of injury can it be targeted in safeguard actions. Even then, imports cannot be reduced below their trend rate of growth. This preferential treatment could be quite helpful to Mexico if these measures proliferate.

In the case of subsidies and anti-dumping duties, Canada attempted to gain total exemption from US fair trade laws. Even though this unrealistic hope was not accomplished, the two countries made the commitment to develop, over a five-to-seven year period, a mutually acceptable set of trade remedy laws. While this was accomplished, both countries agreed to establish a "binational dispute settlement mechanism" to fulfil two roles:

• The first was a legislative watchdog function which provided for a bilateral review of any proposed changes in either country's current regulations. Any new law one country passes must specify the other country explicitly by name or else the law would not apply to that country. Also, all changes must be consistent with the GATT and the Agreement.

• The second function of the binational dispute settlement mechanism was the operation of a binational review panel to replace domestic judicial review. Final decisions made by the panel are binding on both parties.

It is improbable that any US Administration will ever agree simply to exempt Mexican goods from the possible application of anti-dumping or countervailing duties. Nor is it likely that Mexico and the US could agree on a mutually acceptable set of trade remedy laws. A better strategy is pursued through the binational dispute settlement mechanism. This strategy for improving security of access would place principal reliance on the neutrality of a "judicial" panel, composed of appointees from both nations and a neutral chairperson possibly selected from a non-party, or chosen by agreement between the national appointees. Mexico would, therefore, be well advised to get involved in the process established in Chapter 19 of the Canada-US FTA.

In the case of NTBs, there is no doubt that one of the more difficult areas in the US-Mexico trade relationship is in the use of physo-sanitary requirements on animal and plants, and health and safety requirements. Given that the negotiations on the physo-sanitary requirements agreement are the most advanced in the agricultural area in the Geneva discussion, they may provide an MTN-based solution to this very sensitive and difficult area. But even if the agricultural negotiations in the Uruguay Round fail, the progress that has been made can still be transferred into the Mexico-US-Canada agreement.

Other important NTBs in the US-Mexico trade relationship are the quantitative restrictions on textiles, steel, apparel and agriculture. As part of the negotiations that have taken place under the umbrella of the US-Mexico framework agreement, Mexico has made some progress in expanding its quotas on textiles, apparel and steel.[8] The US intends these quotas to disappear by early 1992. Even if some of them are extended due to political pressures, Mexico should get expansions well above its present levels.

In agriculture, the US uses import quotas to restrict trade in poultry, dairy, and some meat products, and uses a variety of subsidies in support of its domestic supply-management program. Canada also maintains these same restrictions and imposes seasonal tariffs on fresh produce in order to support farm income. Mexico continues to maintain import licensing controls for 60 agricultural tariff categories, including grains, oilseeds, dairy goods and certain agricultural products. In addition, Mexico determines quotas for almost all major imported agricultural commodities. These controls are used to encourage domestic consumption of local products.[9]

The removal of these quotas and import licensing controls would necessitate a coordinated approach to the supply management and other agricultural support policies currently maintained by the three countries. The task of harmonizing these policies through extensive negotiations with the United States and Canada is likely to be technically complex and politically difficult. In the Canada-US FTA, negotiators came to an understanding that reforms need to be pursued in the GATT setting of multilateral trade talks rather than in the bilateral setting. This same logic should justify deferring free trade for agricultural products. After the Uruguay Round, one can conceive that detailed agreements could be worked out concerning supply management and other subsidy practices.

Another topic which will appear in the FTA package is intellectual property. Here, there has been substantial progress. Mexico, stimulated by bilateral negotiations with the United States, has introduced very significant changes in its intellectual property and transfer of technology legislation in the last few years. In January 1990, Mexico announced its intention to introduce legislative changes in the intellectual property law which would include increasing the patent term to 20 years (that used by a number of developed countries), offering product patent protection for products and processes not previously subject to patent protection, and strengthening its trade secrets law. If the Mexican Congress approves these and other amendments, Mexico will then have greater intellectual property protection than Canada. What was a very difficult issue - one that was handled on the side in the Canada-US legislation - will thus largely be resolved before the FTA negotiations are concluded.

The same process is taking place in regard to foreign investment. The Mexican regulatory liberalization of May 1989 has created a more liberal foreign investment regime that provides for greater transparency, increased foreign participation and greater efficiency in the application process. The need for foreign investment will probably accelerate the pace of liberalization and produce a smaller number of exempted sectors.

Problem Areas: Services

One of the major attractions of an FTA for Mexico is the fact that, within the framework of a general free-trade agreement, it would still be possible to exclude certain sectors or industries from the scope of bilateral or trilateral negotiations. Article XXIV of the GATT has been interpreted to authorize the exclusion of up to 20% of the total trade in goods among the members of a legitimate free-trade area. This interpretation of the "substantially all trade" rule has permitted the EFTA countries, for example, to limit the scope of their free trade agreements to trade in industrial goods only: agriculture, a sector rife with state intervention, is excluded; heavily regulated services such as banking, transport, and insurance are not included; and free movement of labour is not provided for.[10]

Another area requiring special rules in the negotiation

142

of an FTA is trade in services. The US and Canada consider it one of their top priority negotiating objectives and, it has become an increasingly important component of Mexico-US bilateral trade. Including it in the agreement is considered highly desirable. Mexico has expressed and has given proof of, its interest in negotiating trade in services.[11] This attitude is largely explained by the relatively large share of services in the Mexican economy. They represented about 62% of GNP and 10% of total employment in 1985. From this perspective, Mexico is a service economy.[12] In turn, exports of services represented about 30% of total non-factorial receipts in current account in 1985. Imports represented a similar amount. These percentages are relatively high for developing country standards. They are explained mainly by trade in services between Mexico and the United States.

Nevertheless, even if a given country is willing to negotiate, it has to define what, and how, to negotiate. In the case of services, this is not easily done. The services sector is one of the least studied economic activities in developing countries. Not only is the data not sufficiently detailed but in many instances it is simply unavailable.

Even less clear are the likely effects of negotiating a "liberalization" of services. Certainly, liberalization of trade in services leads to similar results as liberalization of trade in goods. However, in the latter instance, the magnitude of the effects upon production and trade can be gauged according to the change in the level of tariffs. No such easy estimate can be made in the case of services.

Moreover, there is still insufficient reliable information on the economic consequences of existing national regulatory barriers to trade in services. Mexico, the United States and Canada maintain entry controls and other regulations that exclude foreign controlled enterprises or limit their allowed share of the domestic market in service sectors such as banking, transportation and communications. Other barriers operate in particular sectors. Any useful analysis of service trade issues must focus, therefore, on the national regulatory arrangements specific to each particular type of service. For example, government procurement preferences for local suppliers are major impediments to trade in engineering and construction services, while restrictions and cost-increasing regulations on the transborder transmission of business data are a major irritant to those who trade in financial and business consulting services.

The negotiations on this diverse set of problems will be further complicated by considerable differences in the national regulatory policies that currently apply in many service sectors. Free trade in transportation or in financial services, for instance, will require the harmonization of diverse national rules governing price competition, service quality, consumer protection and other equally contentious matters. The fact that each particular service industry is affected by regulations that are virtually unique suggests that future negotiations on services should be conducted on a sectoral basis.

In spite of these difficulties, Mexico has been making rapid progress identifying what to negotiate and defining with more precision its interest in this area. To this effect, a survey was conducted by the ministry of Trade and Industrial Promotion in consultation with the private sector. According to the results, Mexico would be willing to negotiate in 14 service sectors.[13] According to the official declaration, negotiations would only consider trade in services but not investment flows, since these are a different matter to be negotiated separately. All participants in the exercise agreed that it was necessary for Mexico to become more efficient and competitive in services and that, to attain this, there was need to open its market to external competition. The main areas where Mexico would be willing to grant concessions are tourism, insurance, telecommunications, informatics and engineering services. Likewise, the areas where Mexico is interested in obtaining concessions are engineering, construction and other labour-intensive sectorial activities such as agriculture.

144

There is one main stumbling block to a negotiation in services between Mexico, the US and Canada. In the negotiations the US and Canada are likely to focus on areas such as financial services, telecommunications, and informatics. They are likely to resist liberalization in services that involve the actual displacement or utilization of labour, where Mexico has a comparative advantage. The large disparity in national wage levels will undoubtedly raise serious concerns from industries and workers likely to face increased competition. This will make it quite difficult for the US and Canada to include this issue in an FTA. However, recent reforms in financial services and Mexico's apparent willingness to provide more open access to its services market in areas of special interest to the US and Canada, could well put pressure on the US and Canadian governments to accommodate Mexican concerns about trade in labour-intensive services in an FTA. Nevertheless the issue will be contentious. Even the US-Canada agreement only yielded provisions dealing with trade in certain white collar services.

Problem Areas: Energy, Labour and Environmental Standards

One of the most difficult areas in which to achieve free trade is energy. This is a sector where a particular bilateral agreement will have to be struck between Mexico and the US. The Mexican government has insisted that this area should be kept out of the negotiations. This does not mean that there is no need for special rules to govern bilateral trade in energy. Mexico's main concern regarding natural resources is whether a free trade arrangement would constrain its ability to impose production quotas, taxes and export controls, and to further national security and industrial policy objectives. The GATT specifically provides for such controls, unless they are discriminatory or act as disguised restrictions on international trade. It is possible that the United States will seek to negotiate some legal assurance of access to future Mexican energy supplies, akin to those contained in the Canada-US FTA. Any guarantee to US energy consumers must, however, preserve Mexico's authority to limit exports in order to meet anticipated domestic requirements for such resources. Article XX(g) of the GATT permits signatories to maintain non-discriminatory measures "relating to the conservation of exhaustible natural resources if such measures are made effective in conjunction with restrictions on domestic production or consumption". A similar provision could be included in any general agreement covering trade in non-renewable resources.

Even though the American and Canadian governments, as well as many economists and business groups in both countries, favour a NAFTA that would include Mexico, the issue of free trade with Mexico has become contentious in the US and Canada. The US and Canadian labour movements were generally opposed to the Canada-United States FTA. They are expressing even stronger concerns about the inclusion of Mexico. Foremost amongst labour's concerns are the issues of low wages and the lack of stringent environmental regulations. Assembly operations in Mexico occur primarily in maquiladora industries, begun in 1964 and traditionally located on the border with the United States. In these, American companies transport partly completed products to Mexico and then pay maquila employees (many of whom are women) lower wages to assemble the components or complete the manufacturing process. The labour movement in the US and Canada have noted that the maquiladora are set up to replace American and Canadian workers in various areas of production and that there has been a serious erosion of Mexican social standards, human rights, and maquiladora wage rates. Labour leaders, therefore, suggest that any trilateral agreement with Mexico should contain a social charter based on common standards for labour, social policy and the environment.

It is not realistic to expect Mexico to sign a social charter guaranteeing equality of wages, as some American and Canadian labour leaders would like. It is difficult for a developing country, such as Mexico, to attract industry without the incentive of low wages. Wages in the maquiladora are about double wages elsewhere in Mexico. Furthermore, the nature of the maquiladora is changing. In recent years, the maquiladora program has attracted more sophisticated forms of production in automobile-related manufactures and advanced electronics assembly. This "second wave" of maquiladora plants have made substantial investments in complex technology and are using growing numbers of male workers.[14] Overall, the number of men employed in maquiladora plants has increased from less than 20% ten years ago, to about 35% in 1991. In some sectors, such as transportation equipment, men now comprise up to 50% of the workforce.[15]

These "new" maquiladoras are significant because they demonstrate that sophisticated, high quality exports can be produced in Mexican plants using advanced production technologies. Whereas the "old" maquiladoras typically were export enclaves that generated employment and foreign exchange but used few local materials inputs and had limited spread effects on the rest of the country's industrial structure, the "new maquiladoras" may help Mexico move to a higher level of development by fostering greater technology transfer and the training of a skilled and well-educated workforce. The maquiladoras have now moved to other areas in Mexico, such as Guadalajara. This has provided Mexican producers with more inputs, and local content in the maquiladora has increased from about 1.7% to 6.0%.

In the case of environmental standards, it is important to recall that international distinctions in tolerable levels of environmental risk are created because the weight attached to environmental standards tends to vary with the income levels of different countries. In low income countries, even if environmental and health risks are acknowledged, the income levels do not permit a structure of environmental regulation comparable to that in rich countries. In view of the differences in levels of economic development and national priorities, it is clear that environmental standards cannot be wholly uniform. Some mechanism must be found to accommodate differences in national priorities linked to levels of economic development and cultural factors. This suggests that negotiators should aim at what may be called "intermediate standards," in the same sense and for the same basic reason as that which underlies the widespread advocacy of intermediate technology in the Third World. This would not imply a "downgrading" of US and Canadian regulations. Rather, it would imply an "upgrading" of Mexico's norms, together with the recognition that the social costs of regulation are relative to national income.

Conclusion

There is already a considerable amount of integration among the economies in North America. The convergence of commercial policies among the three countries, especially marked in the case of Mexican liberalization efforts, makes a NAFTA more feasible today than at any time in the past. However, there is also considerable opposition to an agreement from labour unions and threatened industries in the United States and Canada. It is to be hoped that the outcome of the negotiation will not depend on the actions of special interest groups, but on a calculation of the benefits and costs to the three societies as a whole.

References

1.   The range of economic sectors expressly open to wholly foreign-ownership has been broadened significantly. Foreign investment of up to 100% is allowed in unclassified activities, which account for 72.5% of the 754 economic activities that comprise the Mexican economy. Included are certain industries (such as glass, cement, iron, steel

and cellulose) for which administrative restrictions had previously restricted majority foreign participation. Of the remaining 207 classified activities, 40 more are open to 100% foreign investment, with prior approval. The implications in several areas of the new regulations are especially noteworthy. For example, telecommunications is now considered a classified activity in which foreign investment is allowed up to 49%. Prior to the 1989 regulations, foreign participation in telecommunications services was prohibited. See UNITED STATES INTERNATIONAL TRADE COMMISSION (1990) *Review of Trade and Liberalization Measures by Mexico and Prospects for Future United States-Mexico Relations* (Washington, DC: USITC) Publication 2275, April.

2. This approach has been considered by Michael Hart, who concludes it is feasible. But he observes that the negotiation would require ingenuity in dealing with aspects of the chapters on border measures and safeguards and would face technical difficulties in the chapters dealing with rules of origin, agriculture, energy, government procurement, business travel, investment, financial services and dispute settlement in the case of antidumping and countervailing duties. Hart notes that the success of the negotiations in this option would depend largely on the degree of flexibility that the United States and Mexico could bring to the table. Hart even suggests the chapters and themes where Mexico could get differential treatment without hurting the integrity of the agreement (i.e. agriculture, government procurement and financial services). See HART, MICHAEL (1990) *A North American Free Trade Agreement: The Strategic Implications for Canada* (Ottawa and Halifax: Centre for Trade Policy and Law and the Institutes for Research on Public Policy) p.129.

3. This general approach is suggested in LIPSEY, RICHARD AND SMITH, MURRAY (1989) "The Canada-US Free Trade

Agreement: Special Case or Wave of the Future?" in SCHOOT, JEFFREY (ED) *Free Trade Areas and US Trade Policy* (Washington, DC: Institute for International Economics). A particular application of this approach to Mexico's Free Trade Initiative can be found in LIPSEY, RICHARD *Canada at the US Free Trade Dance.*

4.   See SMITH, MURRAY (1990) "A North American Free Trade Agreement: Agenda and Modalities for the Negotiations" Paper prepared for discussion at a Meeting of the Council of Foreign Relations, New York City, November, 5.

5.   See ROSEN, HOWARD F "The US-Israel Free Trade Agreement" pp. 97-120; also JAMES, DENNIS JR "The Agreement on Establishment of a Free Trade Area between the Government of the US of America and the Government of Israel" pp. 121-130.

6.   See BENNETT, TIMOTHY "Lessons for Mexico of the Canada-US Free Trade Agreement" Paper prepared for the International Forum: "Mexico's Trade Options in the Changing International Economy" p.284; also SCHOOT, JEFF AND HUFBAUER, GARY C "The Realities of a North American Economic Alliance" p. 22; and HART, MICHAEL "The Elements of a North American Free Trade Agreement" Paper prepared for the International Forum: "Mexico's Trade Options in the Changing International Economy" p. 339.

7.   It is estimated that US tariffs, as well as those of other developed countries, have been reduced significantly in successive rounds of GATT negotiations. Nominal (stated) US tariffs, weighted by imports, are in the 3-6% range. By 1990, 85% of Mexican exports to the US entered in the duty range of 0-5%. However, according to Mexican government officials, some Mexican products still face high tariffs: 150 items have over 20% tariffs; 190 items have tariffs of 15-25%; and 244 items have 10-15% tariffs.   The value of

Mexican exports under these categories was estimated at $1.6 billion in 1989. But it probably would have been much higher, had the tariffs been lower. See BLANCO, HERMINIO *Senate Hearings* op cit.

8. The US government agreed to eliminate quotas on 52 Mexican textile and apparel products and to expand quotas by an average of 25% for other products in February 1990. According to the estimates of the Mexican government, this would imply that Mexican exports would double from their 1989 level. In steel, the US doubled its annual Mexican import quota from 400,000 to 800,000 tons. In 1989, Mexican steel exports came close to $400 million. US INTERNATIONAL TRADE COMMISSION (1990) op cit.

9. According to a recent report by the US General Accounting Office (GA), licensing requirements are the most significant barriers to US agricultural exports to Mexico. About 59% of the value of US agricultural exports to Mexico are covered by Mexican licensing requirements. See US GENERAL ACCOUNTING OFFICE (1990) *US-Mexico Trade: Trends and Impediments in Agricultural Trade* January.

10. See CURZON PRICE, VICTORIA (1987) *Free Trade Areas, The European experience. What Lessons for Canadian-US Trade Liberalization?* (Scarborough: CD Howe Institute) pp. 48 ff.

11. Mexico was one of the few developing countries that supported the inclusion of trade in services in the Uruquay Round. It continues to participate actively in these negotiations. Other countries, however, continue to maintain a "hard line" and only ruefully participate in the negotiations following the lead of Brazil and India.

12. See DEL MATEO, FERNANDO Y CARNER, FRANÇOISE (1989) "Mexico frente a las negociaciones de servicios an la Ronda

Uruquay" in Torres, Blanca et al *La Adhesion de Mexico al GATT. Repercusiones Internas e Impacto sobre las Relaciones Mexico-Estados Unidos* (Mexico: El Colegio de Mexico) pp. 359-388.

13. This refers to negotiations in the Uruquay Round and not particularly with the US and Canada.

14. Carillo, Jorge (1989) "Transformaciones en la Industria Maquiladora de Exportacion" in Gonzalez-Arechiga, Bernado y Barajas-Escamilla, Rocio (Eds) *Las Maquiladoras: Ajuste Estructural y Desarrollo Regional* (Tijuana, Mexico: El Colegio de la Frontera Norte-Funcacion Friedrich Ebert) pp. 37-54.

15. Shaiken, Harley (1990) *Mexico in the Global Economy: High Technology and Work Organization in Export Industries* (La Jolla, CA: Center for US-Mexican Studies, University of California, San Diego) Monograph Series 33, p. 12.

13
The European Community Experience
Jacques Lecomte

His Excellency Jacques Lecomte is the Head of the Delegation of the Commission of the European Communities to Canada. Since joining the EC Commission in 1964, he has been involved in the development of agricultural policy; prepared the Commission's actions for EC membership of Denmark, Ireland, Norway, and the United Kingdom; been a member of the Commission's representation in London; worked as the personal assistant to the Director General for the External Relations of the EC Commission; been in charge of information for the Commission's 50 delegations to Africa, the Caribbean and the Pacific; been in charge of the implementation of the steel production control in the steel plants; and been responsible for the management of 91 external offices of the Commission.

Ten years ago, the EC Commission had very limited competence in environmental policy. The 1986 *Single European Act* modifying the founding Treaty of Rome did not yet exist; the 1985 White Paper outlining the program required to complete the internal market by 1992 had yet to appear; and the EC had scarcely a skeleton of an environmental policy. Neither the political changes democratizing the countries of Eastern Europe nor the EC's own increasing political cooperation had yet occurred, nor were they even foreseeable.

Yet within a decade, the EC has taken numerous actions in the field of the environment and is moving toward the realization of a common EC environmental policy. It is well under way to achieving its goals for the 1992 Common Market. The Commission has begun to examine closely the related issues of trade and the environment particularly in the context of the GATT negotiations. Moreover, the

Commission has been given the lead role in coordinating assistance to Eastern Europe. However, the EC is currently facing tremendous challenges, both internally and externally, in its efforts to address environmental concerns. In 1990, in its Dublin Declaration, the European Council stated:

> "The Community must use more effectively its position of moral, economic and political authority to advance international efforts to solve global (environmental) problems, and to promote sustainable development and respect for the Global Commons."

The EC must demonstrate, by its choices and behaviour, that the more prosperous countries of the world, which in their time have contributed to the creation of global environmental problems, are now prepared to take the necessary concrete steps for the resolution of not only domestic and regional environmental problems but also wider international or global problems. In this context, the Commission is proposing that its fifth Action Program on the Environment will be an important step in the promotion of a more coherent strategy geared toward the achievement of sustainable development. This can best be achieved by a proper appreciation of the importance and value of the environment to present and future economic, social and cultural life, and an effective sharing of responsibility for its guardianship among all sectors of society.

To accomplish this objective the Community must make special efforts externally. It must act at the pan-European level, incorporating the European Free Trade Area (EFTA) Member States, with whom it now shares a European Economic Area, Eastern and Central Europe, and the Mediterranean Region. It must expand its relations with developing countries including, in particular, the African, Caribbean and Pacific countries covered by the Lomé Agreements. And, it must operate at a global level in the

GATT, at the United Nations Conference on Environment and Development (UNCED) Conference in Rio, and within the growing number of international environmental conventions in which the EC participates.

The EC recognizes that the clean-up of the environment in Eastern and Central Europe is essential for the development of those countries' economies. It also offers tremendous benefits to the countries of Western Europe, through reductions in transboundary pollution, notably through acidifications and international rivers such as the Elbe, Danube and Oder, and the Baltic and Adriatic seas.

At present, there is an enormous gap in financial, technical, educational, scientific and human resources between the East and the West in Europe. The Community can contribute best to closing this gap through the PHARE program launched by the G-24 countries.[1] This program, originally intended to assist the economic restructuring of Poland and Hungary, has been extended to include Czechoslovakia, Bulgaria, Romania, Yugoslavia, Albania and the Baltic countries of Estonia, Latvia and Lithuania, as well as the former territory of East Germany. In 1990, its first year of operation, the PHARE program was granted 500 million ECU (or about $700 million by the EC to fund projects related to economic restructuring, agriculture development, human resources and the environment.

Over one-fifth of these funds was spent on projects to improve the environment. Each project was defined in close collaboration with the countries receiving the aid, and on the basis of their proposals. Every aspect of the environment was covered: water, air, waste, nature protection and even, in some cases, nuclear safety (for example, at the nuclear power plant near Rostock on the Baltic Sea in the former East German territory). In addition, in 1990, one regional project was launched with the financial backing of the EC: the Regional Environment Centre in Budapest. In 1991, the EC has budgeted 785 million ECU (over $1 billion) for the entire PHARE program, of which, once again, probably 20% or more will go toward environmental projects.

The first conference of Environment Ministers, convened under the umbrella of the PHARE program, took place in Prague in June 1991. The EC Commission, the UN Economic Commission for Europe, Canada, Japan, the USA and, most European countries participated. At that Conference, the EC Commissioner responsible for the environment, Carlo Ripa di Meana, outlined the EC's environmental action plan for the region.

That action plan has six major elements:

• The *first* within the PHARE program, is the support of additional regional projects reflecting the fact that pollution does not respect boundaries (an example of this is the effort to reduce air pollution in the Sulphur Triangle region of Poland, Czechoslovakia and eastern Germany);

• The *second* element is the preparation of the ground for consolidating the actions taken under various international environmental conventions to clean up the Elbe, the Oder, and the Danube river;.

• The *third* element is the gathering of statistical information on the extent and nature of pollution in the region to determine priorities better, monitor progress and evaluate projects;

• The *fourth* element is encouraging and facilitating scientific research on the causes of and cures for environmental damage and pollution;

• The *fifth* element is the definition of codes of conduct for investors in Eastern Europe, to avoid causing further damage to an already devastated environment (e.g. in November 1991, the Commission together with the Regional Environment Centre in Budapest, hosted a conference for investors to help them make the right decisions); and

• The *sixth* element is the exchange of views with Eastern European countries on global environmental problems such as the greenhouse effect, the depletion of the ozone layer and genetic diversity, with a view to seeking the support of those countries for the Community's own approaches to these problems.

Clearly, the EC is only at the beginning of its combined efforts to improve the quality of the environment in Eastern Europe. But the Commission of the European Communities has every intention of persevering in these efforts with the help and support of all the countries in the region.

References

1. PHARE is the Commission of the European Communities Programme of Assistance to the countries of Central and Eastern Europe.

14

Eastern Europe: The Experience of Ukraine
Yuri Scherbak

The Honourable Yuri Scherbak is the Minister of the Environment for Ukraine and head of the Green Party. He is the first non-communist Minister elected. He was also a Member of Parliament in the Supreme Soviet prior to its dissolution. A doctor of epidemiology by training, he is also a writer. His account of the nuclear reactor accident at Chernobyl was the first to be published in the Soviet Union.

The newly-independent Ukraine faces formidable economic and environmental challenges. Its first Ministry of the Environment was created on May 13, 1991 by Cabinet and approved by the Parliament on September 14, 1991. The Ministry was thus created very shortly after Ukraine proclaimed its independence from the former Soviet Union, on August 14, 1991. It had been under Soviet domination since the Revolution in 1919.

Ukraine was the second largest Republic after the Russian Federation in the USSR. It occupies approximately 604,000 square kilometres, or 2.7% of the total territory of the USSR. It has as much land as France and the United Kingdom combined. Its population is 55 million, composed of 73% Ukrainians, 22% of Russian origin, 1% Jewish, and 4% other minorities.

Ukraine accounts for 25% of the total manufacturing sector of the former USSR. Energy production equals 300 MKWH of electricity, of which 22% is nuclear energy. Its production and export of other basic items are as follows:

- 160 MT/year of coal, of which 8% is exported;
- 190 million cubic metres/year of gas, of which 25% is allocated for domestic consumption, and the rest is allocated to other Republics;

- 100 MT/year of iron ore, of which 16% is allocated for exports;
- 4.5 MT/year of minerals;
- 20 MT/year of cement;
- 50 MT/year of wheat;
- 4 MT/year of meat; and
- 7 MT/year of sugar.

Ukraine contributes approximately 5% of the world's sulphur production. In terms of natural resource reserves, Ukraine has about 14% of the world's iron ore, 8% of its coal, and 50% of its titanium. There are other natural reserves of lesser magnitude. In 1990, it exported approximately $14 billion of minerals and other products to satellite republics.

The industrial sector in Ukraine is very large and complex. Its largest sector is steel production, which provides material for the military industry of the USSR, an industry which manufactures tanks, missiles, submarines, electronics, aircraft, televisions, and warships. Agriculturally, Ukraine is known "as the bread basket of the USSR".

The environment of the Eastern Bloc, as a whole, has suffered enormously in the past several years. Because of the complexity of its industrial sector, Ukraine has probably suffered environmentally more than any other country in the former Bloc.

There is a need for major remedial actions in the very near future because the environment of Ukraine is devastated:

- the land, water and air are polluted;
- the rivers are so polluted that hardly any biological life exists in them;
- fish are polluted by chemical and toxic substances, such as DDT, PCBs, dioxins, furans and others;
- industry dumps waste into the water without regard for the environment;
- pesticides are the greatest agricultural pollutants in the environment;

• the steel and coal industries are major causes of atmospheric pollution;

• adding to this are automobile emissions. Although the Ukraine does not have as many cars as the West, its cars do not have catalytic converters, and thus emit SOx and NOx without limit.

Chernobyl is not only Ukraine's problem - it is a global catastrophe. It is a warning to the world's civilization of what advanced technology can do to humanity; and even scientists are unable to predict the consequences.

In order to cope with these problems, the Ministry of the Environment is proposing several actions:

• It will establish an Environmental Advisory Council. This body will consist of approximately 10-12 renowned scientists, primarily from abroad. The Council will advise the government on remedial actions to take.

• The Ukrainian Ministry of the Environment is developing strict environmental legislation based on Western technology in order to improve environmental conditions.

• It intends to obtain modern analytical equipment, and to train scientific staff to use it efficiently.

• The Ministry will further establish an Environmental Inspection System to enforce the legislation and Environmental Funds to do the Research and Development for abatement technology. The funds will be paid for by industry and tax revenues.

The opportunities for the environmental industry in Ukraine are tremendous. The market is virtually untapped - there exists a population of over 100 million within a 1000 km radius. Ukraine is inviting western industry, research organizations, universities, and individual companies to visit Ukraine, to look for joint ventures, licensing agreements, and technology transfer. The Ministry is available to facilitate contacts for foreigners with companies, universities, and research institutions in Ukraine. They have enormous scientific staff (available for a fraction of the cost that would normally be incurred

161

in the West) to do the research, the development work and to act as Western representatives, not only in Ukraine but also in other countries, such as Poland, Hungary, Romania, the Russian Federation, and other republics.

15

The Pacific Basin: The Experience of Japan
Makitaro Hotta

Makitaro Hotta is a Professor of Anglo-American Law at the College and the Graduate School of International Relations at Ritsumeikan University in Kyoto, Japan. He is also Associate Director, International Centre at Ritsumeikan University, a member of the American Bar Association (International Associate), the Law and Computer Association of Japan, the Japanese American Association of Legal Studies, and the Japanese Association of Real Estate Studies. He received his LLB and LLM from Waseda University in 1971 and 1973, and an LLM from Harvard Law School in 1977.

Japan's experience demonstrates that there is no definitive answer to the question of how to harmonize and/or coordinate two seemingly polar issues such as trade and the environment. Trade occurs, ideally, in an environment free from governmental or private regulation. The GATT system has been promoting international free trade and Japan has been one of the greatest beneficiaries of the system. Under the GATT, Japan has become one of the richest nations in the world.

Environmental issues, by their very nature, require government regulation. This proved true during the 1960s and 1970s when Japan suffered from severe environmental degradation: notably the massive air and water pollution that generated the so-called Big Four Pollution Suits. Following a series of judicial decisions, the Diet enacted several anti-pollution measures. Administrative and penal sanctions were imposed on industries and individuals as a means of environmental protection. Industries installed facilities for waste reduction and recovery of industrial by-products, such as chemicals, heat and water. Trees were planted around factories. These activities were supplemented by financial contributions industries made to a fund that was established in order to compensate victims of pollution, among other things.

In the early 1970s, Japan suffered its first oil crisis. Japanese industry managed this crisis by introducing "energy-saving" strategies, thereby reducing the consumption of oil and other energy sources. Thus, the problem of trade versus environment was first solved by a series of strong environmental regulations imposed by the local and national governments in Japan. Faced with these difficulties, industry tried to incorporate environmentally friendly technologies in their production processes and products. This approach was a major breakthrough for Japanese industry but it generated increased competitiveness in Japanese trade internationally.

As a result of strong government regulation, many industries began to invest substantial amounts of money into research and development activities. New production facilities were installed and new technologies were introduced. These changes coincided with the government's policy of "structural coordination" of industries, which changed the national industrial structure from the "heavy and hard" industries, to the "light and soft" ones. Investments were made mainly in such industries as electrical goods, textiles, other miscellaneous products, in the Newly Industrializing Entities (NIEs) and ASEAN. In the late 1970s, Japanese investments thus shifted from labour intensive industries, such as textile and electrical, to capital intensive industries such as chemical, machinery and automobiles. This change took place not only in East Asia but also in the advanced industrial nations.

In the early 1980s, and particularly since 1985, Japan faced a second set of economic difficulties arising from the favourable exchange rate of the yen against the dollar. Responding to these difficulties, private industry began relocating plants and factories in the NIEs and ASEAN countries. Most interestingly, labour intensive industrial investments shifted from the NIEs to ASEAN, particularly to Malaysia and Thailand. In the relocation process, there were claims that Japan was exporting pollution to foreign countries. Those claims were not groundless but the real issue was a different one: small and medium Japanese industries found it difficult to stay in business, not because of environmental considerations but because of a lack of competitiveness. For example, the forestry industry in Japan had become one of the weakest and most troubled industries. Under the liberalization of the wood trade, Japanese industry could not compete with imported timber from countries with tropical forests.

This competitive disadvantage resulted mainly from shifting the location of production and the economic consequences of doing so. Virtually all industries in the world are facing similar economic considerations. Furthermore, in all countries in the 1980s, both government and industry were not as environmentally aware as they are now. In some instances, the industrial relocations were welcomed by recipient countries. To some extent they contributed to the well-being of people in those countries. Most Japanese industrial activities have been based on the firm belief that their past experience in Japan could be applied directly to foreign countries. Criticisms were voiced about the attitudes of Japanese corporations but a good, corporate decision-making mechanism which could absorb the "high politics" of the international environment had not yet emerged. This is still true, even now, in virtually every corporation in the world.

In 1985, the NIEs increased their investment in the ASEAN countries. Some have charged that the management of these companies from the NIEs has not been conscious of environmental issues and of further environmental degradation in ASEAN. If such is the case, there will be serious environmental concerns in the ASEAN countries because the region is emerging as the centre of production in world trade, particularly in tripartite trade relationships between the NIEs, ASEAN and Japan.

Over the next forty years, a global shift of the paradigm of trade, the environment and development are likely to evolve as specified in Table 1 (see opposite page).

Currently, there is no common agreement about the proper measures to define the relationship between trade and the environment in Japan. The following ten measures are being proposed as the required measures for Japan but they have yet to be incorporated into governmental policies:

- Pay greater attention to the environment than to profit from trade;
- Create a framework in which environmental businesses are more profitable;
- Provide subsidies to environmentally creative businesses;
- Apply sanctions to businesses responsible for environmental degradation;
- Contribute business profits to an environmental fund;
- Impose an environmental tax on corporations (for an environmental fund);
- Restrain development which is environmentally destructive;
- Promote recycling activities by business (via subsidies);
- Incorporate environmental "cooperation" into business "competition";
- Develop an environmentally sustainable social structure.

These measures can be classified into three categories:

- the *first* consists of measures striking a better balance between trade and the environment through more favourable treatment of the environment;
- the *second* comprises measures which impose a burden on business activities, and in extreme cases, impose a ban on international trade and development; and
- the *third* are measures introducing sustainable as well as self-supporting development.

These measures could be implemented in both negative

Table 1 - *General Agreement of Trade and Environment (GATE)*

		1980s	1990s	2000s	2010s
TRADE	Principle	Competition Profit >Environmental Cost		Competitiveness Profit< Environmental Cost	
	Institution	GATT unilateral bilateral	GATT multilateral regional	GATE multilateral global	GATE global universal
ENVIRONMENT	Issue	Exploitation Degredation	Conservation	Amelioration	Creation
	Principle	CCP consumers pay	PPP polluters pay	TPP tax pay	TPP tax pay
DEVELOPMENT	Principle	Free	Sustainable	Growth managed	Balanced Self-supportable

and positive ways. For instance, if an environmental consideration overrides a business interest in trade, then trade in that area could be banned. This is a negative expression of the first proposition. Such an approach actually forms the framework of the Washington Treaty, which basically prohibits trade in environmentally endangered species.

Japan has identified several reservations with respect to the species protected by the treaty. Six of the reserved items concern whales, two concern lizards and two concern turtles. However, Japan has already publicly stated that it will consider withdrawing its reservation on a particular lizard in 1992, at the next conference of contracting states which will be held in Kyoto, Japan. With regard to turtles, several import measures have been taken, including a limitation on the number of imported Taimai turtles and a total import restriction on another turtle.

There is no clear policy from Japan to indicate that it will propose a revision of Article 20 of the GATT in order to incorporate the environment as one of its general exceptions. It is reported that the GATT will start to examine environmental measures and international trade in its revived working group, which was created in 1971. Ambassador Ukawa, the Japanese representative to the Geneva International Organizations, will be appointed as the chairman of that working group.

GATT should consider drafting a General Agreement on Trade and Environment, to be known as the GATE . The GATE would be a mechanism by which future trade would be regulated and developed. The concept of competition should be changed to that of "competitiveness", where competition will only be permitted by paying greater attention to the environment and by rejecting the externalization of environmental costs. The concept of competitiveness should also take into consideration the need for an environmentally level playing field.

The Japanese Government decided, in October 1990, to establish the Global Warming Prevention Action Program.

Starting in 1991, the Program will cover the next 20 years. Its specific goal is to maintain the emission level of CO_2 after the year 2000 at the 1990 level. The Program promotes changes in urban and regional structures, transportation systems, production structures, energy supplies and national life style in order to reduce the emission of CO_2. It also includes other measures, such as scientific observation and research, education and international cooperation.

With regard to research activities, the Japanese Government established two programs:

• the Comprehensive Promotion Program on Research and the Study for the Preservation of the Global Environment; and

• the Basic Plan of Research and Development of Earth Science Technology.

The Global Environmental Research Centre was established in the National Environmental Institute. Funding measures were also taken for the promotion of a comprehensive study of the global environment.

Finally, in order to construct a "recycling society", several bills were submitted to the Diet. These bills restrain the inputs of new resources, minimize the waste emitted into the environment, and aim at the re-use and renewable use of resources.

The role of local government in the protection of the environment in Japan is an important one. Comparing the GDP of major local governments in Japan with those of foreign countries reveals that the Tokyo Metropolitan Government has a larger GDP than Canada and Spain. The Osaka Prefectural Government has a GDP similar to that of the Netherlands. Aichi Prefecture produces more than Australia. Most of the local governments have their own measures for the protection of the global environment.

Several industrial organizations have also issued their views on the problems associated with the preservation of the global environment. Within companies, several sections relating to the world environment have been organized

169

under names such as the "world environment section" and the "environment related business branch". This movement is expanding in each company's marketing and consumer related activities. The environmentally sound activities of industry, and its assistance to the benevolent activities of citizens and of local governments, will be important in order to form an environmentally sustainable society.

At the mass public level, the United Nations' World Environment day is celebrated every June 5th by large numbers of citizens and civic organizations. This activity is important in demonstrating citizens' concern for the environment. Though the number of NGOs active on the international stage is relatively small, those engaged in community activities are many. It can be expected that these community-oriented, non-profit organizations will contribute to environmental protection activities. Government agencies - such as the Ministries of Foreign Affairs, Agriculture, and Post and Telecommunications - support voluntary activities by NGOs through various cooperative and funding programs.

Finally, the "Ecomark" has been adopted by the Japanese Environmental Association, to encourage the preservation of the environment. It has a purpose similar to the "Ecolabel" which has been used in Germany, Canada and the Nordic countries. In addition, the Ministry of Education has prepared materials for use by teachers in environmental education. Local governments, such as the Osaka Prefectural Government, have published supplementary reading materials for use in environmental education in elementary schools.

16

The Pacific Basin: The Experience of Thailand
Juanjai Ajanant

Juanjai Ajanant is a Professor of Economics at Chulalongkorn University, Bangkok. Prior to that he held a number of positions with the Government of Thailand, including Policy Advisor to the Prime Minister, Chief Economic Advisor to the Minister of Commerce, and Advisor to the Ministry of Foreign Affairs. He has worked on a regular basis for the National Economic and Social Development Board, the United Nations ESCAP, the World Bank, UNIDO, UNDP and the United Nations University in Tokyo. Dr Ajanant studied Economics at the University of Lancaster, England; International Economics at the University of Surrey, England; Econometrics at the University of Pennsylvania, Philadelphia; and Economic Development at Temple University, Philadelphia. He is the author of numerous articles and books.

The experience of Thailand illustrates many of the difficult issues that arise in considering the links between economic growth, environmental protection and export access from the perspective of a third world country.

Following a period of slow growth from 1982 onward, the Thai economy took off in the late 1980s and from 1988 to 1990 real economic growth averaged more than 10% per annum. Projected economic growth for Thailand is 6.5%-7.2% for the next 5 years. Economists are confident that the real economic expansion in Thailand can be sustained at that level for the next decade.

In an attempt to industrialize the agrarian-based economy in the early 1960s, the government decided to adopt an import-substitution policy. This trade regime has been maintained to the present day. Thai manufacturers did not expect their products to be exported but, by a stroke of good fortune, Thai exports entered world markets in the mid 1970s, after the first oil shock.

The emergence of Thai exports forced the government, in 1980, to review its trade measures and related administrative practices. Following an extensive study on trade performance and the export system in 1984, the government began to adopt pro-export measures. These measures included exchange rate policy, fiscal measures and monetary instruments and had the result of boosting Thai exports. With an average growth of over 20%, Thai exports have made a significant impact on the economy. Japanese investment has made Thailand's economic growth even more impressive. By 1990 it was the major source of investment from abroad and the growth of Thailand has been largely fuelled by exports and Japanese investment.

As the Thai economy took off in the late 1980s, the world economic environment began to change dramatically, due to the paralysis of the GATT talks and the proliferation of unilateral trade measures implemented by major trading nations. Moreover, interest in environmental issues has grown tremendously in the last decade. Since many environmental issues are global issues, domestic pressure groups have become international pressure groups and have become a real political force. Greenpeace has grown from a humble base into an international movement. Likewise, concern for animals has made an impact on consumer choice. It is no longer sufficient to discuss resource use in terms of production, consumption and exchange in stylized neoclassical economics. Policy makers have been made aware of the consequences of both private decisions and public policy on resource arrangements. International concern for the environment has left a dent in the commerce of virtually every nation.

Thai Environmental Concern

The type of industrialization which Thailand has been

pursuing says much about its concern for the environment. Being a well-endowed country, in the early 1960s manufactured goods consisted of resource-based and processed products. At the same time, the agricultural sector relied on low-tech and rain-fed production. Increases in agricultural production depended on the expansion of acreage. The government remained unconcerned that farmers slashed and burnt virgin forested areas (mainly national forest) in the 1960s in order to enlarge farm acreage. Nor was it concerned with the loss of mangrove areas. The primary concern was to develop fast enough to catch up with the rest of the civilized world.

Throughout the last thirty years, as policy-makers focused on growth per se, it was very difficult to insert new objectives in the government's agenda. More recently, environmental issues have divided the public into two groups: those who want growth at any cost and those who are concerned with resources for future generations. The growth at any cost group has prevailed most of the time. A close look at the poor record provides testimony of Thailand's miscalculation.

In order to generate sufficient electricity to meet growing demand, the Electricity Generating Authority (EGAT) of Thailand built hydro-electric dams during the last two decades. The construction of the dams meant resettlement of thousands of villagers to new areas, loss of forested areas and loss of natural habitat for wild animals. The EGAT maintains that hydro-electric dams keep the unit cost of electricity down but they have never calculated the costs of resettlement and the social costs of environmental loss. Vested interest in the EGAT - from suppliers of credit and equipment - grew so much that it became impossible to convince them to search for an alternative way to generate electricity.

In the logging industry, Thailand's forested areas have been reduced at the rate of 16% throughout most of the 1980s. Areas that have been previously harvested have not been replanted due to an archaic system of concessions.

173

As trees of legal size disappeared from concession areas, companies began to harvest smaller size trees. In fact, many began to cut trees illegally in the national forests. Law enforcement has been weak and sometimes government officials are involved in wrong-doings. Forested areas are fast disappearing in Thailand, resulting in changing rates and patterns of precipitation. The National Environment Agency (NEA) has noted that the level of water in the country's rivers declined by at least 2-3 centimetres during the 1980s. In order to welcome foreign investors to Thailand, several regulations relating to effluent charges made by the Ministry of Industry have been overruled at the cabinet level. The cabinet rulings have enlarged the areas that companies can pollute. Only when the designated areas affect the fresh supply of tap water are the rulings set aside. Therefore, in certain areas the BOD level from the nearby rivers has been reduced to a critical level. Moreover, the level of noise and air pollution from Bangkok's traffic is critical.

During the last civilian administration, before the coup ousted the government in February 1991, Thailand had begun to re-arrange its development objectives. The government, armed with new inputs from NGOs and various agencies, began to deal squarely with the environmental issues. In 1989, it passed legislation to ban all logging in the Kingdom. While that legal document became an important milestone, the government had to contend with political harassment throughout the entire period. In the search for alternative clean power, several dam construction projects were reviewed. Many were put on the back burner until the World Bank made an environmental assessment. In fact, the previous government's record on environmental concern is probably the best among all governments in the post-war period. Still, Thailand has not gone far enough in re-arranging its national agenda to fit with world expectations. And across Indochina and the ASEAN region, environmental issues have often been bypassed for development's sake.

New Agenda for Development

The 1991 World Development Report defines economic development as a sustainable increase in living standards. The concept encompasses material consumption, education, health and environmental protection. By that World Bank definition, Thailand is not on a sustainable path. Public awareness of environmental issues in Thailand has been low, as if the environment is not an urgent matter. Government agencies have failed to deliver the message to the public and business sector. Worst of all, policy-makers from political parties have not had to make environmental concern one of their platform policies. Their explanation is that they are not concerned with the environment as long as there are poor people in their constituencies. Yet a new direction and policy guidelines can be set even without a call from the public. The government may have to set the tone.

There are several changes that must be institutionalized to save the environment:

• the Government must define national objectives that include environmental concerns;

• the National Environmental Agency (NEA), which remains an office in the Prime Minister's Office, must be upgraded to a department within the Ministry of Science, Technology and Energy;

• the NEA should be reinforced by a new bill that regulates environmental issues;

• the new legislation should be drafted by people from all walks of life- designing a new bill should not be left to lawyers whose concern is to regulate behaviour using obscure legal clauses;

• the NEA should develop its capacity to measure pollution levels scientifically (i.e. levels of carbon monoxide, decibels, BOD and others);

• the NEA should be given sufficient funds from the national budget to perform necessary functions; and

• the NEA should campaign at the lowest level of the

populace and in elementary schools to make people aware of environmental issues.

This is a short list of measures which the government can initiate in order to make a serious and concrete effort on global issues. Even this list may prove to be too much for the Thai people to implement. While the government is concerned with environmental issues and would like to be among the civilized nations that take the issue seriously, environmental issues have not been advanced on the political agenda by any Thai party. Only scholars have articulated the merits of a sound environmental policy. In designing environmental laws, there are very few legal experts in the country. In Thailand, human resources are in short supply in areas related to power conservation and the environment, and this is the same for most developing countries. It takes more than international pressure groups to mobilize the new agenda in some developing countries; it requires time, money, human resources, and the right political climate to realize a comprehensive plan. Developing countries usually have time but they lack resources to strengthen their capacity to control their own environment.

The International Dimension of the Environment

Supporting policies that protect the environment does not mean bringing environmental issues into international commerce in all cases. The rush to protest against certain products is well taken but the rush of major governments' policies to exchange a good environment for market access is tantamount to harassment of the developing countries. Market access is already complicated by several administrative manipulations that prevent easy penetration. In recent times, several other issues have been clouding international trade. Issues such as workers's rights and environmental laws have been used as a pretext for protection.

While policy makers everywhere are concerned with

workers' rights, they are more concerned with job loss. In the on-going North American Free Trade Agreement (NAFTA) negotiations, some Canadians have been trying to bring Mexican environmental laws in line with Canadian laws. The people who advocate this are neither environmentalist nor business-oriented; they are the people who would lose their jobs from the shift of production elsewhere. Environmentalists in Mexico should be arguing the case for a clean environment in their country but it appears that a domestic boundary is no longer safe from environmentalists from abroad.

As the major developed countries begin to insert environmental concerns into their trade policies, the struggle for survival in the developing countries becomes more onerous. Without earnings from manufactured exports (the usual cause of pollution) those industries will not be a leading sector of the economy. Forcing these industries to become cleaner means that many industries will simply move from one country to the next and the agricultural or traditional sectors will not be enough to sustain the economy if and when environmental issues become impediments to commerce. This scenario is not far-fetched; it could become a harsh reality very soon.

There is a fine line to be drawn on the environmental issue. Yet it is possible to differentiate between global issues and those which are specific to a locale. Environmentalists should pursue those issues that have global impact, such as global warming, acid rain, loss of rain forest and air and water pollution that lead to international conflict. Those issues which are specific to a locale and fit with the social norms of the society in question should be left to local pressure groups. Campaigning against these specific issues can be done effectively through domestic political systems. Too much pressure on developing countries will prove to be counter-effective, merely leading to conflicts without resolution.

E
Multilateral Regimes

17

The General Agreement on Tariffs and Trade (GATT) [1]
Piritta Sorsa

Piritta Sorsa is an economist with the World Bank, Geneva Office, and currently works on issues related to the GATT and the Uruquay Round, including trade and environment. She has also worked as an economist with the OECD and UNCTAD. She has an MA from the Turku School of Economics, Finland, and a PhD in international economics from the Graduate Institute of International Studies in Geneva.

In recent months, the environment has become a major topic of discussion at meetings of the GATT Council. At the same time, the GATT has raised much passion among environmentalists, many of whom accuse it of being anti-environment and propose modifications to its rules.[2] In contrast, trade officials want to clarify the relationship between trade, GATT and environmental policies in order to prevent a rise in environment-related trade friction and also to address environmental issues with the most appropriate policies.

The present discussion has revealed one fundamental point: once it is acknowledged that trade, as such, is not the source of most environmental damage, it follows that trade policies are not the best vehicles for dealing with environmental problems. The GATT is not against the environment: in fact, by setting limits to the use of trade instruments[3] for environmental purposes, the GATT rules encourage the search for more appropriate environmental policies.

The role of the GATT in relation to most environmental issues is indirect:

- *First*, a well functioning international trading system is important for growth, and growth is important for the environment because growing economies find it easier to allocate additional resources for environmental protection. The GATT was set up to promote the smooth functioning of the international trading system and setting environmental policies has never been regarded as part of that task.

• *Second*, although the GATT rules and environmental policies do interact indirectly in many areas (GATT rules bear on border adjustment of domestic policies, on the application of standards in trade, on the use of subsidies, and on the use of trade measures with public policy goals), the application of some GATT rules with environmental ramifications is subject to varying interpretations. The concepts applied are unclear and they have rarely been tested in case law. This can lead to trade friction and protectionist abuses that undermine the GATT's primary function as guardian of the international trading system. Uncertainty can also affect environment-related investments.

Most legitimate environmental policies are not in conflict with the GATT rules. Therefore, there is no need to modify the GATT on environmental grounds but there is a need to clarify some of the relevant rules. The main sources of uncertainty in regard to environmental policies under present GATT rules include the extraterritorial application of certain types of domestic environmental policies, the use of trade sanctions to deal with international problems and the overall relationship of international environmental agreements to the GATT.

A closer look at the existing rules also reveals certain anomalies in relation to the application of efficient environmental policies, which should be discussed within the GATT. Some sharing of the costs of environmental policies can be constrained by the GATT subsidy rules. As the environment is not mentioned in the public policy goals in Article XX, some legitimate environmental policies may fall outside the scope of the GATT. The border adjustment rules may encourage the use of indirect taxes to address all types of environmental problems. This can lead to double taxation of environmental costs or the imposition of domestic environmental costs on imports.

Environmental Policies: Some Basic Issues

Understanding the links between the GATT and the environment requires a brief consideration of the source and nature of environmental problems, environmental efficiency issues, problems of environmental enforcement, and cost sharing:

• *Environmental problems* arise from various types of market or government failures. If prices do not reflect the costs of environmental damage, over-consumption may lead to unsustainable use of common resources like clean air, water or the ozone layer. Similarly, "bad" policies like subsidies to forest clearing or transport can have an adverse impact on the environment. Sustainability, or the appropriate state of the environment, can be difficult to assess or estimate. Many problems are subject to scientific disagreements or differing value-judgments. The restoration or maintenance of a sustainable balance between economic activity and the natural environment in the most efficient or least-cost manner is one of the main tasks of environmental policies.

• *Efficient environmental policies* should correct the problem as close as possible to its source by equalizing marginal costs and benefits. This can be achieved by government intervention or through the assignment or exercise of property rights. Many surveys[4] have concluded that, once the real life complexities of environmental policy making[5] are accounted for, no explicit ranking of policies can be made. Nevertheless, most studies confirm the greater overall efficiency of market based instruments over regulations, and direct over indirect instruments. The main problems with regulations are non-transparency and disregard for cost differences associated with alternative approaches to, for example, emission reduction.

With international environmental problems, whether transnational or global,[6] efficiency requires action by all concerned. Measures by one country alone can be costly and can only partially reduce global damage.

While trade policies are not as efficient as environmental policies, their use may arise in the real world of the second-best. If less distorting policies are not available or do not work, trade policies may have to be used - either alone or to complement other policies. For example, if trade is a major mechanism of transmission of an environmental problem, some control of trade may be needed and restrictions may be especially necessary where high risk elements, such as contagious diseases or nuclear wastes, are involved.

- *Enforcement* of environmental policies can be induced either through punishment or reward. National sovereignty sets limits to international enforcement and calls for cooperation. Adoption and enforcement of policies across countries can be enhanced by moral suasion, compensation, and trade or other sanctions. Moral suasion is easier in countries with higher environmental awareness. Compensation is becoming common in practice. Debt-for-nature swaps and environment-linked aid have increased. Some countries are offering to pay for the clean-up of pollution or environmental threats in other countries.[7] Some countries are punishing others with unilaterally determined sanctions. Bans on imports of furs killed with leg-hold traps and timber from unsustainably-managed forests have been proposed within the EC, to take effect in 1995. Some international environmental treaties punish "free-riders" with trade sanctions.

The use of trade measures to enforce international environmental policies is clearly second best to negotiation and compensation. With global issues, the need for common action to ensure efficient outcomes can justify trade restrictions as a last resort. Otherwise "free-riders" undermine the efforts of others. A threat of sanctions can also induce participation but any unilateral use of trade measures, even as a second best alternative, should not be allowed. Their efficiency is doubtful, not only because trade with third parties can continue, but also because unilaterally inflicted punishment carries no guarantee of cooperative behaviour in the future. Moreover, the difficulty of detecting the source and extent of environmental damage, in many situations, can lead to the threat or use of trade restrictions for harassment purposes.

• *Sharing the costs* of environmental policies requires judgments about the distribution of property rights. The question of who has a right to pollute or to be polluted has a bearing on who bears the cost of environmental protection and who receives the revenue. A company may claim that its acquisition of assets includes rights to pollute.[8] Tribal groups may claim traditional ownership of common resources. Policy makers have to decide whether polluters should be taxed or subsidized in order to secure compliance with environmental policies. Many countries have strong feelings about their exclusive right to decide on the use of their natural resources, and want compensation for any interference. Environmentalists, on the other hand, often feel that natural resources, such as forests, are a global common asset and countries over-exploiting them should be punished for destroying them. These are difficult issues that have to be decided both nationally and internationally.[9]

The GATT and Domestic Environmental Policies

In general, the GATT rules are not in conflict with the pursuit of efficient domestic environmental policies. The GATT is concerned with how, not why, policies are applied. The most relevant parts of the GATT dealing with domestic environmental issues are the basic rules on border adjustments (Articles I, III), certain exceptions for public policy goals (Article XX:b,g), the Standards Code and rules on dumping and subsidies.

The distinction between product and production related environmental problems or policies is central to an analysis of the interaction of domestic environmental policies with the GATT rules:

• Product related policies address consumption issues. They cover both imports and domestic goods. The GATT rules require the relevant domestic policies to be applied in a non-discriminatory manner between imports and domestic goods.

• Production related policies, or production and process methods (PPMs), address production issues. Their scope is limited to domestic production. The GATT has no say in purely domestic policies. Subjecting imports to domestic production methods would threaten the very basis of specialization through trade. It would undermine the capacity of countries to benefit from their comparative advantage. In practice, however, the distinction between product standards and PPMs may be difficult to make, which can, in turn, raise doubts about the interpretation of the GATT rules in this area. For example, the extent to which a process related chemical leaves a trace in a product can determine whether the problem is product or process related. Finally, if the GATT cannot dictate to countries what their PPM choices should be, it follows that the GATT would not permit compensatory trade restrictions aimed at eliminating international differences in pollution abatement and control costs.

a) Basic Rules
There are two basic GATT rules regarding the treatment of imported products.

• *First*, imported goods must be granted the same treatment at the frontier (in relation to tariffs and any permitted non-tariff restrictions) irrespective of their source. These are the non-discrimination (most-favoured nation or MFN) rules of Articles I and XIII.[10]

• *Second*, the national treatment provision of Article III requires that, once an imported product has crossed the frontier, it must be subject to treatment no less favourable (regarding taxes, regulations, etc.) than that enjoyed by the like domestic product. Article III provisions refer to products, not the permissibility of trade measures to enforce particular production methods or to adjust for differences in costs of alternative methods (PPMs). The imported and domestic products in question must be "like" products, and the taxes and charges referred to in the Article are those falling directly on the product concerned.[11]

Most product-related environmental policies should not be in conflict with the non-discrimination requirement of national treatment and unconditional MFN, if they are applied uniformly. For example, both imported and domestic cars can be required to carry catalytic converters, or to meet certain exhaust emission limits. There has been some concern whether differentiated tax rates, according to some criteria like chemical content, would be compatible with the MFN.[12] As long as the basis of taxation is transparent and the same for all, a problem should not arise.

Some environmental policies may conflict with the stipulation against disguised protection under the national treatment provisions. This could be the case with deposit-refund-types of policies or some regulatory measures that cause relatively higher costs of compliance for imports. For example, a requirement that all soft-drinks must be sold in returnable bottles can give an advantage to domestic producers. Within the EC, a requirement by Italy that all pasta sold in Italy should be made of hard wheat (grown mainly in Southern Italy) was considered a non-tariff barrier (NTB). Any intent to grant implicit protection to domestic goods in such cases as these may be difficult to prove.

Environment-related trade disputes of this type have already emerged and are likely to increase. A recent law in Germany will soon oblige retailers and manufacturers to take back packaging material on their products. This measure has been challenged as a NTB by the international packaging industry.[13] A similar case concerning a Danish requirement on recyclable bottles was first rejected by the

EC Commission as an NTB, but was later upheld by the European Court on environmental grounds. Some EC countries are currently planning legislation to make recycling of numerous products like cars or appliances goods a responsibility of their producers.

As the basic GATT rules are not concerned with the purpose for which policies are applied, some environmental measures may be considered incompatible with the rules. Nevertheless, some of these policies can still fit the GATT public policy exceptions in Article XX, or fall within the scope of the Standards Code (see below).

The adjustment of taxes at the border is subject to special rules.[14] By convention within the GATT, indirect domestic taxes can be levied on imports, and rebated on exports. The adjustment also applies to indirect taxes on inputs, if these are physically incorporated in the product. This reflects both practical convenience and shifting assumptions of tax incidence. Indirect taxes (sales, turnover, value-added, per unit input or output charges) are assumed to be shifted to the consumer, whereas direct taxes (income tax, social security charges, profit taxes) would be "borne by the producer".[15] The physical incorporation requirement for inputs reflects the difficulties of measuring the share of other inputs in the final product.

With environmental policies, the main impact of this taxation rule is that it can create a bias in favour of excise taxes. Although indirect taxes are sub-optimal from an efficiency perspective for production externalities, producers are still likely to lobby for such taxes in order to ensure that imports are liable for the same environmental costs as domestic goods. Such taxes would be in full compliance with the GATT and as they can be rebated on exports and levied on imports of the same good, the impact of the cost of the environmental policy on domestic industry's competitiveness is reduced.

The use of indirect taxes can also make imports pay for domestic environmental clean-ups regardless of whether they are the source of the problem. The rules could also lead to double taxation of environmental costs, depending on how countries use environmental taxes. If an exporting country levies direct taxes, and an importing one indirect taxes, to correct for the same externality, the imported good will pay twice the environmental cost. These problems could partly be avoided by the application of the Polluter Pays Principle or international policy coordination. Although PPP it is not a GATT principle, most OECD countries have adopted it as a guideline for domestic policies.[16]

b) PPMs and the Basic GATT Articles

The GATT concept of "like product" and the unconditional MFN principle go some way in clarifying the relationship between basic GATT rules and PPMs (the permissibility of trade measures to enforce particular production methods or to adjust for differences in costs of alternative methods). Essentially, MFN and national treatment rules limit environment related compensatory adjustments to policies affecting products, as opposed to production methods. The GATT text specifically restricts border adjustment to "like products". The purpose of the concept is to prevent protectionist measures on the basis of an artificial differentiation of products. Differing methods of production do not make the final products different - no differentiation at the border is justified on this basis. Beef is beef regardless of the method of killing the bull; tuna is tuna regardless of the types of nets used to catch it. This means that countries cannot devise taxes or regulations for imports based on differing methods of processing.

The GATT offers no definition for "like products". A case by case approach has been considered most appropriate. Commonly used indicators in the GATT Panels have been: end uses in a market; consumer tastes and habits; and a product's properties, nature and quality.[17] Another test applied in some cases has been whether domestic and imported items are included in the same tariff schedule. In past cases, various types of coffee (robusta or arabica), or domestic "whisky" and a Scottish brand whisky were considered like products, and thus ineligible for different customs treatment.

The word "unconditional" used in association with the MFN principle also argues against any discrimination at the border based on differences in production methods. Entry of a product at the border cannot be made contingent upon environmental conditions in the exporting country - either in relation to a production process or in general. The fundamental intention of the drafters of the GATT was to provide stability and maintain the comparative advantage enjoyed by the lowest cost foreign producers, without regard to value judgements in the importing state about the desirability of policies that give rise to low costs.[18]

In practice, however, the distinction between product and process characteristics is not always easy to establish. This makes the application of the rules more difficult. In many food and pharmaceutical industries, the "product concept" can be interpreted to include a certain element of risk influenced by the method of production. Hygiene standards in slaughterhouses influence the health risk embodied in the final product - meat. In international trade, it is common that importing countries inspect production methods in some food and pharmaceutical industries. On site inspection with perishable products can also be less costly than a blunt rejection of the product at the importer's border. In some cases, the "likeness" of a product may depend on whether additives like hormones or chemicals can be detected in the product or pass a certain threshold level of risk. Some of these problems are addressed in the GATT Standards Code (see below).

c) Exceptions - Article XX (b,g)
Most problems of interpretation of GATT rules in relation to environmental policies are linked to the exceptions. Article XX allows countries to deviate from their basic GATT obligations for certain public policy goals, but under relatively strict criteria.[19] The text requires countries to

adopt the least trade-distorting policies available and to apply them in a non-discriminatory way. The application of the Article to environmental issues has been the subject of considerable debate because many of the concepts and definitions used are vague and have rarely been tested in disputes.[20] The main problem the Article raises in regards to domestic environmental policies is whether it allows countries to restrict imports on account of differences in environmental policies (PPMs).

The PPM issue is directly linked to extraterritoriality considerations. As the headnote of the section does not specify where the object of the public policy measures is to be located, some argue that a country has a right to worry about health problems in other countries as well. Therefore, importing countries could require that imported goods are produced in a certain way. If accepted, such an approach would not only work against the realization of comparative advantage, but would lead to a power-led imposition of values across countries and the disruption of trade world-wide. This would undermine the rule-based nature of the GATT and would reduce the opportunities for gains from specialization through trade. The scope of the Article should, therefore, be clarified and limited to product-related public policy goals only within each country's territory.

What amounts to a contrary interpretation of Article XX has been apparent in a number of recent (or contemplated) trade measures. The EC has plans to forbid imports of furs caught with leg-hold traps. The US has banned tuna imports from Mexico because the drift-nets used kill dolphins. This case was recently brought to the GATT and the Panel ruled against the extraterritorial application of the Article. Whether this is enough to prevent the adoption of further similar measures remains to be seen.

Another problem with Article XX is that it does not specifically mention the "environment" among the public policy goals. Protection of "human, plant or animal life or health" may cover most environmental issues, but not all.

Contrary to many national applications of similar laws, this may leave some potentially legitimate environmental policies outside the scope of the Article and the GATT. For example, various recycling schemes (legitimate as environmental policies) may not be considered to fall within the rubric of protection of "animal, human, plant life or health" and, therefore be ruled GATT-inconsistent both under the basic rules and under the exceptions.

Uncertainty, and potential for abuse, may also arise from a lack of specificity as to the types of measures that can be applied on environmental grounds. One question is whether trade restrictions may only be applied to products directly implicated in the environmental problem at hand, or whether restrictions can be applied to other products as well. This issue arises basically from the fact that trade measures may be applied for enforcement and retaliation, and not directly to give effect to a solution to a specific environmental problem.

In principle, Article XX favours the adoption of efficient environmental policies, with trade measures being applied only as last resort. Policies have to meet three criteria:

• they must fit the scope of the Article;
• they must be "necessary" to (or related to) the stated objectives; and
• they must be non-discriminatory and non-protectionist.

The criteria of "scope" means that the use of Article XX must be related to the public policy objectives enumerated. The GATT has no role in judging the desirability of the objectives per se, but rather the appropriateness of policies applied to meet the declared objectives.[21] Nevertheless, a judgment has to be made on whether the purpose of the exceptional policies is within the public policy area. In the Thai cigarette case,[22] the Panel did not consider whether a reduction in smoking was desirable, but ruled that smoking was hazardous to health. The Panel referred to an expert report requested from the World Health Organization (WHO). In the Mexican-US dolphin/tuna case, some questioned whether dolphins were an exhaustible natural resource (as scientists disagree on the issue), which is required by Article XX (g). Purse-net fishing can, however, be harmful to "animal life or health" (but so is fishing itself) and fit within the scope of Article XX(b). It could be a matter of judgment whether discarding rather than recycling glass bottles poses a danger to "human, animal, plant life or health".

The "necessary" condition under Article XX(b) is fundamental in setting limits to the use of trade measures for public policy goals. The importer has to prove that an exceptional measure under Article XX is the least trade-distorting alternative available. The Article thereby promotes the search for efficient environmental policies to address the source of a problem. In the Thai cigarette case, the Panel concluded that information campaigns, and other measures against smoking were more appropriate than trade restrictions for the stated goal - the reduction of smoking. In the Tuna/Dolphin Panel it was argued that initiating an international agreement limiting dolphin kills would be less trade-distorting than trade restrictions to achieve the environmental objective.

For many environmental problems, trade restrictions may not meet the necessary criteria. It should be relatively easy to demonstrate that policies related to the management of animal herds are more "necessary" than export bans for "protection of animal life". In ivory trade, for example, a total trade ban is unlikely to meet the "necessary" test. Less trade-distorting alternatives available would be conservation policies. Hazardous waste is a case where the necessity of trade bans would be easier to justify.

In the case of domestic issues, the "necessary" condition should also limit the scope of the Article to product-related measures. It would be difficult to demonstrate that restrictions on imports of products that pollute in another country are "necessary" for health protection in the consuming country.

The "necessary" requirement in Article XX(b) may, on

193

the other hand, become a source of concern for the international trading system. Implicitly, it requires the GATT Panels to judge on countries' choices of environmental policies, which indirectly may force the GATT to take a stance on certain environmental issues. In the Thai cigarette case, the GATT Panel sought expert advice from an outside organization - WHO. If the German packaging law was brought to the GATT, the Panel might have to decide whether the "take-back" requirement was the least trade-distorting policy available. To do this would require some expertise on environmental matters.

The "relating to" concept in Article XX(g) has a more precise meaning, because of the requirement in the text that the trade measure be taken in conjunction with similar domestic restrictions on the use of the same non-exhaustible natural resource. It should be relatively straightforward to show that, unless accompanied by similar domestic measures, bans on exports of logs or other resources do not meet the test. For example, Thailand has banned all logging to protect certain forests, whereas Indonesia applies a ban on exports of tropical logs only. The latter is unlikely to be GATT-compatible.[23]

The non-discrimination and "no-disguised-protection" requirements in Article XX are linked, through the use of the words "arbitrary" or "unjustifiable" in the headnote, to the purpose of the measures applied. Thus, there may be a justification for some discrimination or measures seemingly favouring domestic producers. For example, the requirement of refillable bottles, if accepted in terms of the scope of the Article, could fit the criteria here.

d) Standards Code
Certain types of environmental measures can be justified under the Agreement on Technical Barriers to Trade (TBT), commonly called the Standards Code. It is a free-standing agreement and applies to signatories only, who number approximately forty. Like Article XX, the Code recognizes the precedence of public policy goals over free

trade under certain circumstances. It also aims at preventing the use of these standards and regulations as NTBs.

Contrary to Article XX, "environment" is explicitly mentioned in the text in addition to protection of human, plant and animal life or health. This makes its theoretical scope wider than that of Article XX for its signatories. The Code promotes transparency, and signatories are required to notify all planned policies to other signatories in the GATT.

The Code creates a presumption in favour of the use of harmonized international standards, and spells out the principles of non-discrimination and the use of the least trade-distorting measures available. The Uruguay Round has developed some of these concepts further. Proposals include: more precise rules for risk assessment; more explicit need for scientific evidence as a basis for standards; and a proportionality principle.[24]

The Code raises similar issues as Article XX with respect to PPMs, or extraterritoriality. The text is sufficiently unclear in several areas to allow for varying interpretations. Like Article XX, the Code does not mention where the protected environment should be located. PPMs are addressed only indirectly in the dispute settlement provisions. PPMs can be invoked if a party is considered to have circumvented its obligations in relation to product standards. This has led some to conclude that PPMs are covered in the Code and that countries can require imported products to have been produced in a certain way. The Standards Committee has discussed the matter in the past, but has not come to any conclusions. Case law offers little help as there have been no formal disputes.

The Standards Code carries implications for the efficiency of environmental policies through its bias in favour of harmonization of standards internationally. The harmonization of product standards can, in some cases, improve efficiency by reducing the costs of compliance with different standards and by increasing their transparency. However, as efficient environmental policies often require differentiation according to local conditions - especially with production or emission related standards - harmonization of PPMs, if covered, may be inefficient and may undermine comparative advantage.

e) Subsidies and Dumping

The GATT subsidy and dumping rules touch upon some aspects of environmental policies. They can limit the options to finance environmental policies or influence attempts to restrict trade on account of differences in environmental policies across countries.

The GATT set limits to the use of subsidies to finance environmental policies because of the potential impact of subsidies on competitiveness. Export subsidies on manufactured products are, in principle, prohibited. Production subsidies can be countervailed, if they cause injury to an industry in the importer's market. Environmental or other subsidies of a general nature (i.e. production subsidies) can be GATT compatible, if they do not have major trade effects.

Some sharing of the burden of environmental costs through general subsidies can help mitigate demands for protection. Problems with the identification of polluters may also put the burden of financing clean-ups on governments. Countries do use many types of general direct or indirect subsidies, and their reasonable use is likely to pass unchallenged.

Within the Uruguay Round, it has been proposed that certain types of environmental subsidies could be included in a category of non-countervailable subsidies.[25] These would be, for example, part of a one-time adaptation or the acquisition costs of environment-friendly equipment. But, subsidies are not without side-effects - polluters may be encouraged to pollute more in order to obtain more subsidies, or their use may encourage entry to the industry.

The use of countervailing duties to offset differences in environmental standards or costs across countries has been proposed by some environmental groups.[26] There has never been a test of whether this would be allowed by present GATT rules.

Countervailing duties can be imposed if there is injury to domestic industry and evidence of a subsidy. Key concepts under the rules, such as "injury", "industry", and "subsidy" are not very clearly defined. This has led to the abuse of the provisions for protectionist purposes. Past attempts at clarifying the use of subsidies in the Subsidies Code have done little to reduce the problems.

Proof of an implicit subsidy would run into difficult measurement problems. The investigator would have to identify the optimal or sustainable level of environmental protection of the firm in the exporting country, which is a formidable task for anyone. A true environmental subsidy or dumping investigation would also have to take account of differences in environmental conditions in the two countries. Furthermore, it could be argued that "the lack of subsidy" is generally available and therefore not countervailable.

The use of anti-dumping actions on environmental grounds would be difficult to justify, since dumping is what firms (and not governments) do. Lower environmental standards in one country as opposed to another would generally be regarded as the result of government inaction on the regulatory front. The treatment of certain cost-increasing regulatory constraints on firms as a countervailable (implicit) subsidy would represent a new departure in the use of anti-subsidy provisions, both in the GATT and at the national level.

It would be an unfortunate innovation, considering the precedent it would set for regarding anything that gave rise to differential cost structures (fewer holidays, different tax levels, fringe benefits, etc.) as countervailable.[27]

The GATT and International Environmental Policies

The relationship between the GATT and international

environmental agreements has been the subject of some controversy. International environmental policies interact with the present GATT rules in a number of ways:

• In the absence of a GATT waiver, both the instruments and enforcement mechanisms applied under international agreements could fall foul of the GATT.[28] The problems with instruments used are similar to those discussed above in relation to domestic policies. The use of trade measures for enforcement under international environmental agreements (global or transnational) raises some untested issues for the present GATT rules (moral suasion and international financial transfers are outside the scope of the GATT).

• Within the GATT, the unilateral use of trade sanctions raises the extraterritoriality issue under Article XX. The multilateral use of trade sanctions in global treaties on the environment can test the non-discrimination requirement in Article XX.

a) Instruments

Commonly agreed international environmental policies (in or outside a formal treaty) can contain instruments that fall within the scope of the GATT (QRs, non-discrimination etc.). For example, the total trade ban on ivory in the Convention on International Trade in Endangered Species of Wild Fauna and Flora (CITES) could be against the GATT rules that forbid quantitative restrictions (Article XI). The ban's justification under the exceptions in Article XX could be difficult, unless it is accompanied by a similar domestic ban or it could be shown that other less distorting measures were not available. The requirement of prior informed consent for trade in hazardous materials in the Basel Convention on the Control of Transboundary Movement of Hazardous Waste and Their Disposal (not yet in force) would be easier to justify under Article XX, because of the imminent danger to human health in the product.

An environmental treaty can also define common

objectives but leave the choice of instruments to the signatories. Then the measures applied individually by signatories (unless waived) can fall within the scope of the GATT. The issues raised with the GATT are then similar to those with the national policies discussed above. For example, in the Montreal Protocol on Substances that Deplete the Ozone Layer, the treaty defines a common goal for reducing the use of chlorofluorocarbons (CFCs) in production and consumption, but countries have a choice of instruments to use in order to reach the target. Problems with the GATT can arise, for example, if countries start banning imports produced with CFCs (a PPM). Trade friction may also arise from differences in the types of taxes applied (direct or indirect) or in the standards used across countries.[29]

b) Sanctions
The main GATT issue that arises in the context of transnational environmental problems is the unilateral use of trade sanctions. Whether their use is compatible with the present rules is linked to the interpretation of extraterritoriality in Article XX. The transnational nature of some environmental problems brings a new element to the extraterritoriality issue in the GATT. In this case, the method of production in one (exporting or neighbouring) country can cause direct damage in another (importing) country (e.g. smog). This has led some to argue that, in the case of transnational pollution, Article XX would justify trade restrictions (if less trade-distorting means are not available) because there is damage to "plant, human, animal life or health" inside its borders. Furthermore, as constraints on extraterritoriality also limit the influence of an importing country on its neighbours' policies, trade measures would be the only means available. For example, Sweden could argue that production in Poland sends acid rain inside Swedish borders. Sweden could use moral suasion or offer to pay for the clean-up in Poland. If Poland refused both alternatives, Sweden could claim that trade

measures against Poland would be the only available alternative to reduce acid rain in Sweden. Others contend that any kind of unilaterally determined extraterritorial application of Article XX to PPMs is illegal under the GATT, because the GATT rules only refer to product-related measures within a country's borders.

The nature of many transnational environmental problems calls for caution in the unilateral use of trade sanctions, even as second-best alternatives. Within the GATT, they should be banned for several reasons:

• *First,* the existence and extent of many (transnational) environmental problems is subject to difficult measurement problems, subjective value-judgements and uncertain scientific evidence. For example, whether dolphins are in danger of extinction is debated among experts. Whether this is a transnational environmental issue or an attempt by the US to impose its PPMs on Mexico is debatable.

• *Second,* in many cases the exact source of any transnational environmental damage can be very difficult to establish. How much of the acid rain in the Nordic countries comes from Germany, Poland or the USSR, or how much of it can be attributed to specific goods, may be impossible to establish. Trade sanctions in these cases would seem disproportionate and difficult to target.

• *Third,* in many cases unilateral trade measures are unlikely to be effective. If the importer is a small market in the total exports of the polluter, it can always divert sales to other countries. Re-exports can also undermine a trade ban against a polluter.

• *Fourth,* to comply with the non-discrimination requirement of the GATT, it seems that the importer would have to apply the measure to all sources of environmental damage. Non-discrimination would be very difficult to manage, as production methods do not show in the product.

• *Fifth,* any attempts at devising special rules within the GATT, to justify unilateral trade measures to combat transnational sources of environmental damage, could lead to serious problems of definition, and the abuse of the system for the purpose of protectionism. Express formalization of a practice can also lead to its increased use. Experience with other "unfair trade" measures, like anti-dumping, and countervailing duty investigations clearly illustrates the problem. A more productive and efficient way to deal with these issues would be negotiation and compensation, as suggested by theory and experience.

An important outstanding issue in international environmental treaties and the present GATT rules is whether discrimination against non-signatories is GATT-compatible. Some claim that the text of the headnote to Article XX "where the same conditions prevail" would allow countries to make environmental agreements that discriminate against third parties. This is because obligations undertaken by signatories are different in time and substance from those of non-signatories. This was the interpretation of the drafters of the Montreal Protocol, for example, when a trade ban on third parties was adopted. The supporters of this view sometimes also invoke paragraph (h) of Article XX, which under certain circumstances exempts international commodity agreements from general GATT obligations. However, Article XX would require the discrimination to be proved necessary - it has to be the least trade-distorting measure available. This would put the burden of proof on the signatories as to the need for trade sanctions. Thereby, the GATT and international environmental treaties could coexist - the GATT rules would discipline the use of trade measures for environmental protection but allow them selectively in the enforcement of international treaties.

A stricter view contends that discrimination cannot be allowed under a strict interpretation of Article XX. Thus, any discrimination against nonsignatories would be against the GATT. The only way out would be to negotiate a waiver from basic GATT obligations, or amend the GATT to allow for specific exceptions for environmental purposes. The conclusions of the Tuna/Dolphin Panel point in this direction.

As GATT rules are in little conflict with the pursuit of efficient environmental policies, there seems to be limited justification for major amendments of the GATT in response to international environmental concerns. The existing GATT rules would discipline the use of trade instruments for global environmental problems and lead to caution in their application as sanctions. Existing problems of interpretation can be solved by clarification of certain concepts in Article XX. The other option, the use of waivers, can pose problems if the number of relevant treaties or GATT-inconsistent policies involved is large. Furthermore, extensive use of trade instruments outside GATT disciplines (through waivers), could lead to a serious disruption of trade and do little for the environment due to the second-best nature of trade instruments in these circumstances.

Conclusions

The GATT is likely to be subjected to a protectionist attack, on environmental grounds, in the 1990s. This conclusion is suggested by a number of trends:

• *First*, the costs of compliance with environmental measures in the future are likely to increase. The proposed carbon taxes alone can amount to the equivalent of a $10 per barrel increase in the price of oil. Higher standards and recycling requirements are also putting new financial burdens on producers. This can trigger demands for protection against competing imports, especially if exporters are not seen to be making similar efforts to protect their environment. Lack of environmental measures abroad may have political appeal as a basis for unfair trade actions. But, as awareness of environmental problems and environmental quality differ across countries, so, too, are policies and their costs likely to differ. International efforts to coordinate environmental policies may help, but many differences will remain.

* *Second*, with the overall reduction in tariffs over the past decades, the use of NTBs has increased in response to changes in comparative costs. Abuse of anti-dumping and countervailing duties, and grey-area measures like Voluntary Export Restraints, have become more commonplace. The GATT may not be ready to confront these pressures. The above discussion of the GATT rules and the environment points out that many of the relevant rules are subject to varying interpretations, thus causing uncertainty and friction in trade. There is a need to clarify existing rules vis-à-vis environmental policies.

In summary, three conclusions stand out:

* *First*, the GATT has little conflict with the pursuit of most legitimate environmental policies but some relevant rules are subject to varying interpretations. The resulting uncertainty can lead to protectionist abuses and poor environmental policies.

* *Second*, the GATT may have some anomalies in relation to efficient environmental policies (limits to subsidies, bias for indirect taxes, coverage of all relevant environmental issues) that need to be discussed.

* *Third*, the present uncertainty may challenge the role of the GATT as the guardian of the well-being of the international trading system but there is no need to amend the GATT. The present problems can be solved by clarifying some of the rules, or by a selective use of waivers in exceptional cases.

Looking ahead, three guidelines recommend themselves:

* *First*, trade should not be restricted because of differences in environmental policies - the scope of Article XX and the Standards Code should be clearly limited to product-related measures.

* *Second*, the unilateral use of trade sanctions to deal with international environmental problems should not be allowed - the scope and use of Article XX extraterritorially need to be clarified, and moral suasion or compensation encouraged instead.

* *Third*, the relationship of international treaties with

the GATT needs to be clarified. They can coexist and reinforce each other. The GATT rules would encourage the application of efficient global environmental policies and allow for a limited use of trade sanctions in enforcement, and participation under strict criteria, only if negotiation and compensation are exhausted. This could be achieved by a clarification of Article XX or by a waiver under Article XXV.

References

1. An earlier version of this paper was published in *The World Economy* Vol. 15/1 (January, 1992).

2. See, for example, ARDEN-CLARKE, CHARLES (1991) "The GATT, Environmental Protection and Sustainable Development" (World Wildlife Fund) Discussion Paper; and SHRYBMAN, STEVEN (1990) "International Trade and the Environment: An Environmental Assessment of the GATT" *The Ecologist* Vol 20/1, January/February.

3. GATT forbids the use of quantitative restrictions (QRs) and changes in bound tariffs.

4. ESKELUND, G AND JIMENEZ, E (1991) "Choosing Policy Instruments for Pollution Control (World Bank) A Review - PRE Working Paper 624; MUZANDO, T R, MIRANDA, K M AND BOVENBERG, A L (1990) "Public Policy and the Environment: A Survey of the Literature" (International Monetary Fund) Fiscal Affairs Dept Working Paper 56; NICOLAISEN, J AND HEOLLER, P (1990) "Economics and the Environment: A Survey of the Issues and Policy Options" (OECD) Economics and Statistics Dept Working Paper 82.

5 Environmental problems have many peculiar characteristics. Sustainability can be location specific - it depends on nature's capacity to absorb damage. Environment can be a superior good. It is a wide concept

- issues range from chemical pollution to biodiversity. The existence of a problem can be subject to great uncertainty, value judgements or difficult technical identification and measuring problems. Many environmental problems concern more than one nation state. Domestic, transnational and global problems raise different issues for policies.

6. The distinction is not always straightforward, but is linked to the number of players involved: global problems affect most of mankind (global warming or depletion of the ozone layer), whereas transnational ones are limited to a few countries (acid rain or river pollution).

7. The EC, for example, has offered 70 million FF to improve the safety in a nuclear plant in Bulgaria (*Le Monde* July 7, 1991).

8. This has recently become an issue in privatization in Eastern Europe. Buyers want assurance of no-liability to clean up past pollution by the companies.

9. The OECD countries have supported the polluter pays principle (PPP) with national issues and victim pays principle with international issues. The PPP decision was strongly influenced by a desire to avoid trade and investment distortions from subsidies and to promote R&D for cleaner technologies.

10. Except in certain defined circumstances, many of which are temporary in nature, GATT members are not permitted to use quantitative (non-tariff) import restrictions. The non-discrimination provisions of Article XIII only refer, therefore, to a narrow range of situations where quantitative restrictions may be applied (the Article XI prohibitions of such measures notwithstanding).

11. These are normally referred to as indirect taxes, to be

contrasted with direct taxes falling on the factors of production (wage and profit taxes).

12. KIRGIS, F (1972) "Effective Pollution Control in Industrialized Countries: International Economic Disincentives, Policy Responses and the GATT" *Michigan Law Review* April, Vol 70/5.

13. *Financial Times* (1991) June 28.

14. Report of a Working Party, L/3464, 1970, GATT: Basic Instruments and Selected Documents, 18th Supplement.

15. Who actually bears the taxes depends on such factors as the structure of competition in the market etc.

16. The problems were raised in the Superfund Case between the US and some of its trading partners. A US indirect tax levied both on imports and domestic goods on certain chemicals to finance toxic waste clean-ups was considered GATT-compatible.

17. Border Tax Adjustments, Report of a Working Party, L/3464, 1970, GATT : Basic Instruments and Selected Documents, 18th Supplement.

18. KIRGIS F (1972) *supra* note 11.

19. Most relevant for environmental issues are sub-paragraphs (b) and (g). Article XX (B) covers measures "necessary" to protect "human, animal or plant life or health". It was originally drafted for health quarantine purposes. Article XX (G) covers measures that "relate to" the conservation of exhaustible natural resources, if taken together with restrictions on domestic production and consumption. The headnote to the Article requires the measures to be applied without "arbitrary or unjustifiable

discrimination" between countries where the "same conditions prevail", and so that they do not constitute "disguised restrictions on international trade".

20. Seven cases have been subject to formal Panels in GATT under the Article.

21. This has been stressed in several Panel reports.

22. The US challenged Thailand's import ban on cigarettes, which Thailand defended on health grounds (Article XXb).

23. GATT would, however, allow Indonesia to impose a tax on exports of logs.

24. Trade restricting measures should be proportional to the stated objectives.

25. The three categories of subsidies proposed in the Uruquay Round are prohibited subsidies, permissible but countervailable subsidies, and non-countervailable subsidies.

26. ARDEN-CLARKE, CHARLES (1991) *supra* note 1.

27. A similar duty on imports could be levied under Article III, provided it is an indirect one.

28. Contracting Parties can waive their GATT obligations under Article XXV with the approval of a two-thirds majority of GATT members representing over one-half of the full GATT membership.

29. In this case, the small share of CFCs in total costs (an estimated 3%) and easy availability of substitutes should reduce potential for trade friction. Nevertheless, the potential is there for other treaties.

18

The Organization for Economic Cooperation and Development (OECD)[1]
Candice Stevens

Candice Stevens is an economist and the Principal Administrator for trade and environment issues in the Environment Directorate of the OECD in Paris. She previously worked on trade and industry issues in the Industry Division of the OECD. Prior to coming to the OECD, she worked in the United States Government - for the Environmental Protection Agency, the Department of the Interior, the Department of Commerce, and the Office of Technology Assessment of the US Congress.

The OECD is the successor to the group that administered the Marshall Plan after World War II. In the early 1960s, when work with the Marshall Plan was complete, member countries decided to form the OECD. There are now 24 member countries in the OECD, the Partners in Transition program with East European countries promises to expand this number and Mexico and Korea have applied for observer status. The OECD coordinates, negotiates, discusses and debates the economic and trade policies of member countries. In April 1991, it formed a Joint Trade and Environment Working Group, made up of representatives from each of the trade and environment ministries of each member country. The Group's purpose is to develop joint trade and environment guidelines. It is addressing the question of how environmental policy makers take into account the impact of their policy measures on trade and, equally, how trade policy makers take into account the environmental effects of their policies. The Joint Report of the Group was published in June 1991 and a Progress Report in June 1992.

Originally, the Joint Working Group had agreed on a completion date of June 1993 but in August 1991, following the release of the GATT Tuna-Dolphin Panel Report, sufficient pressure mounted to change the deadline to June 1992. Many working in this area are not optimistic, however, of the feasibility of this new deadline, particularly as the work unfolds. At the heart of the issue is the direct use of trade measures for environmental purposes. It is anticipated that discussion will become more controversial and a divergence of views more apparent.

The work program of the Group addresses two components that embrace the issues the guidelines will ultimately affect: the effect of environmental policies on trade and the effects of trade policy on the environment.

The Effects of Environmental Policy on Trade

This is the standard area of work done in the past. In the first instance, the possibility that environmental standards can be non-tariff barriers is approached by the OECD from the perspective of national policy harmonization. To date, the greatest focus has been on testing and regulating industrial chemicals and this may extend to pesticides and pharmaceuticals.

Harmonization is being examined with a view to developing an agenda that would:

a) prioritize policies from an environmental perspective (for instance, those that aim to solve global environmental problems such as the use of CFCs) and

b) prioritize policies from the trade perspective (through the identification of environmental policies that are causing the most concern from the trade point of view).

The Environment and Trade Group is also looking at economic instruments within the realm of harmonization and non-tariff barriers. One OECD group is looking at the trade impacts of environmental taxation, for instance. There is also an analysis of eco-labelling and how this can be harmonized at the international level. There is much support of this work from the business community.

The Environment and Trade Group is also working on the question of competitiveness - how environmental regulations affect industry costs and how the use of environmental technologies can contribute to industries' competitiveness.

The key to the Trade and Environment Program, however, is the direct use of trade measures for environmental purposes. There is a sense that the next round of the GATT will be the "Environmental Round". It will look at what the OECD is calling trade-related environmental measures (TREMs).

The OECD has categorized TREMs into four different types:

• *First* there are complementary measures. This issue was raised by the GATT Tuna/Dolphin dispute. These measures are applied to product standards and may be applied to process or production method standards. Many OECD countries want more freedom to discriminate against products based on the methods by which they are produced. Countries would then not be required to buy products that may have been produced contrary to their own methods of production or even contrary to their own environmental preferences. This is a very controversial issue. Current Working Group negotiations are concerned with the criteria and circumstances under which complementary measures can be applied to production processes.

• *Second*, there are coercive measures. These may be stronger than complementary measures because there may not be a corresponding domestic regulation in place in the importing country. The most prominent examples are the proposed import bans on tropical timber. For example, in the European Community, a law will go into effect in 1995 that will disallow the import of tropical timber that has not been harvested on a sustainable basis. This raises questions of national sovereignty, extraterritoriality, and how far one country can apply their environmental regulations to other countries, particularly when the first

211

does not have the commodity in its own territory. This area is under question in the GATT and is defended on the environmental side under the banner of the "global commons". Such measures may be justified in certain circumstances when the goal is the protection of a global resource such as the ozone layer.

• *Third,* there are countervailing duties. Currently, under trade law, a country can countervail unilaterally. The question of concern to the Working Group is whether a lack of environmental regulation constitutes an implicit subsidy that can be countervailed with a trade action. This measure is popular among environmental NGOs but needs to be looked at more closely.

• *Fourth*, there are cooperative or multilateral measures, such as trade provisions in international agreements, their implementation, and enforcement. There is quite a wide range of views as to when they are effective in an environmental sense and when they are acceptable in the trade sense.

Because, in the OECD, members of the Environment and Trade Group sit down as equals, none of these measures is totally ruled out. The question is not "Can we use these measures?", but rather, "When can each measure be justified and how can rules be provided for their use?".

The Effects of Trade Policy on the Environment

The other side of the work program deals with the second component of the trade-environment link - the effects of trade policy on the environment. This is much less understood and much less studied than the first component and, because the idea is relatively new, extensive research is only now beginning.

The OECD is starting from the position that, overall, trade liberalization is beneficial for the environment but can also have some negative effects. It recognizes that free trade and trade liberalization need to be carefully examined and monitored for their environmental effects, and that

212

there is a need for further development of measures that can mitigate any negative effects.

The work of the Environment and Trade Group is concentrating on sectoral studies of the effects of trade on the environment in forestry, fisheries, agriculture, energy, transport and endangered species. Workshops are also being held in a parallel effort to understand these. In February 1992, the meeting of the Working Group on Trade and Environment discussed the effects of trade policy on the environment, and how policy makers can examine these when formulating new trade policies.

The environmental implications of free trade agreements - such as the North American Free Trade Agreement, Europe 1992, the Australian-New Zealand agreement (ANZERTA) - and commodity and preferential agreements are under study. The purpose of these studies is to devise common checklists for trade policy makers of the environmental implications of trade agreements and how they can be taken into account and mitigated.

The value of the OECD in this process is to ensure that neither the environment lobby nor the trade lobby of each country is locked into one position or another during the negotiation period. Open minds should prevail as the OECD forges into this new and important area.

References

1. This presentation represents the views of the author and not necessarily the OECD.

213

F
Future Challenges

19

The UNCED Challenge: The View from the North
Pierre Marc Johnson

*Pierre Marc Johnson, medical doctor and lawyer, teaches
and conducts research at McGill University's Law School
and Centre for Medicine, Ethics and Law. He is also a
Special Advisor to the Secretary-General of the United
Nations Conference on Environment and Development. He
is Vice-Chair of the National Round Table on the
Environment and the Economy and on the boards of the
International Institute on Sustainable Development,
Winnipeg; Unimedia; the SNC Group Inc; the Québec
Medical and Legal Society (Honourary Chairman); and
Oxfam (Founding member). From 1985-1987 he was
Premier of Quebec and Leader of the Opposition.*

In addressing the issue of trade and the environment from
the perspective of northern developed countries within the
context of UNCED, it is important to be as concerned as
much with solutions as with problems. One of the biases
in dealing with environment and development issues
today, is the tendency to dwell too long on the description
of problems because of the difficulty of finding solutions. It
is possible, however, to begin to identify solutions.

In dealing with government intervention, the notion of
integrating environmental and economic concerns is an
obvious solution. Direct fiscal incentives and subsidies for
research and development leading to a more efficient use
of resources are also part of the solution. Technological
progress and efficiency are also essential instruments of
competitiveness in external markets.

Industries have to be pro-active in the exploration of new
markets which spring out of environmental concerns and
regulations around the world. This initiative is required
whether it be new technologies, the elaboration of new

217

products, specific training or even the use of innovative marketing techniques. Industry must also anticipate the advent of new regulations, including forthcoming international regulations, and plan well ahead.

At the international level, it is important to recognize the new balance of power between the North and the South emanating from our common need to address environmental challenges. The recourse to multilateral institutions derives not only from an ideological choice, but also from a recognition that it may be the only intelligent way of managing the very complicated issues of trade and environment globally.

For most citizens in developed countries, there are three levels from which to address the nexus that binds international trade and environmental concerns:

• *First*, for better or worse, the developed world has the expertise, the awareness, and some would say, the paternalistic frame of mind to see itself as the custodian of the international debate on the environment. Pressured by public opinion, northern governments will demand a more ecologically-rational management of natural resources and environmental protection. Perhaps they will even adopt elements of sustainable development policy at home as well as in their relations with foreign countries, particularly with the developing world. In fact, it is not unthinkable that the difficulties and the hard choices for politicians in making these decisions at home may cause some northern governments to be more active in the international arena, motivated purely by domestic and political reasons. As northern governments assume the leadership within the international debate on the environment and sustainable development, and even if most developed countries' representatives are sincere, much of the rhetoric on the global environmental agenda will be used to satisfy political audiences at home and to justify barriers to trade as well as controversial interventions in the affairs of economically weaker states. While the North may have the right to drive the international environmental agenda on issues such as climate change, the preservation of biodiversity and the reduction of atmospheric pollution, it has the inescapable and corresponding responsibility to make this agenda acceptable to the developing world by ensuring that development is a central part of this agenda. Through its commitment of sufficient resources, and through the acceptance by the international political system and the economic order that these substantial terms may often be unfavourable to the wealthy, the North must also make the agenda possible and implementable.

• The *second* level at which these issues are to be addressed is that of trade globalization and liberalization. The potentially irreversible trends towards trade liberalization, whether globally through the GATT or through regional treaties and organizations, forces protracted and painful debate upon the northern world. The debate will focus on the desirability and necessity of harmonizing and synchronizing environmental standards between trading partners who want to provide corporations with a more level regulatory playing field. Just as the Europeans have had to wrestle for years with the question of the European Social Charter as a result of European commercial integration, North Americans now have to ask themselves what will be the environmental America of tomorrow in a potential North American Free Trade Agreement. They have to agree on the meaning of "national treatment" in the context of differing environmentally-friendly production methods between countries. In opening this Pandora's Box, states and governments will find themselves dealing with the complex and difficult issues of extraterritoriality. This issue and that of "state sovereignty" (the fundamental building block of the international political system) are pitted against interdependence and foreign intervention, unavoidable givens of the international commercial system and of global environmental issues.

• *Third*, is the more pragmatic level of national interest.

At stake here are the practical aspects of "realpolitik" or "realeconomics" and the instinctive, almost Pavlovian, reactions of Western societies: their predilection to conflict on trade issues. The ecological imperative will be used recurrently for a variety of purposes. The episode of the American restriction on imports of tuna, prompted by the environmental unfriendliness of fishing methods, is a forerunner of things to come. The ecological rationale will also be used by states to tell other states how to manage their resources. Governments in the North are very sensitive to the moods of domestic public opinion. One has only to think of the episodes of the baby seals, where the Canadian government was put on the defensive, essentially for the sake of European public opinion, through very well organized campaigns in Europe by Greenpeace and others. The next target could be the Brazilian, the Malayan, or the Canadian timber trade, or perhaps hydroelectric production in Northern Quebec.

More often than not, and unfair as that may be, the victims of green protectionism will be the poorer countries from the South. As the level of sophistication of the Northern decision-makers on global environmental issues increases, the challenge will be to keep the green-protectionism trend under control. That is largely what UNCED is all about. UNCED is the United Nations Conference on Environment and Development, held in Rio from June 3 to 15, 1992. It is an attempt to implement elements of the Brundtland Report. It is a World Summit, designed for heads of states and governments (between 70 and 120 of them) to consider massive amounts of documentation, studies prepared by the UNCED Secretariat, "national reports", and an unending series of international meetings.

In practice, UNCED is an attempt to examine solutions to the extraordinarily difficult issues of the world's inescapable interdependence and the pervasiveness of environmental issues:

• *First*, it is to be hoped that UNCED will result in the

signing of international agreements, protocols or treaties on climate change, biodiversity, forestry and biotechnologies - recognising that classical instruments of negotiation among states usually take much more time to prepare than has been allotted to the negotiating of these agreements.

• *Second*, a document entitled the Rio Declaration or the Earth Charter contains basic principles of the definition of a sustainable relationship between humankind and nature, a recognition of the necessity to adjust development to the essential solidarities required between the North and the South, and a promise to fully use the world's capacity to regenerate the resources it needs to develop now while permitting future generations do the same.

• *Third*, UNCED saw the presentation of a document called Agenda 21. It is a comprehensive compilation dealing with poverty, water access, recycling, environmental assessment and auditing, land-based pollution, education and environment, and many other issues. All development and environment issues discussed are included in Agenda 21. This does not mean that all the states and governments will subscribe to it but itis a document which outlines what should be done for the future and what are the commitments, whether multi-lateral, bilateral, regional, sub-regional, or domestic, which can be made by various governments.

UNCED should not be seen as a point of arrival for what has been going on in the two years that preceded it. Rather, it should be seen as a starting point to face the turn-of-the-century with hope bolstered by a few good solutions. However, Northern countries will not be able to do this if they do not address the fundamental and central issues of large-scale technological transfers and financial transfers to the South:

• *First* and foremost, a net transfer of financial resources to developing countries on concessional and preferential terms cannot be avoided. This has become necessary to enable southern countries to promote national development and acquire the technology, expertise and the gigantic pool of capital goods essential so they can depart from the path of wasteful and polluting development which the North started 200 years ago.

• *Second*, there is an imperative and inescapable need for the transfer of the most recent, cleanest and most environmentally friendly technology for industrial production and manufacturing to Third World countries. The terms of these transfers must not undermine the international system of protection of intellectual and industrial property, but must realistically address the issues of expediency and affordability.

All of these issues bring the North and the South together, whether they like it or not.

20

The UNCED Challenge: The View from the South
Nural Islam

Nural Islam is the Senior Policy Advisor, International Food Policy Research Institute, Washington, DC. He was Assistant Director-General, Economic and Social Policy Department, Food and Agriculture Organization (FAO) Rome; Deputy Chairman / Minister, Bangladesh Planning Commission / Ministry, and Chairman, Bangladesh Institute of Development Studies. He has an MA and PhD from Harvard University. His recent publications include: "Poverty in South Asia: Approaches to its Alleviation" Food Policy (April 1992); "South Asia Regional Perspectives on the New World Interdependence" Development Journal of the Society for International Development (1992); and (co-edited with Alberto Valdes) The GATT, Agriculture and the Developing Countries International Food Policy Research Institute (September 1990).

It is now widely recognized that market failures, policy failures, population growth and poverty all contribute in a complex, interactive way with environmental degradation in both developing and developed countries. The resulting environmental degradation ranges from soil erosion, water and oil pollution, and land degradation, to a loss of biological diversity and climatic change.

The environmental problems are not only local and national in character; they are also transnational in character and global in nature. The number of global environmental problems and issues have been increasing in importance over the years. The distinction between environmental problems that are confined within national borders, and those which spill over national borders and are of either a regional or a global nature, is very important from the point of view of policy. Sharing environmental

223

responsibility amongst nations differs, depending upon the nature of the environmental problems. However, this distinction is sometimes contested by environmentalists, who believe that no environmental problem - however local its origin or nature may be - does not have global ramifications. They believe that pollution or environmental degradation of any kind, anywhere, causes degradation everywhere.

The distinction between national, on the one hand, and global, on the other, becomes blurred when cross border spillover is non-physical in nature. This includes aesthetic, ethical or moral considerations, such as the concern of the citizens of one country for the preservation of species in another country.

In addition, the distinction between environmental degradation that is reversible, and that which is not, has very important policy implications. When environmental degradation is reversible, it can be sustained in the short-run interest of rapid growth, provided that - as resources accumulate and technical knowledge expands - the country is able and willing to devote resources to reclaim the degraded environment and reverse the process after a certain period. This option is not available when the environmental degradation is irreversible and natural resources are lost forever.

The relative emphasis placed on the acceleration of growth and development, on the one hand, and the enhancement of the environment, on the other, differs in poor and rich countries. Greater emphasis and a higher priority is attached to growth, as opposed to environmental preservation, in the developing countries.

The interrelationship between poverty and the environment is complex. The poor suffer most from environmental degradation, and poverty often presents a constraint on dealing with environmental issues. With economic growth and increasing population, pressure is exerted on natural resources. Given current technology, such pressure is fraught with the possibilities of environmental stress.

As income increases, there is an increase in both resources and the opportunities at the disposal of poor people and poor countries to combat environmental degradation. Pressures to discount the future are reduced and readiness to preserve resources for the future tends to increase. While the developed countries have, in the past, contributed predominantly to the degradation of the global environment, the contribution of the developing countries is going to rise in the future, as their economic growth picks up and the pace of their industrialization quickens. At present, their ability to deal with environmental problems is restricted by their limited access to both technology and financial resources.

It is in this context that the interrelationship between trade and environment, as seen by the developing countries, is best viewed. Trade and trade policies affect the patterns and intensity of their use of resources. Given an undervaluation of natural resources (whether due to market failures or policy failures), an opening up of trade with expanded market opportunities and an increased demand for natural resource-based products may lead to an intensive use of resources and may cause their over-exploitation. Given the acute shortage of foreign exchange in many developing countries, and their urgent need to meet mounting debt service burdens and import requirements for development expenditures, they are under considerable pressure to expand exports, through special incentives if necessary.

However, to the extent that prices of resources and inputs are not below the level dictated by competitive markets and to the extent that the divergence between social and private cost and benefits is offset through fiscal and other means, environmental degradation is not likely to follow the opening up of trade. At present, in many countries, domestic price policies for inputs and outputs lead to over-use of chemical inputs, and over-exploitation of marginal lands, including the depletion of forest resources. It is frequently alleged that export trade contributes to deforestation but, in many instances, this is an exaggeration. Deforestation stems from a multiplicity of causes, such as the settlement of forests for agricultural purposes that is often generated by increased population pressure in the areas surrounding forest regions, as well as by slow growth and productivity in agricultural land. Both these factors drive the poor to encroach upon forest lands in order to seek sustenance and enlarge food supply.

The process of settlement of forest lands by small and poor farmers is facilitated by commercial logging, which opens up infrastructure, roads, transport and communication to the forest lands. Often, it is accompanied by government policies, such as subsidies and tax and credit programs, that encourage large-scale cattle ranching or commercial farming. Frequently, small herders in search of grazing lands and pastures when existing pastures are exhausted or community properties are appropriated, move to clear additional forests. In many areas, especially in tropical drylands, the major source of deforestation is the need for fuelwood for household and rural energy need.

In the context of this myriad of factors contributing in different ways to deforestation, it is not easy to generalize about the role of foreign trade, such as the export of logs. In a few instances, where tropical forests constitute a major source of foreign exchange earnings, it is conceivable that trade, combined with inappropriate domestic policies for logging, has contributed to excessive deforestation, thus threatening the future capacity of the rain forest to regenerate itself. However, on average, today's industrial raw wood production is a small proportion of the forest output in developing countries. Moreover, exports are a small proportion of their total industrial raw wood production.

The protectionist policy of developed countries - with their tariffs and import restrictions escalating according to the degree of processing of primary exports - works against the establishment of processing industries in developing countries. Under these circumstances, a given amount of foreign exchange earnings requires a greater input of natural resources than would be the case if it was exported in processed form. The higher the degree of value added, the lower is the pressure on natural resource exploitation for earning a given amount of foreign exchange.

In many instances, through export taxes, developing countries depress the domestic price of their exportable natural resources in order to lower the cost of the domestic processing industry. However, such processing industries are often inefficient. They are highly protected from import competition and suffer inadequate utilization of capacity. In view of this inefficiency and inadequate capacity utilization, net foreign exchange earnings (the gross foreign exchange earnings, minus the foreign exchange sacrificed through loss in raw material exports) are often low.

It is alleged that the differences in environmental standards relating to both products and processes of production, in developed and developing countries, lead to differences in comparative costs. This, it is said, gives undue advantage to developing country industries subject to lower environmental standards and, therefore, adversely affects the competitive advantage of developed country industries. While the subject has raised much controversy, there is only limited empirical knowledge about the impact of differential environmental standards on comparative cost advantage.

There are several aspects on which further research is urgently needed:

• *First*, what are the costs of environmental measures in different economic activities in different countries? They need not necessarily be the same measures. To use findings (derived from data in the United States) on the environmental control costs of different industries and apply it uncritically to other countries - especially developing countries - does not seem to be justified. Moreover, the proportion of pollution abatement costs in the total gross output of different industries appears to be very low, except for a few selected industries involved particularly in processing raw materials or mineral resources.

• *Second*, a question that may legitimately be asked is whether it is either efficient or equitable to have uniform environmental standards regarding the processes of production or products. There are several reasons why this is not necessarily so:

a) Consumer preferences vary among countries. Preferences based on environmental quality should be treated as much as a basis for trade as preferences for other goods and services. In countries with poor per capita income, the preference for environmental quality receives a low priority.

b) At the present low level of environmental degradation or pollution in developing countries, the ability to assimilate environmental degradation is higher than in developed countries. The developing countries, therefore, do not require as strict environmental standards as the developed countries.

Differences in preferences for environmental quality and in levels of environmental stress should be considered as factors governing the flow of trade or the basis of comparative advantage in the same way as differences in the endowment of other factors of production. There is no reason, therefore, to interfere with the comparative advantage of developing countries in this regard, either by enforcing uniformity of standards or by imposing restrictions or the exports of developing countries.

• *Third*, even if it was agreed that it was desirable to reduce differences in environmental standards across various countries, the question remains on whether the search for uniformity should be made through trade measures or through international agreements on environmental regulations. Trade restrictions against developing country exports, either to improve their environmental standards or to enforce higher environmental standards similar to those prevailing in developed countries, will be counterproductive. They will delay growth in developing countries and consequently delay their ability to deal with environmental problems through the acquisition of better technology and higher investment. There is an analogy with the case of low wage industries in developing countries. Restriction against exports from the low wage industries in developing countries is neither a desirable nor an effective means of improving the income of their workers.

The problem of differences in "product" and "process" standards needs to be handled through international negotiation and agreement. A complete harmonization of standards is not possible. Individual countries will necessarily impose standards that are different from, or higher than, those in other countries. This does not justify a country with high environmental standards imposing restrictions on exports from countries with lower environmental standards. Consumers should be free to choose between products from different countries, given full information on the standards imposed.

In cases where a country imposes restrictions to protect higher standards within its borders, a legitimate case can be made for compensation to be provided to exporting countries if such higher standards cannot be justified on scientific grounds. The developing countries would need technical and financial assistance to improve their standards insofar as scientific evidence requires such an improvement. They would also need a longer time frame to meet such standards in view of their technical and institutional inadequacies. International agreements on environmental measures and policies should incorporate provisions for such assistance.

In dealing with both "product" and "process" standards across borders, the developing countries prefer international arrangements and agreements rather than unilateral action. In a game of unilateral action, the big trading partners can retaliate against each other. They can therefore stop a proliferation of trade measures designed to force uniform environmental standards. The developing countries do not have the economic strength to retaliate. Therefore, they require international rules and regulations that will be observed by all countries.

To enforce international agreements through trade measures, as in the case of the Montreal Protocol, need not necessarily be the best available alternative. There are other ways of enforcing international agreements, which secure both penalties and inducements. These relate to other areas of international economic transactions, such as access to capital markets, commercial bank loans, or development assistance to poor countries. An appropriate combination of "sanction" and "inducement" depends on the particular circumstances of each agreement. Sanctions are always an unstable means of inducing compliance with international agreements. They create uncertainty in international relations. Compliance through persuasion and inducement creates a more stable framework.

Among the inducements available to facilitate the implementation of environmental measures to deal with the problems of the global commons, two mechanisms stand out: one is "debt for nature swaps" and the other is the Global Environmental Facility of the World Bank, United Nations Development Program and United Nations Environment Program.

• The "debt for nature swap" was initiated originally by environmental organizations. It focuses on heavily discounted commercial debt. The international environmental NGOs purchased heavily discounted commercial debt and swapped it for the domestic resources of an indebted country, on the condition that the resources so mobilized were devoted to projects to preserve the environment. Increasingly, "debt for nature swaps" have been extended beyond commercial credit to government credit as well.

• The Global Environmental Facility, on the other hand, seeks to mobilize additional resources to finance such projects as those relating to the emission of greenhouse gases and global warming, international waters, and the preservation of biodiversity. Projects which confer environmental benefits exclusively within the boundaries of a nation do not qualify for the Global Environmental Facility. Projects which are not attractive in terms of costs and benefits to a single nation, but would become attractive if global benefits were included, do qualify for financing under this Facility. Similarly, this Facility covers projects which are found attractive in domestic terms but can confer global benefits if additional costs are incurred.

If developing countries are to cooperate by investing in projects with global environmental benefits, they must receive resources in addition to, and separate from, traditional or general development assistance ("new funding"). The additional resources are not meant to promote development in a traditional sense, but to promote global environmental welfare. Such assistance might be considered an effective way to deal with global environmental problems.

In order to ensure that environmental development assistance is truly "new funding", it is necessary to establish and maintain separate accounts of environmental and development assistance and to monitor them over time to ensure that the benefit does in fact materialize. The aim is to ensure that existing development assistance is not diverted to achieve global environmental objectives.

G
Conclusion

21

Canada's Contribution to a New Trade-Environment Regime
John Kirton

John Kirton is Associate Professor in the Department of Political Science, University of Toronto, a fellow of Trinity College, and a member of the Foreign Policy Committee of the national Round Table on the Environment and the Economy. He is the author and editor of numerous books and articles on Canadian Foreign Policy, including Canadian Foreign Policy: Selected Cases *(Prentice-Hall, 1992) and* Canada as a Principal Power: A Study in Foreign Policy and International Relations *(Toronto: John Wiley, 1983).*

The complex relationship between trade and the environment has clearly become the issue of the 1990s for those seeking to enhance economic competitiveness and ecological sustainability in Canada and throughout the world. As the decade opened, Canadian business saw the staples of their resource-based export economy assaulted by environmentally-motivated or mantled groups and governments abroad. Simultaneously, Canadians concerned about the environment faced the prospect of their cherished domestic initiatives coming under attack from an international trading system which accorded too little value to ecosystems now under severe stress. As alarmed exporters and environmentalists were forced to confront each others claims, they began to see how a greater ecological and economic awareness on both their parts offered new possibilities to promote the values of each.

Propelled by this sense of threat and opportunity, the question of trade-environmental links has been thrust onto the agenda of the major governments and international institutions managing the world's international economic and ecological interdependence. Federal governments in Canada, the United States and elsewhere have moved rapidly to improve the environmental capacity of their trade bureaucracies, the trade expertise of their environmental organizations, and the integration of the two communities in their national decision-making process.

Within North America, negotiations for a North American Free Trade Agreement and the prospect of even wider hemispheric extensions have offered the opportunity to embed environmental concerns effectively within a major trade liberalization agreement, and thus provide a working foundation and model for broader trade agreements to come.

Within Europe, the 1986 Single European Act and the 1992 program have increased the environmental competence of a European Community and Commission that had long exercised the trade policy responsibility for its member countries, just as the liberation of Eastern (and formerly Soviet) Europe has presented formidable economic and ecological challenges next door.

At the broader international level, the 1987 Montreal Protocol on ozone and the 1989 Basel Convention on hazardous waste have launched a decade in which direct, and at times discriminatory, trade-related measures appear to be the instrument of choice in ensuring effective enforcement of international environmental agreements. The Organization for Economic Co-operation and Development (OECD) has begun work through the combined efforts of its Trade and Environment Committees. The General Agreement on Tariffs and Trade (GATT) has followed with the reactivation of its stillborn Group on Environmental Measures and International Trade. Through their annual Summit, trade ministers' Quadrilateral, and now environment ministers' meetings, the world's seven major industrial democracies and the European Community have taken up the subject in concert, starting in 1991. And the United Nations has moved to address the issue through its United Nations Conference on Trade and Development (UNCTAD) and the United Nations Conference on the Environment and Development (UNCED) in June 1992.

This collision of trade and environmental concerns and the resulting proliferation of activity has forced the Canadian government and international community to address a new subject for which there exist few established principles and little underlying empirical analysis.[1] To some extent the process of integrating trade and environment concerns has unfolded (in a form all-too-familiar to students of sustainable development) with long established, broadly accepted, relatively powerful, economic institutions and regimes (in this case for trade) attempting to understand, accept and accommodate the newer, less entrenched, and apparently more strident claims of the environmentalists. In the encounter it is relatively easy for both communities to acknowledge intellectually that particular forms of trade liberalization and management are but a means of enhancing efficiency, and thus promoting the ends of both economic growth and ecological integrity in an equal and equitable way. However in practice, it is more difficult to accept that threats (often invisible, severe, and potentially irreversible) to the global ecosystem might now require rethinking a half-century old multilateral trade system that has generated such enormous wealth for the North, and replacing it with a fundamentally new regime in which the claims of an endangered biosphere and impoverished South have equal weight. The challenge is all the more difficult for recession-ridden Canadians, who have long understood the vital importance of open international markets and suppliers for their prosperity but have only recently come to comprehend that the health of the ecosystem (which sustains their open, resource-based economy) constitutes an even more basic national interest.

It is important, but relatively easy, for members of both

237

the trade and environmental communities to recognize the intense physical and policy interdependencies between their respective domains, to conclude that they must "share the file", to assert that liberal trade and environmental protection are complementary and mutually reinforcing imperatives, and to sit down together to construct a mutually acceptable new trade-environment regime.[2] Both in Canada and internationally, these challenges are currently being met. What remains are the more difficult steps of deciding upon whose home playing field the integrated edifice should be erected, what particular mixture of materials should be employed in what combination, and what the ultimate purpose of the structure should be. Is the established multilateral trading system, with its proven record of wealth generation in the face of ever-potent protectionist pressures, the foundation into which greater environmental sensitivity should be injected? Should this injection take the form of "add-on environmentalism" by conceding new but narrowly-defined environmental exceptions to venerable trade principles? And is it Northern economies, rather than Southern societies or global ecosystems that are under the greatest threat now and in the foreseeable future? Answering these questions from the standpoint of sustainable development suggests many instances in which Canada can help create a closer integration of, and more equitable balance between, trade and environmental values, both at home and abroad.

Canada's Position in the International Trade-Environment System

In identifying Canada's interests in the trade-environment debate, and an appropriate Canadian approach to shaping a global regime reflecting those interests, it is important to recognize Canada's peculiar position as a global trade and environmental power. As the country with the world's seventh largest economy, import market, and export share, Canada is a global trading power of the first rank.[3] Yet, as

238

the smallest of the major powers and as a developed country with an exceptionally high dependence on trade and a heavier than usual reliance on resource-based rather than highly-manufactured or service exports, Canada is far more vulnerable than its G-7 peers to rising international protectionism, particularly in the form of restrictions on environmental grounds.

In the environmental domain this unusual mixture of strength and vulnerability reappears. As the country with the world's second largest territory - encompassing vast natural resources and a medium-sized population, and located at one of the critical regulators of the planetary biosphere, the Arctic - Canada has world-leading environmental resources and responsibilities.[4] However, as the country with the world's longest coastline, a location on three of the world's great oceans (the Atlantic, Pacific and the Arctic), modern technologies and rich populations to exploit the natural resource base, and uniquely fragile northern and Arctic ecosystems, the Canadian environment remains unusually vulnerable to the predatory actions of outsiders and citizens alike.

In both the trade and environmental domains, then, Canada has both the power and incentive to play a leading role in international efforts to define a new trade-environment regime, and to do so in a way which accords relatively equal weight to each interest. Canada is also very well positioned to engender a widely-supported international consensus on this regime, given its status as perhaps the most well-connected country in the world.[5] Its special relationship with the United States, reinforced by inter-penetrated political systems and a multitude of bilateral economic and environmental agreements and institutions, its privileged relations with the United Kingdom and France, and its full-fledged membership in all G-7 institutions, give it influence in the world's most powerful capitals and countries.[6] Its status as a charter member of, and preferred coalition partner within, the world's major multilateral institutions link it closely with the influential middle powers of the world. And its position as one of the two leading, financially dominant powers in the Commonwealth, la Francophonie, and most recently the Organization of American States, endows it with contacts and credibility among developing countries throughout the world. Moreover, its character as a rich industrialized country, but one with an export-oriented, resource-based economy focused overwhelmingly on a single metropolitan centre (the United States), gives it a first hand awareness of the sensitivities of developed and developing countries alike.

Taken together, these features of Canada's position in the international scale of power and the institutionalized processes of international governance challenge the instinctive, self conception of Canada as a relatively environmentally-secure but economically-vulnerable middle power, dependent on defending the existing rules-based, multilaterally-embedded trade system against environmental assailants and the unilateral, discriminatory, extraterritorial weapons they sometimes wield. It inspires a more searching look at how Canada, as a first-rank economic power with important national environmental vulnerabilities and special global custodial responsibilities, might work to modify the world trade system, through individual initiative if necessary, to secure greater environmental benefits in the short term and the more durable economic benefits that flow from them.

Canadian Policy Approaches

Such a position provides a foundation from which Canada can calculate its approach to the welter of issues currently on the table in the burgeoning trade-environment debate. Three general questions are of central importance:
• the impact of national environmental action on Canada's international economic competitiveness;
• the role of unilateral trade measures to promote international environmental protection; and

• the breadth of agreement among countries about environmental threats and trade remedies required to make new multilateral agreements.[7]

The first of these issues arises from a fear that the current international economic system, with its emphasis on trade and investment liberalization, may threaten national efforts to enhance the environment at home. The concern is that competitors in, or moving to, foreign jurisdictions with less stringent and costly environmental standards will, thereby, be able to gain a competitive advantage by exporting products from "pollution havens" abroad to "environmental sanctuaries" back home. This behaviour would disadvantage competing producers, their workers and perhaps even consumers in the "sanctuary", as well as the environment in the "haven". Such a threat generates calls to "level the playing field" by lowering environmental standards at home, by introducing trade measures to protect the relatively clean and green domestic market, or by forcing an increase in environmental standards abroad. The issue is of immediate importance to Canada as the prospect of a North American Free Trade Agreement, and eventually the Uruguay Round of the GATT, promise to introduce two new, major waves of trade and investment liberalization on the Canadian economy and environment.

There are clearly a few high profile cases in which the economic costs of stricter environmental standards at home are a powerful, and even appropriate, deterrent to their introduction. For example, in the current debate over measures to control greenhouse gas emissions, a "carbon tax" on gasoline at the pump in Canada, in the absence of one in the United States, could well further encourage Canadian consumers to shop south of the border, to the harm of both the economy and the environment in Canada. However, such examples highlight the central fact that the overwhelming potential "threat" to Canada comes from the prevailing and prospective environmental standards in the United States, and its northern states in

241

particular, rather than those in jurisdictions further afield.

In general, the jurisdictions that constitute Canada's front line competitors have environmental standards that are as high, on balance, as those faced by Canadians just north of the line. Moreover, in the overall production mix, the cost of meeting enhanced environmental standards is generally very small relative to such other factors as: transportation costs for inputs and products, labour costs and productivity, and the quality of available infrastructure. Even for competitors in states on the Mexican border, and in Mexico itself, it is likely that ever-rising standards and enforcement performance in those jurisdictions, the corporate codes and cost calculations of larger corporations, and the environmental consciousness of consumers in Canada, will deter any attempts to rely on "dirty" products or production processes for competitive advantage. Indeed, many industries may well want to gain a competitive advantage by moving to ever higher environmental standards in advance, and in anticipation of, their competitors and of government regulators at home and abroad.

In the face of such a limited threat from "dirty" competitors, there is little need for such major new border defences as the introduction of systems of environmental dumping or countervail. This is particularly true given the potential, based on past experience in cases such as softwood lumber, for such systems to spread to other countries and do more economic damage to Canadian exports than good for its environment.

Indeed, strengthening the existing border defences seems to be a superior option. Canada already has a world-leading environmental product labelling system in its Environmental Choice program. Existing trade law allows countries to impose "environmentally-friendly" labels on imports, on a non discriminatory basis.[8] Thus, domestic incentives and border measures are already in place in Canada to encourage a de facto upward adjustment of environmental standards through market dynamics.

There is, however, one domestic defensive measure where innovation is urgently needed. This is a reform of international trade law to permit national and subnational government subsidies to domestic firms to introduce best-available environmental technologies, and thus meet or surpass higher government-mandated environmental standards more rapidly and readily. The creation of such a genuinely "green" box of environmentally-allowable subsidies, in both NAFTA and the Uruguay Round of GATT negotiations, would allow governments to offset any competitive disadvantage their higher environmental standards might impose on their firms, without fear that such actions would endanger their export markets by attracting countervailing suits from governments abroad. It would also promote the development and dissemination of environmentally friendly technologies throughout the world.

A further set of desirable measures are actions to ensure the enforcement of existing, if lower, environmental standards in foreign jurisdictions. This could involve the publication of comparative cross-national standards (for the benefit of Canadian consumers and others). It could include the provision, by Canadians governments and firms, of more money, technology and training to meet existing standards and teach the value of higher ones.[9] It could also extend to the negotiation of agreements to allow, on a reciprocal basis, joint or even trilateral inspection teams to visit the production facilities and processes in each others' jurisdictions, to assess the extent to which these meet each country's national standards or those jointly or regionally agreed upon. At first glance this might appear to represent an extension of existing trade rules from product to process standards, and an extraterritorial intrusion into a foreign jurisdiction.[10] Yet there are precedents in existing trade practice for out-of-country process inspections.[11] Moreover the joint and reciprocal features of such an arrangement render any surrenders of sovereignty routine. Such an arrangement

243

would also encourage jurisdictions within Canada to avoid any lax enforcement of their own environmental laws, with consequent direct benefits to the Canadian ecology.

Canada could also usefully negotiate a common set of internationally-harmonized environmental standards that reflect the highest levels existing in Canada and allow for increases to which Canada might wish to upgrade in the future. Devising a system with a high base and upgrade bias does mean that Canadian firms would face the prospect of having to meet ever higher standards dictated by environmental enthusiasts in the United States - even the California component. However, as the experience of the automotive sector suggests, the large share of US ownership of Canadian firms, and the importance of the US market to Canadian firms in many sectors, means that the market mechanisms of an integrated North American marketplace already work powerfully in this direction. Because there may be some tendency for standards to be set at a high level - for precautionary purposes - when initially introduced, and lowered as more data becomes available, some provision should be made for the possible lowering of standards, but only when genuinely "sound science" supports such an action.

The second major issue facing Canada in the trade-environment complex concerns the circumstances in which unilateral trade action to protect the environment should be allowed. "Never" is the instinctive response of a country whose citizens and corporations can readily recall the recent plethora of cases in which unilaterally imposed "green protectionism" (by groups and governments in much larger entities, such as the US and the European Community) has damaged Canada's staple exports. It is also the ideological and intellectual answer of those whose commitment to multilateralism is grounded in a calculation that a merely middle-power Canada is destined to lose to the unilateralism of the major powers, in a world in which relative national power rather than internationally-agreed rules prevails.

There are, however, sound logical reasons for environmental activists - particularly in major powers such as the United States - to look to unilaterally-imposed trade measures as an effective weapon in their arsenal. Because major powers often have unique scientific capabilities, they tend to be in the vanguard of discovering and reacting to global environmental threats, such as that to the stratospheric ozone layer. Waiting for an international consensus to develop before permitting action would deprive the global community of:

a) timely remedial action by a major player;

b) a clear environmental activist to serve as a leader around which an international coalition can be assembled to address the problem; and

c) an empirical basis on which to assess the best response strategy to be adopted in an international agreement.

Moreover, in the real world of international politics, the mere possibility or threat of environmentally-inspired unilateral trade measures by the United States has brought otherwise overlooked environmental problems to the attention of governments and publics in the targeted jurisdictions, and led to accommodating, environmentally-friendly responses without unilateral measures actually being imposed. It may even be that the particularly open, participatory political systems of the United States and of European countries, where green parties are influential, might enable environmental concerns to have an appropriately large voice and weight that they would lack if held hostage to the consensus produced by a global common denominator, or by the least open, least democratic, least participatory country in the international system. In this sense, the recent US-Mexican agreement to eliminate dolphin-unfriendly harvesting methods in the Mexican tuna industry - as much as the environmental provisions within and accompanying the North American Free Trade Agreement - is a product of the uniquely easy access of environmental groups to the US Congress. At the other end of the spectrum, the cumulative ecological devastation caused by decades of communist rule in Eastern Europe stands as a grim reminder of how closed political systems systematically suppress ecological values.

Within Canada itself, there has been at least one occasion upon which the Canadian government concluded it was necessary to act unilaterally, in defiance of an economically sound set of international law, to protect an endangered ecosystem of critical value both to Canada and the world.[12] In the *Arctic Waters Pollution Prevention Act of 1970* (AWPPA), the Canadian government withdrew from the compulsory jurisdiction of the International Court of Justice to impose standards unilaterally on vessel construction that, while non-discriminatory on paper, restricted primarily foreign vessels in practice. Despite the sustained opposition of the US, and an international legal regime created by maritime powers well before the pollution threats to the world's oceans had become serious or known, Canada succeeded in having its unilateral actions subsequently endorsed by a strong majority of the world's countries. They eventually served as the basis for a new international law of the sea, far more supportive of environmental values that its predecessor. Those recalling the success of the AWPPA, and concerned about the diminishing fish stocks on Canada's Grand Banks, might well conceive of circumstances in which the possibility, threat, or even use of unilateral action with trade implications, could serve the national and international interest again. And it is possible that foreign pressure, backed by unilateral trade action directed against Canada, has brought some environmental benefits to Canada, even if at painful, short-term economic cost.

It might, thus, be unwise for Canada to dismiss absolutely the use of unilateral action with trade implications in defence of the environment, or to declare that the use of such measures has done only damage to Canada, or to assume that in a world of allowable unilateralism Canada is always destined to lose. At the same time, it is important to be clear about the particular set of circumstances that were necessary for unilateralism to succeed in the AWPPA case:

• there was a clear, scientifically compelling, and publicly visible danger to an ecosystem of critical value not only to Canada but to the global community as a whole;

• unilateralism was resorted to only after the failure of repeated efforts to modify an obsolescent international regime by using the existing rules of the game;

• an overwhelming number of the world's countries, including those from the developing world, were prepared to endorse the Canadian action;

• the restrictions were limited;

• the enforcement measures and the trade effects were light and indirect; and

• the unilateral measures were applied within a territorial domain that did not lie within the jurisdiction of another sovereign state.

If convoy-like internationalism remains preferable to consensus-creating unilateralism in all but the most desperate circumstances, how many ships should be required to join the convoy before it can legitimately set sail? The ideal of universalism is almost never attainable in a world of over 175 sovereign states. Holding to it would therefore give a veto to "dirty" or distracted countries, or those willing to hold the environment hostage to unrelated political demands. Even that assumed exemplar of multilateralism, the GATT, has only 108 contracting parties, and international environmental agreements with trade measures often have far fewer. With 108 signatories, the 1973 Convention on International Trade in Endangered Species of Wild Fauna and Flora (CITES), and its restrictive trade measures, has as equal a claim to represent broadly accepted international law as the GATT itself and is, thus, not open to challenge on the grounds that it lacks minimum multilateral legitimacy. But over the past several decades Canada has seen fit to join the 33 member Montreal Protocol on ozone, the 5 member Polar Bear Convention, and the 4 member North Pacific Fur Seal Convention, and thus endorse the international legitimacy of the trade measures they contain. With several decades of success in using very limited plurilateralism - in practice - to protect the environment, there is no reason for Canada to be trapped by the mythical world of broad multilateralism now.

Strengthening National Decision-Making Structures

The need to translate these general approaches into detailed policies raises the question of the adequacy of the Canadian federal government's decision-making structures and processes: can they integrate trade and environmental considerations in an appropriately balanced and effective way? Since the creation of a combined Department of External Affairs and International Trade in the early 1980s, Canada has enjoyed a comparatively tight institutional link between its trade ministry and those organizations responsible for international development and international affairs. More recently, the onset of the OECD's trade-environment work and the NAFTA negotiations has brought the trade and environment ministries into a much closer relationship with each other and with outside organizations. In 1991, the government formed an Interdepartmental Committee on Trade and the Environment, chaired by EAIT and involving seven departments, to help formulate its policies on these matters for the OECD.[13] Canada's OECD delegation maintains regular contact with interested ENGOs before and after the Canadian delegation attends meetings on trade and the environment in Paris. Representatives of environmental non-governmental organizations have been appointed to the government's senior International Trade Advisory Committee (ITAC), and to a majority of the 15 Sectoral Advisory Groups on International Trade (SAGITs) advising the government in the NAFTA negotiations. These individuals have had the opportunity to provide detailed comments on the draft NAFTA text. And other environmentalists have also been brought into the NAFTA advisory process.

Such changes, however, still generally involve the incremental addition of environmental representatives and concerns into bodies created, and still dominated by, the trade bureaucracy. Moreover, they lack, in some respects, the many institutional innovations that have brought trade and environmental representatives much closer together in the United States. There, too, a large inter-agency group on trade and the environment has flourished, with officials from dozens of organizations actively involved. Environmental representatives have been added to the NAFTA advisory committees as well. But, in addition, the United States Trade Representative (USTR) has equipped herself and her organization with a dedicated environmental advisory committee, created a full time Deputy Assistant Secretary for the Environment, added representatives of the US ENGO community as observers on the US delegation to the OECD, and personally consulted environmental groups on the NAFTA negotiations. At the same time, the Administrator of the Environmental Protection Agency has created his own trade policy advisory committee, despatched officials to work within the USTR's office, and secured for the EPA the joint lead, with the USTR, on the NAFTA standards negotiating group. Although much of the stimulus for these moves may have come from Congressional pressure, as the necessary price for securing an extension of negotiating authority for trade deals dear to administration's heart, this politically-inspired process of integration has, on the whole, generated benefits for the US trade policy community and been received with goodwill.

Many of these innovations warrant close scrutiny in regard to their potential applicability and value in the Canadian situation. In conducting this evaluation, however, it is important to note that the Canadian government is already notably more advanced in the integration of trade and environmental concerns at the senior levels of government, as a consequence of the cabinet system and the current cabinet committee design. Moreover, both the current trade and environment ministers, in part through their participation in the work of the National Round Table on the Environment and the Economy, have had opportunities to become aware of the claims of each other, and of sustainable development, that their counterparts in the United States still lack.

Institutionalizing the International Trade-Environment Regime

In the larger task of building an international trade-environment regime that reflects Canadian interests and values, it is important to assess which of the many available international institutional forums are best equipped to deliver the preferred results. The inherited instinct of many Canadians is to rely, in the first instance, on the venerable multilateral organizations created in the immediate post world war two period - the United Nations and the GATT. Yet there are concerns about the ability of such traditional favourites, confined by charters based on the priorities and scientific knowledge of distant decades, to adapt to such new issues as the trade-environment relationship. In this instance, reliance on Canada's instinctive internationalism should be avoided in favour of a systematic, competitive appraisal of the relevance of the many international institutions now available to define a modern trade-environment regime.

In practice, that regime will be partially shaped by a North American Free Trade Agreement among Canada, the United States and Mexico.[14] It is this triad that, like the European Community, is inventing and implementing operational trade-environment relationships that other, more broadly-multilateral institutions are still merely talking about. At a minimum, NAFTA offers a fast start up and field trial for new trade-environment practices. Because it embraces two of the world's largest trading powers and one of its most environmentally open political systems, NAFTA could provide a rich laboratory, likely to generate a regime encompassing many of the relevant issues (and one with political impact as well as intellectual influence on the world beyond). And because it includes a developing country whose political leaders have cast off the sterile rhetoric of the North-South confrontation of the 1970s, it is likely to incorporate the concerns of poorer countries in a meaningful and productive way. So, despite the current unpopularity of NAFTA in Canada, few are arguing, as they did in the Canada-US Free Trade debate of 1988, that Canada should abandon NAFTA and rely instead on the more multilateral GATT system to deliver a new trade-environment regime.

Given its centrality, it is important that the trade-environment model NAFTA sets be an appropriate and forward-looking one. The proper referent for evaluating NAFTA is, thus, not how much more it has taken account of, or done "for", the environment than the Canada-US Free Trade Agreement which preceded it. Rather it is the extent to which NAFTA's integrated trade-environment regime realizes the ideals of sustainable development. At a minimum, a prospective NAFTA agreement should be reviewed by Canadians against all of the core principles of sustainable development articulated in the Brundtland Report[15] (and whether it makes substantial progress in meeting them) and not just the current list of demands of environmental groups in Canada or the United States.

Such a review would look in the first instance for the inclusion of the term "sustainable development" in the preamble of the treaty, as a way of injecting the general principle into the spirit of the treaty. Although the preamble does not contain legally binding commitments, it is a very important aid in the interpretation of the language contained in the treaty. There is a developing principle in international law that, although Courts may look to the intention of the parties as manifested by the words used, they will also examine the history and purpose of the treaty as evidenced by the preamble.[16]

A second area of attention is NAFTA's dispute settlement mechanism. US negotiators for a NAFTA have been instructed by their Administration to develop "dispute settlement mechanisms that are sensitive to environmental programs and values".[17]

In the spirit of more open, transparent, balanced and informed decision-making, a NAFTA dispute settlement mechanism could usefully make provision for some form of public participation in panel hearings. Standing might be granted to those individuals and communities whose environment or resource base would be affected by the Panel's decision.[18] Moreover, NAFTA could require that, in cases with environmental dimensions, its dispute resolution panels contain individuals with environmental expertise. Ideally, these individuals would be appointed not only at the discretion of the country which calculates that environmental considerations will work in its favour, but on a more automatic and collective basis.

Finally, NAFTA panels could strengthen their capacity in regard to the scientific evidence which arises in environmental and conservation disputes - both by establishing a new environment-specific dispute settlement mechanism for NAFTA and by employing the capacity of the IJC and the other joint environmental organizations operating on the US northern and southern borders.

A second international institution that has received considerable attention in the trade-environment debate has been the GATT. At their London Summit in July 1991, the leaders of the world's seven major industrial democracies and the European Community declared that they would "look to the General Agreement on Tariffs and Trade (GATT) to define how trade measures can properly be used for environmental purposes."[19] More recently, Prime Minister Mulroney has declared that "once the current Uruguay Round of global trade negotiations is complete, Canada will support a further round of negotiations in which environment will be a focal point."[20]

This apparent choice of the GATT coincides with a Canadian instinct to see that body as the centrepiece of a multilateral trade system that has successfully defended Canada and the world against the ever potent forces of protectionism, including those cloaked in environmental garb. From an entirely trade and economic perspective, the GATT is, indeed, a significant theoretical and sound practical success. From the standpoint of sustainable development, it has the advantage that developing countries are included in an important way among its 108 members. Unlike most International Environmental Agreements (IEAs) it also has a proven dispute settlement capacity, having dealt with 207 cases and rendered 86 rulings from 1948 to 1989. But as an institution likely to integrate environmental concerns into its trade raison d'etre, and to do so in a way that accords the environment equal value, it has several disadvantages

In the international community the GATT co-exists with 127 IEAs which, on the whole, have a strong claim to constitute legitimate international law. Of the 17 IEAs with trade provisions, 3 were freely concluded among countries before the GATT came into existence. Some IEAs, notably CITES, have as many participating countries as the GATT. And, whereas international environmental agreements are duly authorized intergovernmental treaties or conventions, after the deliberate rejection of the International Trade Organization it was initially conceived to be, the GATT remains an historic half measure representing "an essentially contractual relationship without full international status."[21]

Within the GATT itself, there are few openings for environmental considerations to enter or flourish. After 45 years, the term "environment" is still entirely absent from its Articles of Agreement, which enshrine economic values according to a calculus in which environmental costs are largely dismissed as externalities. It thus reflects the political priorities and state of scientific knowledge of 1947 rather than 1992. Although environmental concerns were forced upon it in the early 1970s and resulted in the creation of a Group on Environmental Measures and International Trade in that year, the GATT succeeded in strangling this nascent environmental intrusion at birth. A second attempt at environmental start-up in late 1990 was similarly resisted, resulting in more delay and a work program for the 1990s restricted to terms of reference two decades old.

As an international organization, required to respond rapidly to new priorities, the GATT suffers from extremely weak ministerial management and political oversight, even with the creation of a Trade Policy Review Mechanism in 1990. As a trade organization, it has no provision for including ministers of the environment or their officials in its regular work. Nor does it have particularly strong environmental expertise within its secretariat.

Moreover the GATT's performance to date in dispute settlement seems to suggest that it cannot easily incorporate environmental concerns. Its critics complain that "of the seven GATT panel reports involving an interpretation of Article XX where measures were taken on environmental grounds, not one of them clearly survived" the highly restrictive conditions the GATT imposes on any exceptions to its entirely economic disciplines.[22] Such criticism must, of course, be tempered by a recognition of the tendency of injured states to take to the GATT's dispute resolution processes primarily those cases where a thin veneer of environmental public relations has been used to cloak a hard core of classic protectionist intent.

Far more serious has been GATT's failure thus far to serve as an effective forum for introducing sustainable development considerations into the debate on agricultural trade subsidies, and temper them on these grounds alone. The GATT has similarly been slow to define and authorize an allowable set of national subsidies to facilitate the development and introduction of environmentally supportive products and processes.[23] Nor has it given priority to the elimination of tariff and non-tariff barriers on such items and thus created a stimulus for their international dissemination. The GATT's basic decision that such issues would be taken up after, rather than as part of, the Uruguay Round may have been appropriate when that Round was headed for completion in 1990. However by mid-1992, with no clear end to the Round in sight, the costs of delay have mounted considerably.

Taken together, these features of the GATT suggest:

• *First*, that as currently constituted, it should not be the primary forum for defining or developing the new integrated trade-environment regime. As the home playing field of the trade policy community, devoid of high level political management and ecological sensitivity or expertise, it has neither the will nor the capacity to handle such a transcendent integrative task.

• *Second*, the GATT should give priority to the tasks for which is institutionally well suited but has not dealt with well to date, and which are important for promoting sustainable development on a global basis. These omissions include: disciplining those agricultural subsidies which have the most destructive effect on the environment; defining allowable subsidies for environmentally-supportive products and processes; and reducing tariff and non-tariff barriers to them.

• *Third*, there is no pressing need at present to amend the GATT's Articles of Agreements to better incorporate environmental concerns. Despite the concerns of GATT's critics, there is at present a tolerable state of "peaceful coexistence" between the GATT and the IEAs. Although the latter contain provisions that are - on the face of it - GATT-illegal, the GATT has thus far not moved, or been forced to declare them so, and has confined its acts of "anti-environmental" commission to cases where the protectionist rather than ecological character of national actions prevailed. In cases such as the threat to the stratospheric ozone layer or the trade in hazardous waste, where there has been a clear and present environmental danger and where the environmental response has been undertaken by multilateral rather than unilateral action, the GATT has thus far offered no challenge or constraint. This is not merely because the GATT, or aggrieved parties who might complain to it, have simply been slow off the mark. Rather it is because the GATT has been able to co-exist easily for most of its life with other, restrictive, discriminatory, less-than-fully-multilateral trade regimes when and where the threat was equally clear.[24] Thus the GATT could well be left alone for at least a while longer to impose its disciplines in its home field of normal, non-threatening trade, to sense where values not encoded in its articles have overriding claims, and to interpret its rules in ways that reflect this political reality. While this might make for some tortuous legal reasoning in potential cases in the future, it seems like a manageable price to pay. Moreover, such a pause would provide time to assess more adequately which trade-related measures within the recent generation of IEAs effectively accomplish their environmental objectives, and do so at a sensible economic price.

• *Fourth*, as part of this regime of "peaceful co-existence", those applying trade law on the one hand and those devising and implementing IEA's on the other, should make a particular effort to respect the sacred core of the others' concerns and thereby avoid unnecessary collisions.[25] Environmental negotiators and regulators should look for ways in which trade measures can be encoded and applied in a way that respects the GATT principles, as Sweden did in applying the trade provisions of the Montreal Protocol on a non-discriminatory basis. And trade negotiators can examine how the GATT's existing principles can be applied in practice on a broader and less rigid basis when legitimate environmental values are at stake.

In looking for a forum where a higher level trade-environment regime could be devised, the OECD offers several strong advantages:

• it has regular ministerial supervision, and thus the flexibility to adapt to new issue areas and priorities on the international agenda;

- it involves economic and environmental interests and expertise on a regular basis from the ministerial level on down;
- it has expertise on environmental matters within its secretariat; and
- it has a respectable historical record, notably through pioneering the "polluter pays principle", of successfully injecting environmental concerns into the international economic system.

At first glance the OECD may appear to be merely a closed rich-persons club. But it does have some expansive features on which to build. It includes, as members, countries from most global regions, and certainly all those at the forefront of world trade. It has long made provision for representatives of both the business and labour communities to participate in its work. It could extend this record of broader representation by conducting its work on trade and the environment in closer co-operation with that of the United Nations Conference on Trade and Development (UNCTAD), where the developing countries dominate.[26] Greater openness in decision-making, and increased environmental expertise, could result from expanding the role which environmental non-governmental organizations play in the OECD's work - perhaps in a way that parallels the participation of business and labour. While there are some real costs to having all countries follow the United States' example and include ENGO representatives as observers within their national delegations in the OECD's trade-environment work, the benefits the United States has secured from doing this warrant an exploration of similar action by other major countries.

The work of the OECD in forging the new trade-environment regime will require guidance from political leaders, and ultimately from heads of state and government who, alone, are responsible for ensuring that trade and environment concerns are integrated, and appropriately balanced, in their national governments. It is only these heads who can redress the inherited imbalance between old and strong trade ministries and the less-established environment ministries, and declare that the claims of environmental preservation must become stronger and more integrated in mutually supportive ways with those of economic growth.

The annual summit of the seven major industrial democracies and the European Community provides an appropriate forum for exercising such collective leadership in the trade-environment area. Its members command a strong majority of the relevant capabilities of the global community in the economic domain, and a plurality of most in the environmental field. Because it has only eight members, all of like political and economic composition and all represented by heads of government or state, its prospects of reaching timely agreement are much better than those of larger, more diverse, and more bureaucratically-managed bodies. And because the United States represents a minority of the G-7's capabilities, the regimes the G-7 generates are likely to be an effective control, rather than a mere collective legitimation, of American unilateralism in this domain.

The breadth of the G-7's trade-environment agenda, and the direction it has provided in presenting a reconciliation, suggests it is a productive forum for giving high level guidance in shaping the new trade-environment regime.[27] Moreover Canada's membership as a principal in the summit and all its related G-7 bodies, and its record of leadership on environmental issues within them, make the G-7 a particularly good forum within which Canadian interests can be pursued. In order to realize the full potential of this forum, however, it would be desirable to institutionalize the recently-initiated meetings of G-7 environment ministers, and to tie their work more closely to that of their colleagues in trade ministries, and to that of the heads themselves.[28]

References

1. The initial overviews of the subject from a Canadian perspective are: ST PIERRE, ANTOINE (1991) *Impact of Environmental Measures on International Trade* Report 76-91-E (Ottawa: Conference Board of Canada); HART, MICHAEL WITH GERA, SUSHMA (1992) "Trade and the Environment: Dialogue of the Deaf or Scope for Cooperation?" Paper prepared for the Canada-United States Law Institute Conference on the Law and Economics of Environmental Regulation in the Canada/US Context, Cleveland, Ohio, April 24-26; and the papers presented at the Centre for Trade Policy and Law and the University of Ottawa Faculty of Law's Conference on "International Trade and Sustainable Development" May 14, 1992.

2. The phrase is that of Michael Hart - see HART, MICHAEL WITH GERA, SUSHMA (1992) *op cit*.

3. GATT (1992) *International Trade 90-91* Vol 1 (Geneva) p.11. Under the temporary effects of the recession, Canada's merchandise trade rank slipped to 8th in 1990. The spring, 1992 admission of Russia to the IMF with the 8th highest quota share, just behind 7th ranked Canada, confirmed Canada's overall economic position.

4. For example, Canada has 9% of the world's renewable water supply, 10% of the globe's forests and 20% of the world's forest product exports. It ranks first in the world in newsprint, second in pulp, and third in softwood lumber production. It is also the world's third largest producer of minerals. (Sources: ENVIRONMENT CANADA (1990) *The Green Plan: A National Challenge*; HOUSE OF COMMONS (1990) "Forests of Canada: The Federal Role" Report of the Standing Committee on Forestry and Fisheries (Ottawa) November, p.2.

5. HOLMES, JOHN AND KIRTON, JOHN (EDS) (1988) *Canada*

and the New Internationalism (Toronto: Canadian Institute of International Affairs).

6. In the case of the United States, the work of the Canadian Coalition on Acid Rain and the International Joint Commission are instructive. On the latter see SPENCER, ROBERT, KIRTON, JOHN AND NOSSAL, KIM (EDS) (1982) *The International Joint Commission Seventy Years On* (Toronto: University of Toronto Centre for International Studies).

7. The current international consensus on these issues, as articulated in Principle Twelve of the Rio Declaration on Environment and Development is:
"Trade policy measures for environmental purposes should not constitute a means of arbitrary or unjustifiable discrimination or a disguised restriction on international trade. Unilateral actions to deal with environmental challenges outside the jurisdiction of the importing country should be avoided. Environmental problems should, as far as possible, be based on an international consensus."

8. In the Tuna/Dolphin case, the GATT panel found that the "Dolphin Safe" labelling provisions for tuna products in the Dolphin Protection Consumer Information Act (DPCIA) were not inconsistent with the GATT. The US labelling regulations governing tuna caught in the Eastern Tropical Pacific applied to all countries whose vessels fished in this geographical area. They thus did not distinguish between products originating in Mexico and products originating in other countries. For evidence of the potent catalytic environmentally protective effects of voluntary action by informed consumers, see BENEDICT, RICHARD ELLIOT (1991) *Ozone Diplomacy: New Directions in Safeguarding the Planet* (Cambridge, Mass: Harvard University Press) pp.27-8, which reports that:
"Even before the 1978 aerosol ban, the US market for

spray cans had fallen by nearly two-thirds because American consumers were acting on their environmental concerns."

9. In regard to Mexico both the Canadian government and Northern Telecom have made a promising start in this respect.

10. Countries' continuing concern with the formalities of sovereignty, even in a world of increasingly intense physical interdependence, was recently re-affirmed in Principle 2 of the Rio Declaration, which states that:
"States have, in accordance with the Charter of the United Nations and the principles of international law, the sovereign right to exploit their own resources pursuant to their own environmental and development policies..."

11. The US Food and Drug Administration has the right to inspect food processing facilities abroad in order to assess their compliance with US standards and regulations if the plant exports to the US. In cases, such as hazardous waste or CFCs, where the product, process or pollution presents a clear "security threat" to human, animal or plant life, the appropriate referent is not normal trade law, but the many regimes which exist in the security field. For example, the International Atomic Energy Agency has long had the right to inspect nuclear facilities in member states. See HILZ, CHRISOPH (1992) *The International Toxic Waste Trade* (New York: Van Nostrand Reinhold).

12. MUNTON, DON AND KIRTON, JOHN (1987) "The Manhattan Voyages and their Aftermath" in GRIFFITHS, FRANKLYN (ED) *Politics of the Northwest Passage* (Montreal: McGill-Queen's University Press) pp.67-97.

13. The Departments of External Affairs, Environment, Finance, Energy, Mines and Resources, Fisheries, Forestry,

and Industry, Science and Technology.

14. For background on NAFTA and its environmental dimensions see HUFBAUER, GARY CLYDE AND SCHOTT, JEFFREY (1992) *North American Free Trade: Issues and Recommendations* (Washington, DC: Institute for International Economics) particularly Chapter 7. See also MORICI, PETER (1992) "Free Trade with Mexico" *Foreign Policy* 87 (Summer) pp. 88-104.

15. WORLD COMMISSION ON ENVIRONMENT AND DEVELOPMENT (1987) *Our Common Future* (Oxford: Oxford University Press). For guidance as to how this assessment might be conducted see RICHARDSON, SARAH (1991) *Sustainable Development and Canada's Bilateral Treaties* Background Document prepared for the National Round Table on the Environment and the Economy's Foreign Policy Committee.

16. KINDRED, HUGH M (GEN ED) (1987) *International Law: Chiefly as Interpreted and Applied in Canada* (4th ed) (Canada: Emond Montgomery Publications Ltd) p.160.

17. USTR (1991) "Review of US-Mexico Environmental Issues" Prepared by an Inter-agency Task Force Coordinated by the Office of the USTR (Washington, DC:) October, p.198. This is made more complex by the disparities between Mexico's legal system and those in the US and Canada.

18. This proposal has been put forward in a GATT context by Charles Arden-Clarke in ARDEN-CLARKE, CHARLES (1991) "The General Agreement on Tariffs and Trade, Environmental Protection and Sustainable Development" a WWF Discussion paper (Geneva: World Wildlife Federation) June.

19. LONDON ECONOMIC SUMMIT (1991) "Economic Declaration: Building World Partnership" para.15.

20. CANADA, OFFICE OF THE PRIME MINISTER (1992) "Notes for an Address by Prime Minister Brian Mulroney, Environment Week, Canadian Museum of Civilization, Hull Quebec, June 1, 1992".

21. ELWELL, CHRISTINE (1992) "On the Use of the Trade System to Deliver Environmental Objectives" Speaking Notes for the Centre for Trade Policy and Law and the Faculty of Law at the University of Ottawa, Seventh Annual Conference on Canada and International Trade "International Trade and Sustainable Development" Ottawa, May 14, 1992, p.6. This piece is to be published as part of the Conference Proceedings.

22. ELWELL, CHRISTINE (1992) *op cit* p.4.

23. Included in the Uruquay Round Brussels Draft of the Subsidies Codes there was a non-actionable category of subsidy for one-time environmentally-related subsidy. This has since disappeared and was not in the Dunkel Draft of January 1992.

24. The list includes the Coordinating Committee on Export Controls (COCOM), the London Nuclear Suppliers Group Regime, the Australian Group Regime, and the Missile Technology Control Regime.

25. Perhaps as a preliminary step by ensuring that both communities are represented on the delegations negotiating such agreements and designing implementing mechanism at home.

26. This effort should proceed with appropriate caution, given UNCTAD's record to date on the trade-environment issue. See SAUNDERS, J OWEN (1990) "Legal Aspects of Trade and Sustainable Development" in SAUNDERS, J OWEN *The Legal Challenge of Sustainable Development* (Calgary:

263

Canadian Institute of Resources Law) pp.380-1.

27. MacNEILL, JIM, WINSEMIUS, PIETER AND YAKUSHIJI, TAIZO (1991) *Beyond Interdependence: Meshing of the World's Economy and the Earth's Ecology* (Oxford: Oxford University Press) p.65. Environmental concerns have had an early, easy, and effective insertion into the work of the seven power "economic" summit, as recorded in HAJNAL, PETER (1989) *The Seven Power Summit, Documents from the Summits of Industrial Countries, 19975-1989* (New York: Kraus International Publications).

28. For a similar suggestion see BERGSTEN, C FRED (1992) *Foreign Policy* 87, Summer, pp.17-18.

H
Background

22

Trade, Environment and Competitiveness: An Overview
Sarah Richardson

Sarah Richardson is a lawyer and consultant. She has a BA (Hons) in International Relations from the University of Toronto, an LLB from Dalhousie University, Halifax, and an LLM from Columbia University, New York. She has worked as a consultant in Ottawa and authored the report Sustainable Development and Canada's Bilateral Treaties, *a Background Document prepared for the Foreign Policy Committee of the National Round Table on the Environment and the Economy (Ottawa: 1990). She currently works with the Environmental Assessment Board of the Ontario Ministry of the Environment.*

Introduction

As environmental issues have taken on a greater importance in the minds of the public and politicians during the past half decade, there has been increasing interest in the relationship between environmental protection and international trade. At the international level, in particular, there is now widespread concern about the various ways in which the environmental initiatives of states, acting both unilaterally and multilaterally, may restrict or distort exports and imports.

Reciprocally, given the increasing importance of environmental issues, there is renewed attention to the many ways trade policies affect the environment and, more broadly, the prospects for sustainable development. In light of the importance of trade to the Canadian and global economies and ecosystems, it is crucial that Canadian policy-makers, exporters, environmental groups, and other stakeholders understand more clearly the multifaceted relationship between trade and environmental policies and practices, nationally and internationally. An enhanced understanding is particularly important at a time when Canada and other governments move to implement and build upon the results of the United Nations Conference on the Environment and Development held in Brazil in June 1992.

This chapter provides a factual, descriptive overview of this important and timely international issue. It provides basic information on the central issues facing Canada in the complex relationship between trade and the environment, within the broader context of concerns about competitiveness and sustainable development. It is by no means comprehensive, but is intended to begin an open, ongoing dialogue on a rapidly evolving issue.

The first section reviews, in general terms, the major relationships between trade and environmental policies and practices, and the dominant trade-environment issues on the current international agenda.

The second section examines the challenges Canada's major export-oriented industries face from a growing environmental awareness abroad and at home, and the threats and opportunities this presents.

The third section explores how trade and the environment have come together under the Canada-United States Free Trade Agreement, and how they seem likely to be treated under an expanded arrangement with Mexico.

The fourth section reviews the experience of the European Community in relating trade and environment concerns and the implications for Canadian exporters to the European market.

Finally, the fifth section addresses the relationship between trade and the environment within the major multilateral institutions and plurilateral forums: the Organization for Economic Co-operation and Development (OECD); the General Agreement on Tariffs and Trade (GATT); the Group of Seven major industrial democracies and the European Community; and the United Nations System.

The Trade-Environment Relationship

The Impact of Environmental Protection on Trade
National Measures

Unilateral regulation is the most common way national governments implement their policies for protecting the environment; regulations may affect trade directly, as in the case of environmentally inspired or linked import or export bans. They may also have indirect effects on international competition by increasing or imposing costs, erecting border measures, or by setting product or even process standards that have differential effects.

Environmental regulations can cause trade distortions by varying the costs of compliance which may alter the relative competitiveness of industries and firms in international trade. Regulations may also be "moving targets"- as soon as they are met by industry, costly new standards are imposed by governments which can further jeopardize a firm's international competitiveness.

Competitiveness is also affected by the use of economic instruments in implementing environmental policies: tax rebates, deposit refund systems or marketable permits may, in effect if not in intent, reduce the access of foreign producers to the national market. The growing use of product labelling to indicate the environmental quality of goods also has the potential to affect trade; some countries might distort the otherwise valuable activity of developing standards for "environmentally friendly" products in order to create non-tariff barriers that favour domestic products over competing imported products. Labelling regimes also have the potential to influence consumption patterns, thereby affecting trade, as consumers become more environmentally conscious and show a preference for perceived "environmentally friendly" products - whether imported or domestically produced. Moreover, eco-labelling may impose product testing or certification requirements that are costly for foreign firms to meet, especially because global competition limits the extent to which these cost

269

increases can be passed on to the consumer.

This concern for a country's relative international competitiveness takes on new dimensions when applied to the North-South trading relationship. In the industrialized world, environmental protection has emerged as an issue requiring immediate attention. It comes with associated costs, as industry has to meet air, water, and waste regulations, safety and health regulations, and other environmentally related requirements imposed by law. Over time, these higher costs can, affect Northern competitiveness *vis-à-vis* comparable industries in developing countries.

At present, industries in developing countries are often seen as having an unfair advantage in international trade, due to the lower and less costly national environmental standards they must meet. There is concern in the North at the prospect of losing both export and domestic markets. This concern limits the ability of companies to pass on fully the increased costs of meeting environmental requirements. It also leads Northern industry to press for the implementation of a "level playing field" in environmental matters.

The current debate surrounding the proposed free trade deal joining Canada and the United States with Mexico has highlighted the potential threat from so-called "pollution havens", where lax standards in environmental protection, health and safety, and labour in developing countries lure new investment from jurisdictions with stricter standards, and provide a cheaper export platform from which to compete with producers who remain in the higher-standards and cost locales.

On the other side of the North-South divide, many developing countries are concerned that environmental, health, and conservation restrictions in the developed world will be used to restrict exports to these lucrative markets. From their perspective, the fundamental question is whether the industrialized countries should impose the same standards on imports from developing countries as on their domestic products and processes. Developing countries argue that, in so doing, the North is merely imposing its own ecological preferences on other countries, using trade restrictions and conditions as prerequisites for market access.

Among the unilateral measures taken by states, product bans at the border are perhaps the most onerous of all trade restrictions. Such bans, usually imposed in the name of environmental protection or conservation, are often the result of consumer or industry pressures. Product bans have affected Canadian industry in the past and continue to threaten it. For example, in the early 1980s, the East Coast commercial sealing industry was shut down as the result of a ban on the importation of sealskin, which was imposed by the European Parliament in response to consumer pressure (manifested in an attempted boycott of seal products from Canada) and strong lobbying efforts by environmentalists and others. And in 1989, the US imposed a ban on the importation of asbestos that led to huge cutbacks in the Canadian asbestos industry.[1]

More recently, the US banned imports of tuna from Mexico because the tuna-harvesting methods used by Mexican fishermen killed more dolphins than the level permitted in US domestic legislation. US beef producers have called for restrictions on imports of meat from Brazil on the grounds that Brazilian producers encourage destruction of tropical forests. Some OECD countries require that, before accepting tropical timber exports from developing countries, proper tropical forestry management schemes be evident in those countries. Furthermore, tropical timber exporters worry about the effects of a continuing ban, created as the result of pressure by environmental groups, on the use of tropical timber in a number of European municipalities. Developing countries fear that such restrictions will soon become national policy for countries with strong domestic NGO lobbies and public opinion campaigns. A ban without some form of compensation could be devastating for those Southeast

Asian countries whose economies depend heavily on the export of timber.

A wider concern among industries in Canada is that the lack of internationally agreed standards, and the presence of inconsistent national standards among trading nations, will impede freer trade. There is also concern that, when standards are set, there is a lack of consistency in calculating acceptable levels of risk to the environment.

With the development of technology, very low levels of materials can be detected in the environment. In some cases, there may be an accepted "safe threshold" below which these substances are deemed to be of no harm to the environment — in which case, there is no benefit to setting regulations below the threshold. Other substances may harm the environment at any concentration, and a specified increase in concentration will cause a corresponding degree of harm, regardless of the ambient pollution level. In these cases, benefits from an additional level of pollution abatement are equal at all pollution levels.

There are additional problems concerning the scientific and other evidence on which countries should rely when making these calculations. The scientific basis of an action affecting trade was at issue in the EC-US beef hormone controversy. The issue of the legitimacy of standards, based on non-scientific (generally social) considerations with respect to health and sanitary measures, has also surfaced in the Uruguay Round of multilateral trade negotiations.

Unilateral actions are very difficult to address by the foreign countries adversely affected. All states claim the sovereign right to regulate their own affairs, including promulgating regulations to protect the environment as they see fit and as local conditions warrant. When the domestic regulations of one country impede the free flow of goods, the GATT is ill-equipped to intervene because of its principles of consistency and national treatment, which, in effect, state that as long as a country adopts rules that apply equally to domestic and foreign products, they are

GATT-legal. Moreover, there is no explicit mechanism in the GATT to address environmental non-tariff barriers.

While the 1979 Standards Code deals with the issue of environmental standards, it has not been applied to disputes involving the environment and, in any event, contains a host of substantive and procedural shortcomings. Furthermore, the Standards Code cannot be applied unless the complainant chooses to bring the dispute under the Code. In many instances, a party will choose instead to submit the complaint to the GATT.

International Agreements
Given the regional and global dimensions of many environmental problems, there is an increasing trend toward the direct harmonization of approaches to environmental protection, through the negotiation of international agreements.[2] One reason to include trade provisions in environmental agreements is to address the "free-rider" problem: countries that are not parties to an Agreement benefit from the actions of others, while not incurring the costs of any obligations.

The multilateral agreement with the most far-reaching trade provisions is the Montreal Protocol on Substances that Deplete the Ozone Layer. The Montreal Protocol, first negotiated in 1987 and extensively revised in 1990, controls the production and "consumption" of chlorofluorocarbons (CFCs) and other ozone-depleting substances. It relies extensively on trade instruments to impose and facilitate compliance. Article 4 of the Protocol controls trade with countries not party to the Protocol. Paragraph 1 of Article 4 requires parties to ban both the import and export from non-party countries of CFCs and other substances covered by the Protocol. Paragraphs 3 and 4 of Article 4 threaten future trade restrictions on products containing, or products made using, the controlled chemicals. These provisions could very well be inconsistent with the GATT principles of national treatment and most-favoured nation status.

The provisions of Article 4 apparently were examined in

Montreal by the negotiators in respect of their consistency with the GATT.[3] The negotiators examined the preamble of GATT Article XX and concluded that the Montreal Protocol's Article 4 met the requirements because conditions in countries not party to the Protocol were, in fact, different from those countries who were party to it, all of whom had undertaken significant obligations extending over many years.

However, even if Article 4 of the Montreal Protocol meets the two tests found in the preamble to Article XX (that the measures do not result in arbitrary or unjustifiable discrimination between countries where the same conditions prevail and that the measures do not represent a disguised restriction on international trade), it must still comply with one of the specific exceptions found in GATT Article XX, sections (a) to (j). It is most likely to be defended under (b), which allows countries to be exempted from their GATT obligations if measures are necessary to protect human, animal or plant life or health. However, the term "necessary" has been strictly interpreted by the GATT panels to mean that there is no other GATT-consistent method of implementing the policy. It appears that, in the case of the Montreal Protocol, the policy of protection of the ozone can be implemented in a way that does not conflict with the most favoured-nation principle.

Whether or not the trade-related provisions of the Montreal Protocol turn out to be inconsistent with the GATT, they appear useful in addressing the free-rider problem. They may thus encourage inclusion of similar trade measures in other environmental agreements - as in the framework convention on Climate Change ("global warming") of June 1992.

A second recent multilateral agreement with important trade provisions is the 1989 Basel Convention on the Transboundary Movement of Hazardous Waste. Its aim is to minimize the transboundary movement of hazardous and other wastes; it contains explicit import and export restrictions by requiring countries to trade in waste only with other parties to the Agreement, or with countries with whom a bilateral treaty consistent with the Basel Convention has been concluded. Its effect on trade patterns is potentially even more far-reaching, as a result of onerous and expensive administrative regimes that will be set in place in domestic implementing legislation that requires monitoring of the transport of hazardous materials. Those provisions require prior written notification and consent to the transboundary movement of waste material, detailed information, and heavy insurance. Moreover, hazardous waste must be transported by a hazardous-waste carrier, a requirement that increases transportation costs considerably.

The requirements of the Basel Convention are of particular concern to industries, such as steel, that are involved in substantial recycling. In Canada, the definition of "hazardous waste" in the Basel Convention implementing legislation was vague enough to include recyclables such as scrap steel and other metals. The stringent requirements and procedures of the Basel Convention could potentially render the costs of compliance so onerous that many firms would be squeezed out of the market or encouraged to relocate to the US, where recyclable feedstock is available without the problems and expenses created at the border. The Canadian government has since consulted industry in an attempt to define "hazardous waste" more clearly in its regulations. One alternative is to have recycling and waste governed by an international agreement other than the Basel Convention; the OECD is currently examining the development of an international agreement on recycling. Managing waste efficiently, regardless of the presence of borders, is the ultimate goal.

A third international agreement that contains trade measures is the Convention on International Trade in Endangered Species of Wild Fauna and Flora (CITES). Article VIII, which requires that countries that are party to CITES enforce the provisions of the convention and not engage in trade in species prohibited by the agreement.

CITES uses such trade sanctions as a means of enforcement. However, its enforcement provisions are not as rigorous as those of the Montreal Protocol. Signatories can exempt themselves from provisions with regard to a particular species if they indicate a reservation at the time of signing. The Convention does, however, restrict trade in endangered species that may exist outside the borders of a signatory country, thus extending its impact to include nations that are not signatories to the agreement.

International agreements inspired by the environmental policies of Northern states may be perceived by the developing world as co-ordinated actions against the South. The Montreal Protocol and international action on global warming, which might also impose trade sanctions as a means of enforcement to induce compliance, concern the developing world; it fears that such measures will curtail ambitious schemes for the industrial expansion and production of electricity. Some Southern states also fear that a proposed international forestry convention might affect the ability of developing countries to utilize their tropical timber resources.

Whether or not trade sanctions imposed by international agreements violate the principle of "most-favoured nation", developing countries argue for additional resources and technology to assist them in making the transition from fossil fuels, preserving biodiversity, and reforesting large areas of the tropics. Long-term sustainable development could well require far-reaching changes in order to produce trade flows that are more equitable and better synchronized to environmental imperatives.

How should Canada respond to the increasing trend to environmental awareness and legislation in Canada's traditional export markets, and to the inclusion of trade provisions in international environmental agreements?

One approach is to use existing international trade law, enshrined in the GATT, to combat unilateral and discriminatory trade-distorting outcroppings of the new environmental activism.

A second is to revise international trade law to better absorb the new environmental concerns, while demanding that the trade-related means used to protect the environment be strictly proportional to legitimate ends, impede industry as little as possible, and depart as little as possible from tried and true trade law principles.

A third approach is to relax obsolescent concepts of national sovereignty and trading rules designed almost a half-century ago and adapt to those new environmental standards that are not merely a modern cloak for the old protectionism. In this regard, the Canadian government would have to bear in mind that, in the private sector, there might be trade-offs: while environmental protection measures might be a threat to one sector or firm, others might well seize the opportunity to develop more environmentally friendly products and processes and seize new markets as a result. Indeed, those businesses and sectors able and willing to surpass minimum public policy requirements could well benefit, by not constantly having to replace technologies in order to meet new and ever-higher standards, both at home and abroad.

The Impact of Trade on the Environment and Sustainable Development

A willingness to rethink the sanctity of the existing international trade system involves recognizing the damaging impact it has had on the global environment. In general, trade liberalization has an important, positive role in fostering efficiency and wealth, and, thus, in promoting such environmental values as lower natural resource inputs per-unit of output and the availability of funds for remedial cleanup, technological development, and other ecological purposes.[4] But the existing, inherited trade regime suffers from derogations from this liberal ideal and from other distortions and omissions that produce substantial environmental damage.

The negative effects of trade policies on the environment stem largely from the overall failure of prices and markets to account fully for environmental values and the resulting environmentally adverse patterns of production, unsustainable exploitation of natural resources, and trade in polluting or hazardous products.

Global patterns of production are also distorted more directly through the use of certain tariff and non-tariff barriers to trade, when government intervention on behalf of domestic exporters and importers distorts the market in ways that actively encourage unsustainable development.[5] For example, in the forestry sector, Japan has long favoured the importation of raw logs and penalized the importation of finished products. Because of export embargoes by some suppliers and the increasing use of bans on the export of raw logs by some US states, including Oregon and Washington, countries such as Japan are turning to Malaysia and exploring the possibility of developing new sources of raw logs in such places as the Amazon.[6]

One major impact comes from the use of subsidies that encourage unsustainable patterns of resource exploitation and impose direct physical damage on surrounding ecosystems. In the energy sector, for example, it has been estimated that the US spends more than $40 billion a year on subsidies for conventional sources of energy, including fossil fuels, while countries such as Germany, China, and India provide heavy subsidies for coal.[7]

The environmental effects of trade practices are perhaps most hotly debated in the agricultural sector, which is heavily subsidized in North America, Western Europe, and Japan, to protect domestic supply and agricultural incomes. These subsidies are generally tied to production or even acreage under cultivation. Subsidization leads to the growth of agricultural output and places a premium on production rather than on the environmentally sustainable management of resources. In some cases, agricultural production exceeds the long-term carrying capacity of the environment. Subsidization commonly encourages farmers to cultivate even the most marginal land and make excessive use of pesticides and fertilizers. Subsidization also encourages the clearing of forests, which can lead to soil erosion. One Canadian study suggested that Canadian farmers lost more than $1 billion in 1980 from reduced production due to soil erosion. [8]

Western countries' subsidies to domestic producers not only affect domestic environments, they generate trading patterns that encourage unsustainable practices around the world. Subsidies encourage patterns of production that do not reflect the natural endowments of countries, by making developing countries' exports uncompetitive with the highly subsidized exports of rich countries.

In its 1987 report, *Our Common Future*, the World Commission on the Environment and Development characterized the use of non-renewable raw materials to earn foreign exchange as the main link between trade and sustainable development.[9] The economies of many developing countries depend heavily on export earnings and, increasingly, their governments are placing their hopes for prosperity on export-led growth. The export of natural resources remains a large factor in the economies of many countries, especially those of the least developed nations. The expansion of export markets and GNP in developing countries is often achieved at the price of ecological degradation, leading to the long-term erosion of their natural wealth and infrastructure.[10]

In the 1980s, the situation was exacerbated because deteriorating terms of trade, rising debt-service obligations, stagnating flows of aid, growing protectionism in Northern industrialized economies, and other factors all resulted in severe external payments problems for developing countries. As economic conditions worsened, debt pressures mounted and Southern planners tended to ignore environmental planning and conservation. The urgent need to increase financial flows to supply foreign exchange to service debt repayments completed the cycle of economic necessity leading to environmental degradation. When natural resource exports were used predominantly to meet the financial requirements of industrialized country creditors, the problem was heightened. An over-exploitation of resources for export encouraged unsustainable development policies; for example, the substitution of export crops for traditional food crops on good agricultural land forced subsistence farmers onto more marginal lands.[11]

Another concern of developing and other resource-based countries is the use of trade barriers to reduce market access to the North for processed, higher value-added Southern exports. This can lead to over-exploitation of primary commodities for export by developing countries. Industrialized countries seek to import resources at the earliest stage of processing, in order to add value in their processing industries. Tariffs that are escalated as the level of processing increases contribute, with other factors, to a trading system structured to encourage the cycle of resource exploitation. Many Northern countries feel they have to protect their own domestic processing industries against manufactured exports from LDCs, where some industries are more competitive. Some developing countries respond by restricting exports of unprocessed resources or by making the resources available to domestic processing industries at less than the export or world price. These practices can result in the suppression of resource prices at levels below their long-term value, and also lead to an over-exploitation of the resource base.

While, in the past ten years, there has been less use of tariff barriers by the countries of the North seeking to obtain Southern resources at the earliest stage of processing, protection is maintained in some cases through the use of quotas.[12]

The tradition of Northern protectionism, contributing to an unsustainable over-use of the natural resource base in developing countries, has promoted increased volumes of commodity exports. These trade distortions beg the fundamental question of whether the prices in the market reflect the true long-term costs of natural resources, including resource depletion and environmental impact.

280

The cycle of over-exploitation of the resource base, increasing supply, and decline in the value of commodities, led the World Commission to point out that developing countries are turning the terms of trade against themselves, earning less while exporting more.[13] This form of protectionism has also had the effect of discouraging diversification, which would move from traditional resource exports towards a viable manufacturing industry that could generate wealth and contribute to the alleviation of both poverty and ecological stress.[14]

The Experience of Canadian Industry

At every point, the multiple links between trade and the environment affect Canada, and the competitiveness of Canadian industry, in an immediate and important way. Provincial efforts to encourage the reuse of beverage containers have led to threats of trade retaliation from abroad.[15] Canadian exports of seal and forest products to Europe, and a host of resource products to the United States, have been affected by a wave of "green protectionism" in those jurisdictions. The burden of maintaining subsidies for agriculture and energy is imposing ever-heavier burdens on the federal government's treasury and on the national ecology.

The export, by developing countries, of larger volumes of resources at low prices threatens Canada's resource industries in their traditional markets while degrading the global environment everywhere. Canada itself suffers from the legacy of past decisions to exploit its natural resources in unsustainable ways in order to capture export markets and their short-term economic reward.[16]

Thus, Canada has every reason to become a leader in the international effort to manage trade-environment links in ways that respect the legitimate claims of both interests. But any effort to define an appropriate national policy as the foundation for an international leadership role, must begin with a full recognition of the vital importance to the

Canadian economy of trade, and an open, rules-based trade system; it must also acknowledge that environmental considerations offer both threats and opportunities for the major sectors involved in Canada's international trade.

Environmental Challenges and Opportunities for Canadian Industry

An open global trading system is more important to Canada than to virtually any other industrialized nation because Canada's economy is so highly dependant for its well-being on exports. In 1979, Canada was the tenth-largest exporter and importer of merchandise items in the world. In 1988, Canada's per-capita exports were higher than those of the US, Japan, France, West Germany, Italy, and the UK.[17] By 1989, Canada had become the world's seventh largest trader and, in 1990, ranked as the world's eighth-largest exporter and importer in merchandise trade.[18]

Nearly half the goods produced in Canada are exported and more than 3 million Canadian jobs depend on export trade. Therefore, it is vital that continued secure access to existing markets is maintained. The following tables illustrate the value of Canada's exports by sector, both overall and by major export partners: the United States, the European Community, and Japan.[19]

The following is an overview of the environmentally inspired challenges and opportunities presented to six major sectors of the Canadian economy: the critical export sectors of automotive products, forest products, oil and gas, and mining; and the promising sectors of environmental products and tourism.

Table 1
***Principal Canadian Exports - All Countries* (1988)**

Rank	Commodity Descriptions	Value ($millions)	%
1	Passenger autos and chassis	17,127	12.7
2	M.V. parts, except engines	8,001	5.9
3	Newsprint paper	7,299	5.4
4	Trucks tractors and chassis	7,294	5.4
5	Wood pulp and similar pulp	6,496	4.8
6	Lumber, softwood	5,234	3.9
7	Wheat	4,443	3.3
8	Crude petroleum	4,038	3.0
9	Aluminum, including alloys	3,488	2.6
10	Natural gas	2,955	2.2

**Canada's Major Exports by Trading Partners
(1988)**

Table 2a: United States

Rank	Commodity Descriptions	Value ($millions)	%
1	Passenger autos	16,817	17.2
2	M.V. parts	7,914	8.1
3	Trucks & tractors	7,115	7.3
4	Newsprint paper	6,090	6.2
5	Crude petroleum	3,979	4.1
6	Lumber, softwood	3,415	3.5
7	Wood pulp	2,947	3.0
8	Natural gas	2,886	2.9
9	Aluminum	2,523	2.6
10	M.V. engines	2,293	2.3

Table 2b: European Community

Rank	Commodity Descriptions	Value ($millions)	%
1	Wood pulp	1,658	15.5
2	Lumber, softwood	732	6.9
3	Office equipment	515	4.8
4	Newsprint paper	441	4.1
5	Iron ore	431	4.0
6	Zinc in ores	274	2.6
7	Organic chemicals	249	2.3
8	Wheat	244	2.3
9	Aircraft, parts	229	2.1
10	Nickel in ores	229	2.1

Table 2c: Japan

Rank	Commodity Descriptions	Value ($millions)	%
1	Coal	1,410	16.3
2	Wood pulp	943	10.9
3	Lumber, softwood	859	9.9
4	Precious metals	576	6.6
5	Copper in ores	556	6.4
6	Rapeseed	541	6.2
7	Other fishery food	372	4.3
8	Aluminum	307	3.5
9	Wheat	284	3.3
10	Organic chemicals	221	2.5

The Major Sectors
1. The Automotive Industry
The automotive industry is a vital element of the Canadian economy. Canada currently ranks eighth in the world in total motor vehicle production, behind Japan, the US, West Germany, France, Italy, the former Soviet Union, and Spain. The three major players in the Canadian automotive industry are Chrysler Canada Ltd, Ford Motor Company of Canada Ltd, and General Motors of Canada Ltd. All subsidiaries of US parents, these "Big Three" undertake the vast majority of vehicle assembly in Canada, an industry based in southern Ontario.

Other foreign-owned manufacturers in Canada include Honda and Hyundai, from Japan and Korea respectively. However, there are a number of smaller companies in the automotive sector, largely in the business of producing parts, that are Canadian-owned. In 1989, 156,300 people were employed in the automotive products industry, up from the 103,800 who were employed there in 1975.[20]

The vast majority of Canada's automotive products are exported to the US. Because of this dependence on the US market, it is critical that, as US standards evolve, the Canadian industry is equipped to meet them. However, changing standards in the US are not likely to pose a major threat to Canada's export market there because Canada's major firms have parent companies in the US. Consequently, as long as the technology exists in the US to meet stricter environmental standards, in the normal course of events it will be transferred to Canadian subsidiaries. Nevertheless, opportunities exist for smaller, more specialized manufacturers in Canada to develop technology in anticipation of the stricter standards that will be phased in over the next 15 years.

The following is a brief overview of the types of standards the automotive industry will be required to meet in future. Title 1 of the *Clean Air Act Amendments, 1990* contains provisions that will have a major effect on manufacturers of cars and trucks. These provisions deal predominantly with the control of mobile source emissions from cars and trucks, which currently account for 50% of the ozone pollution and 90% of the carbon-monoxide pollution in urban areas in the United States. Among the issues addressed in the amendments are: more stringent tailpipe standards; reformulated gasoline; an oxygenated fuels program for carbon monoxide non-attainment areas; a California clean car pilot project; and a clean fuels program for vehicle fleets in 22 of the worst areas of air pollution across the US.

As a result of the amendments, auto manufacturers are required to reduce tailpipe emissions of hydrocarbons and oxides of nitrogen, which form smog, by 35% and 60% respectively (Tier I emission standards). These standards will be phased in, beginning with 40% of the vehicles produced in the model year 1994, increasing to 100% of vehicles sold in 1998. Comparable reductions are required for light trucks, such as vans and pickups. By the end of 1999, the Environmental Protection Agency (EPA) will decide on the need, cost, and feasibility of additional Tier II standards for vehicles produced in model year 2004 and later.

Vehicle manufacturers will be required by legislation to install systems to alert drivers when an emission control system is malfunctioning. It will also require that canisters be installed on vehicles to capture hydrocarbons that would otherwise be emitted into the atmosphere during refuelling. This process, to begin in 1995, will be phased in over three years. These devices have not been yet been passed as safe by the EPA and the US Department of Transportation.

The best technology currently available will likely be advanced enough to meet the Tier I tailpipe emission standards for 1994. Technology to meet the 1999 Tier II standards does not exist but, if and when it is developed, it should become readily available to the largest Canadian auto manufacturers; the same is true of the canisters to capture hydrocarbons during refuelling, which are required by 1995. A proviso in the Act states that these will be phased in if and when the devices are identified by the EPA and the Department of Transportation as being safe. Many questions remain about the safety of these devices and (of particular concern to Canadian manufacturers) whether these technologies will perform effectively in cold weather conditions. An opportunity exists for a company to develop and market the technology to meet these criteria.

New emission standards for heavy-duty vehicle engines have the potential to threaten Canadian manufacturers (who do not produce such engines at present). The US has published regulations requiring that low-sulphur fuel be available in that country by October 1993, in order to meet the requirements for the 1994 model year. If this fuel is not available in Canada by that time, misfuelling problems for vehicles from the US could result, adversely affecting the performance of the catalyst used to reduce emissions. This would probably render any vehicle engine warranties void, making it likely that the product's availability would be curtailed in Canada. Because all vehicles for sale in the United States will have to meet these standards, any future Canadian-produced vehicles that do not allow for the use of low-sulphur fuel would not be marketable in the US.

Two clean fuel programs, identified in the US *Clean Air Act Amendments* of 1990, might harm Canadian export markets in the United States, but also present opportunities for industry leaders. "Clean fuels" include: compressed natural gas, ethanol, methanol, liquified petroleum gas, electricity, reformulated gasoline, and, possibly, other fuels. New programs requiring cleaner (reformulated) gasoline will be initiated in nine US cities beginning in 1995.

A pilot clean car program has been established for California; requirements will be set within two years of enactment. The law establishes emission standards and allows the American auto and fuel industries to decide whether to meet the standards by vehicle controls, new fuels, or a combination of both. The program will be phased in in 1996, when 150,000 clean fuel vehicles per year will have to be produced for sale in California. By 1999, this number must have risen to 300,000. Under the law, California must assure that enough clean fuels are produced, distributed, and made available for all clean-fuel vehicles operating exclusively on these fuels in the covered area.

A similar program for fleet vehicles is included in the amendments; vehicles covered by it would be substantially cleaner than conventional vehicles. The fleet program, as agreed on, will incorporate California's low-emission vehicle standards for light-duty vehicles and light-duty trucks by 1988, provided these vehicles are offered for sale in California. By 2001, such vehicles will be required without regard for availability in California; other states with serious, severe or extreme ozone non-attainment areas may adopt the Californian standard.

This aggressive mandate for improving air quality by the use of alternate fuels and electric cars has created opportunities for companies in the business of developing such vehicles. It is predicted that there will be 50,000 non-fuel cars in Los Angeles by the end of the decade. Following in California's footsteps, other states (including New York and Massachusettes) are planning to adopt California tailpipe emissions standards as early as 1993.

A Canadian company has capitalized on this opportunity and developed the first and only battery operated vehicle in North America to be certified by the Federal Motor Vehicle Safety Standards. In December 1990, following a two-to-three year program, Magna, of Markham Ontario, began producing full-sized vans using GM shells, at the rate of one per day. These vehicles cost approximately $50,000 and have a top speed of 52 mph/83kph. Marketing is currently aimed at utilities and fleet organizations and, to date, the major market has been in the US. While there are prototypes for electric cars in Japan and the EC now, these are aimed at a different market; the cars are smaller and are not yet being exported to North America.

The fast-growing market for catalytic converters in Europe creates opportunities there. Mexico, too, is moving towards legislation that will make catalytic converters mandatory in all vehicles. This will produce direct market opportunities for constituent materials: platinum, palladium, and rhodium.

2. The Forest Products Industry

Canada's forest products industry is the country's single largest industrial sector. It accounts for a trade surplus of nearly $20 billion, an amount that exceeds the total trade surplus earned by the agricultural, fisheries, energy, and mining sectors combined.[21] Internationally, Canada is a leading world producer of forestry products, ranking first in production of newsprint, second in pulp, and third in softwood lumber. Canadian export sales of these items represent about 20% of entire world exports.

There are three distinct industrial sectors in Canada's total forest industry:

(i) the timber or logging sector,

(ii) the wood products sector, and

(iii) the pulp and paper industry.

Total direct employment is 349,000 according to Statistics Canada 1989 labour force survey of the forest industry. When combined with those created indirectly by the forest industry, approximately 1 million Canadian jobs are involved.

The logging sector is made up of more than 3,500 companies that harvest timber and ship raw materials to mills in the form of logs, pulpwood or chips. The major business of the wood products companies (which include manufacturers of shingles and shakes, veneer, and plywood) is lumber production, most of which is exported. Canada is the world's largest exporter of lumber, which represents more than 20% of our total sales in the forestry sector. In 1989, some 1,500 wood manufacturing firms and mills employed 135,000 people.

Pulp and paper is the most important sector in the forest industry and a major contributor to the Canadian economy. Total sales represent more than half of all sales in the Canadian forest industry.[22] It is estimated that 145,000 people are employed in some 700 mills across the country, with an annual payroll of $4 billion.

Newsprint is the most important forest commodity produced in Canada for export. Canada services roughly 60% of the world market, with the US as the principal customer. However, new recycling laws in the United States and in Canada mean major challenges for the pulp and paper sector. Many buyers are insisting on specific proportions of recycled fibre to help reduce pressure on municipal land-fills, and to reduce harvesting of forests.

Regulations requiring approximately 35% recycled content in newsprint have been promulgated recently in some US states, a trend that is expected to continue in both the US and Europe. For companies that do not already recycle and do not have access to de-inking facilities, the costs of compliance are enormous.

There is concern that increased production costs in the Canadian industry will render Canadian newsprint uncompetitive in a global market. Apart from the physical costs involved in modernizing plants, other factors will increase costs to Canadian producers of newsprint. For example, Canada will have to become a net importer of waste paper in order to meet the recycled requirements, which will increase transportation costs from mills, most of which are distant from urban centres.

At present new mills in the US are able to produce newsprint that meets the recycled content requirement now and US industry has access to the necessary feed stock. The member states of the EC who are already substantially involved in recycling have a much higher recovery rate than Canadian industry, due, in great part, to the long-standing nature of their recycling programs and their large, concentrated population base.

It makes economic sense for the EC, which must import

significant amounts of fibre for newsprint, to obtain, as it does, approximately 55% of the feed stock to make paper from recycled fibre. This is close to, if not already at, the limit of the recycled content that can be used in paper products. Canadian firms that have the resources and have chosen to move ahead of public policy and/or are based in countries with higher standards of environmental protection, will tend to gain a competitive advantage.

The trend towards recycling could also lead to significant reductions in demand for raw fibre, although that is not yet clear. However, recycling may have job implications, both in the mills and in the forests. Environmentalists have expressed concern that the Canada-United States Free Trade Agreement has emerged as a potential mechanism to defeat resource conservation initiatives, such as the US recycling regulations, by treating them as non-tariff barriers to trade.[23]

Another concern facing the forestry sector is the threat of a possible European consumer boycott of Canadian forest products.[24] Although the threat is not yet well defined, the industry is taking the possibility seriously. In British Columbia, the government is concerned about clearcut logging practices in the province (which have been compared to deforestation in Brazil by those who consider it unsustainable).[25] The current movement seems to be based in Canada, where environmental groups acknowledge they are providing information to their colleagues in Europe.[26]

In order to be successful a boycott must be very well organized and must target easily identifiable commodities. The extent to which the European threat will harm Canadian industry remains to be seen. It will depend largely on the extent to which the European Parliament feels it would be politically expedient to impose a product ban (which is far more effective than an attempted consumer boycott).

Other factors that might threaten the Canadian forest products sector include the possibility that Canadian forest products exporters might have to respond to EC regulations affecting the standards for structural timber: on importation of Canadian green softwood (which EC plant health authorities believe contains a microscopic organism perceived to be a threat to European forests); and on importation of lumber that has been treated with allegedly toxic anti-stain chemicals. An EC ban on pulp produced by processes exceeding certain emission requirements is also possible. German environmentalists want Canadian chlorine-bleached pulp to be banned from their markets. In 1989, Canadian forest products exports to the EC totalled $3.3 billion, making it Canada's second-largest market for forest products. To lose the European market would strike a serious blow to Canada's forest products industry.

3. The Oil and Gas Industry

Export markets are of critical importance to Canada's oil and gas industry; this country's largest export market for these products is the United States. Oil and natural gas are the mainstay among the energy fuels and will, likely, continue to be well into the next century. In 1989, the oil and gas sector contributed about 3-4% of the Canadian economy; in Alberta, where the industry is based, operating companies employ some 43,500 people in more than 400 companies (and these figures do not include the drilling and service sectors). There are no viable cost-effective substitutes to oil and gas on the horizon. The challenge is to supply and use these fuels in an environmentally acceptable manner, especially in today's lower price market, while remaining profitable.

The Canadian oil and gas industry recently faced a tax, introduced for environmental purposes, which impeded Canadian exports of petroleum to the US. In 1988, the American *Comprehensive Environmental Response, Compensation, and Liability Act* ("Superfund") imposed higher tax rates for imported petroleum than for domestically produced petroleum; the taxes were assigned to finance a government clean-up of hazardous waste sites. This tax was challenged by Canada, the European Community, and Mexico and ruled to be in violation of the GATT Article III, which requires national treatment in applying taxes. The US did not seek to justify the measure as falling within the GATT exceptions in Article XX; that would have required it to establish that the purpose of the tax was to protect human, animal or plant life of health, *and* that a GATT-inconsistent tax was "necessary" to achieve such a result.

The threat posed to Canadian industry, which is a primary exporter of crude petroleum to the United States, was enormous. And, although Canadian exports of the finished product are less significant, even they could be threatened by the 1990 US *Clean Air Act* amendments. One element of the amendments, to come into force in 1995, is to mandate the use of cleaner burning ("reformulated") gasoline, in the nine cities in the US with the most severe ozone pollution (and states will be able to require that the rules apply in other cities with ozone pollution problems). When compared with conventional gasolines, the reformulated gas would be required to have 15% lower emissions of volatile organic compounds and toxic chemicals by 1995, and attain a 20-25% lower rate by the year 2000.

In October 1990, the EPA recommended that particulate emissions for diesel trucks be reduced from existing levels by a factor of six. Canada has no diesel fuels specifications and currently obtains its large engines from the US. Nevertheless, without the appropriate fuel, Canadian truckers would not be able to operate the US engines in Canada. The Canadian oil and gas industry is concerned by the cost of converting its fuel to a low sulphur grade: the targets for particulates would require 0.05% sulphur fuels, estimated to cost 2.5 cents per litre more than regular diesel fuel.

Moreover, the possibility of a carbon tax is ongoing. Such a tax might be applied to fossil fuels depending on their carbon content and, therefore, on their CO_2 emissions.

In an international context, a carbon tax would raise the issue of trade and competitiveness: such a tax, unilaterally levied, would put the domestic industry at a disadvantage, while a common carbon tax would not account for the differences between countries in energy use, technologies, and the like.

3. The Mining Industry

The value of Canada's mineral production is substantial: in 1989, $35.4 billion worth of mineral commodities were exported, of which $23.3 billion, or 65.7%, were sold in the United States. The proportion of mineral exports to Japan fell slightly (to 9.7% of the 1989 total), but exports to the European Community, totalling $3.4 billion in 1989, increased from the previous year to 9.6%. In 1989, Canada's net balance of trade (the excess of exports over imports) for all mineral commodities was $15.2 billion, the majority of which was accounted for by non-fuel minerals and coal. In 1988, aluminum and alloys ranked as Canada's ninth largest export, worth $3,488 million and accounting for 2.6% of Canada's total exports.

In 1989, aluminum was the mining sector's largest export, but, in absolute terms, there was a decline in the value of exports of "aluminum" and "lead particles thereof" to the US, as well as to all other countries. Declines were also evident in such commodities as fertilizers, salt, sulphur, ceramic products, plaster, cement, and asbestos.

In that same year, the number of producing mining establishments also declined in all regions of Canada, from a total of 577 at the start of 1989 to 536 by January 1990. Employment in the Canadian mineral industry totalled 106,004 in 1989 - of that number 47,723 (45%) were employed in metal mines and 30,462 (28.7%) in smelting and refining. These employment figures are virtually unchanged from 1988.[27]

The mining sector in Canada is currently facing potential threats, nationally and internationally. For example, a unilateral measure with potentially adverse effects is the

EPA's recent proposal to reduce or eliminate any risks from lead-based products by banning lead products and imposing a tax on virgin lead materials. Such a ban would affect the viability of Canada's entire mining sector and is being examined by the OECD, where it is strongly supported by the American government. Some would argue that such a ban runs counter to sustainable economic development and should be implemented only in extreme cases and then only on the basis of unambiguous scientific evidence.

Recently, the EPA established a committee to recommend a program that would require that lead-acid batteries in the US contain at least 50% recycled material. To meet that requirement, the primary lead industry in Canada would need access to batteries it had previously exported - the vast majority of batteries produced in Canada are exported to the US and used Canadian batteries would not be available in the numbers necessary to ensure production at present levels. Used batteries would certainly be subject to the requirements of the Basel Convention and the substantial expense and administrative procedures involved in having them returned might distort trade.

Moreover, in an international context, the Basel Convention could threaten the viability of the entire mining sector in Canada. Given that natural resources constitute the backbone of Canadian exports, the vague definition of "waste" in the Basel Convention poses a uniquely Canadian problem: by classifying recyclables as hazardous waste, it complicated transport and permit leasing of such materials.

A great deal of recycling takes place in Canadian industry: For example, the primary steel industry includes about 40% recycled content in its products, while approximately 20% of scrap copper is recycled at primary copper smelters. However, the onerous provisions of the Basel Convention threaten the steady supply of feedstock sent back across the border from the US for recycling. The Canadian market is too small to provide industry with sufficient quantities of used materials to continue exporting at its current levels. Thus, the mining industry in Canada, which now exports 80% of its goods to the US, faces a major challenge.

Some sectors of the mining industry might feel threatened by the effects of international attempts to reduce global emissions of greenhouse gases. Carbon dioxide accounts for about half the total greenhouse gas emissions generated by human activity. Because the main source of CO_2 emissions is the burning of fossil fuels, basic industries that depend on these types of energy for their fuel and feedstock will be affected. This would include, for example, electric power generators in Western Canada, where 85% of the power is produced using coal.

A possible carbon tax, discussed earlier, could result in increases in oil and coal prices, which would be especially onerous for energy-intensive industries. Certainly, the production process in the mining sector is highly energy-intensive. For example, a great deal of coking coal is used to produce steel and a substantial amount of electricity is involved in processing aluminum.

5. The Environmental Protection Industry

Increased environmental regulation and standards most clearly create opportunities for the environmental protection industry (EPI). In a general sense, that industry is defined as comprising suppliers of equipment, technologies, products, and services that monitor, prevent or correct environmental damage. It is not clear that the Canadian environmental industry is well placed to benefit from increased environmental protection through the development of environmentally friendly technologies or technologies that make traditional Canadian resource-based industries more environmentally benign.

In large part, the development of a prosperous EPI is dependent on both domestic and international environmental regulations that require compliance with higher standards - standards that call for new and advanced technologies. Over the long term, countries with the strictest domestic environmental standards will likely have a more advanced EPI than those who simply react to environmental regulation that have already become the norm. Those industries that are ahead of public policy will benefit, if they correctly anticipate potential targets and paths.

The controls imposed by the Montreal Protocol in 1987, for example, have been successful in reducing the consumption of CFCs among the signatory states. In fact, initial evidence suggests that the private sector in Canada is exceeding the Protocol's consumption-reduction requirements. Industry realizes that firms who continue to use CFCs in the face of increasing consumer preference for "ozone friendly" products, even when such products are priced at a premium, may incur costs that are higher in the long term than those companies willing to incur the short term costs of conversion. Companies that can afford to invest in research and development, stand to gain, and gain substantially, from developing an environmentally benign substitute for CFCs.

At present, the Canadian domestic EPI market generates $1.4 billion annually, an increase of 43% since 1986. However, there is room for increased penetration of the domestic market by Canadian producers and suppliers: only 44% of the domestic market is served by Canadian suppliers while the remainder is filled by imports, 90% of which come from the US.[28]

Despite the fact that Canada is perceived abroad as a leader in environmental matters, its involvement in this export market has been minimal to date. But the global export market for the EPI is growing at a rapid rate and provides ample opportunity for Canadian exporters. In the US, projections suggest substantial growth in the environmental market while, in Mexico, the EPI is growing at a rate of 10% annually, to $250 million in 1990. In 1987, Western Europe's environmental protection market totalled 40 billion ECU.

Japan is increasing its environmental protection

activities while recent legislation in Taiwan is leading to a $35 billion clean-up plan by the year 2000. Hong Kong officials recently announced a $3 billion environmental clean-up plan. Opportunities in Eastern Europe, with its severe environmental problems, are certainly worth pursuing.

Solid wastes represent a growing opportunity for goods and service suppliers to US markets. It is projected that recycling markets will grow at an annual rate of 13% to 1994. In the US, public spending for solid waste disposal amounts to $7 billion annually, versus $600 million in Canada. Hazardous waste cleanup costs could eventually total more than $200 billion: to date, only six of the EPA's 850 priority sites have been cleaned up. Demand for incinerators in Europe is likely to be high in the short-term but will decrease as clean technologies and recycling programs reduce the quantity of waste being generated.

The projected 1992 demand for air pollution control equipment in the US and Europe is very large. In particular, it is expected that there will be a rapidly expanding demand in the 1990s for equipment to reduce NOx emissions, and FGD (flue gas desulphurisation - the most common means of controlling SO_2 emissions). Ontario Hydro has successfully marketed its flue gas desulphurization technology in the US and is well-placed to take advantage of that market, with its projected worth of $160 million in 1992.

Other successful Canadian firms in this field tend to be small, niche-market players, such as Turbotak (wet scrubbers) or large resource-based companies. Acid rain legislation, alone, could lead to a demand for $80 billion worth of scrubber systems in the US. Inco has successfully marketed in the US the company's flash furnace technology (used for smelting copper sulphide concentrate) - an example of the commercialization of in-house process technology.

These growing environmental markets have a number of features that provide promising options for Canadian suppliers. Canadian capabilities are already well known in such fields as water supply and liquid and solid waste disposal, conservation, protection and environmental enhancement in the forest industries, fisheries management, mine development, pollution control, the development and processing of energy resources (coal, oil and gas, uranium, hydro power), the construction of transportation and transmission facilities (roads, railways, airports, pipelines, transmission lines), and a range of cold weather technologies - not to mention a record of developing, training, and increasing the capabilities of human resources involved in the transfer of technologies.

The developing world will offer opportunities as environmental protection becomes an increasingly important issue. For example, potable water treatment currently represents a major challenge there: only 18% of Indonesia's rural population and 30% of China's have access to safe drinking water. Those countries, as well as Thailand, are making safe drinking water one of their major socio-economic objectives.

One study estimates that $20 to $30 billion would be required annually to provide safe drinking water to all people on earth: a projected 20 million hand pumps will be required while, worldwide, education and training expenditures for water and sanitation will amount to $20 billion annually by the year 2000. Canadian companies, already operating internationally, have a very advanced capability in water and sewage treatment and are well positioned to take advantage of the potential demand.

6. The Tourism Industry

Unlike the others, tourism in not an export industry: customers come into the country, while products and services offered usually do not go out of it. Nonetheless, tourism is a $25 billion a year industry in Canada: foreign visitors spent $7.2 billion here in 1989, making tourism Canada's third-largest earner of foreign exchange and making it, in that sense, an important Canadian "export".[29]

Moreover, Canadians travelling in their own country spent nearly $18 billion in 1989. Tourism generates nearly $16.8 billion in direct income and provides direct employment for more than 622,400 Canadians;[30] the industry grew at 4% per annum between 1975 and 1989, surpassing the growth rates of such major industrial sectors as transportation, construction, manufacturing, and agriculture.

Clearly, tourism's importance to Canada cannot be overstated. The significance of the environment and environmental considerations to the tourism industry becomes apparent when reviewing the "trip types" that have the greatest potential for vacation travel to Canada. A study completed in January 1986 indicated that the two most popular trip types for vacation travel to Canada are touring (which represents 53% of the total trip/nights to Canada) and outdoor/leisure (which represents 29% of trip/nights).[31]

Some 20 million people visit Canadian national parks every year, an indication that travellers are seeking a visually attractive and pristine environment, one relatively free from pollution.

It has been suggested that by the year 2000, tourism will become Canada's leading industry, in terms of income, export earnings and employment.[32] Among the reasons given for such growth are: increases in population, real disposable income, leisure time, and education levels, combined with the desire for self-fulfilment and the physical fitness ethic. There is an emphasis on outdoor vacations as people attempt to escape the pressures of urban life, and look for natural environments.

This is of particular interest to Canada, which is world-renowned for the beauty and variety of its natural environment: the expansive open spaces, magnificent mountains, clean rivers, untouched coastlines, and exotic northern environment, all of which can be considered "environmental capital". However, uncontrolled tourism development, in conjunction with environmental damage from human and industrial activities, can degrade the context in which tourism takes place. Given the importance to Canada of an unspoiled natural environment, unsustainable development is a threat to the industry's ability to generate income from future tourism.

In the 1990s, "ecotourism" is the wave of environmental awareness sweeping industrialized societies. Ecotourism suggests:

> "...travelling to relatively undisturbed or uncontaminated natural areas with the specific objective of studying, admiring, and enjoying the scenery and its wild plants and animals..." [33]

The volume of North American and European ecotourists has tripled over the past five years, reaching $3 billion in 1990.[34] Ecotourism will promote a strong partnership between tourism and conservation and, if successful, will help raise revenue for local and regional economies, heighten local awareness of the importance of conservation, and encourage governments and people to preserve their surroundings.

The relationship between a healthy tourist industry and a clean environment has also been acknowledged by the European Community, and is one of the five priority areas defined in the Community's Fifth Action Plan on the Environment.

The importance of tourism is evident in the other sectors the EC chose as priorities: energy, transportation, industry, and agriculture. The Fifth Action Plan outlines the Community's objectives in environmental planning in those sectors in the short-, medium-, and long-term and incorporates as many constituencies as possible into the decision making process.

The Community predicts that economic growth, leading to more leisure time, will double the number of tourists travelling to Europe and put enormous pressure on its environment - the coastal areas in particular. Already, however, environmental problems, such as algae in the Adriatic caused by pollution and poor treatment of waste water, has cost the European tourism industry 1.5 billion ECU in lost business.

In order to ensure the long-term prosperity of Canada's tourism industry and to achieve sustainable tourism development, it is necessary to find a balance between protecting the environment (the "tourism product"), and obtaining both the social and the economic benefits from tourism. Clearly, environmental protection measures are an important part of this equation.

North American Free Trade Regimes

The trading relationship between Canada and the United States is the largest and most important between any two countries in the world: it now accounts for the flow of C$187 billion worth of goods across the border each year. In 1988, almost 75% of Canada's exports were to the US, while 65% of goods imported into Canada came from the United States. In turn, Canada is the US' largest market, absorbing a quarter of that country's exports.

The commercial aim of the Canada-US Free Trade Agreement (FTA) is to eliminate trade barriers in goods and services between the two countries; it seems certain now that the FTA will be modified and extended with a North American Free Trade Agreement (NAFTA), which will include Mexico.

Because the US is such an important Canadian trading partner and because of the apparent disparities in levels of environmental protection between the three countries (Mexico in particular), NAFTA will have environmental implications that cannot be dissociated from trade and competitiveness. Issues to be considered will affect: the parties' ability to protect their own domestic environments; management, and trade of natural resources; and the resulting danger of the promotion of unsustainable development.

The Canada - United States Free Trade Agreement
Interested Canadian environmental groups and individuals
voiced a number of concerns about the possible effects of
the Canada-United States Free Trade Agreement on
Canada's environment.[35] An issue frequently singled out
is that harmonization of standards could lead to a reduction
of Canadian and American environmental standards. Each
has higher standards than the other in certain areas of
concern, and the argument is that creating a large market
and increasing competition puts pressure on the private
sector to reduce production costs, including the costs of
meeting environmental standards, resulting in a movement
to the lowest common denominator of environmental
regulation.[36] Moreover, there are fears that financial
incentives and other measures, used in Canada to promote
environmental and resource management policies, might
be abandoned, making it increasingly difficult for industry
to take a lead in environmental controls, regulation, and
management.

A number of other specific issues concern
environmentalists, among them: pesticides, hazardous
materials, water, agriculture, fisheries, forests, and energy.

It is argued that the FTA could weaken Canadian
regulation of pesticide, currently based on a demonstration
of safety, and lead to adoption of the risk/benefit analysis
used in the US.

It is also suggested that Canada could become a major
dumping ground for American hazardous waste and that,
under the FTA, the Canadian government is unable to
impose a surtax on hazardous materials that are imported
into the country.

There is also concern that the FTA can create new
obstacles to the so-called "3R" objectives: reduce, reuse,
and recycle, because any Canadian regulation requiring
recyclable packaging or refillable containers can be
challenged by the US as a non-tariff barrier to trade.

Because water is not specifically excluded from the FTA,
some are worried that it will be considered an exportable

commodity like any other. Clearly, there are environmental hazards related to large-scale water diversion schemes.

It is also argued that the FTA will increase economic pressures on agriculture so substantially that it will lead to large-scale corporate farming, which might be destructive to the environment and ultimately unsustainable.

There is also apprehension that the FTA could undermine Canadian prospects for sustainable forest management. At present, the reforestation that takes place in Canada is subsidized by the government, and the US regards reforestation grants as unfair trading practices and subsidies to Canadian lumber exports. Domestic countervail and anti-dumping trade remedies of both parties are left intact by the FTA and continue to be invoked by the US.

1. Structure of the FTA

It is still too early to pass judgement on the specific environment-related concerns raised by the FTA.[37] The fundamental question is how well equipped the FTA is to deal with such issues as those raised in the preceding paragraphs. Article 101 of the FTA clearly states that the Agreement is consistent with Article XXIV of the GATT and, now that the GATT's Contracting Parties have ruled that it does, the FTA constitutes an international agreement within the GATT framework. In FTA Article 407(1), the parties "affirm their respective rights and the general obligations" under the provisions of GATT, Article XI, which prohibits the imposition by states of quantitative restrictions (quotas). To a certain extent, the FTA includes all the protection and shortcomings of the GATT relative to balancing environmental concerns with the philosophy of free trade.

Environmental issues in the GATT have traditionally been dealt with under Articles XX(b) and (g). Articles XX(b) and (g) allow countries to establish measures which will impede the free trade in goods, if those measures are:

• necessary to protect human, animal or plant life or health (b); or

• relating to the conservation of exhaustible natural resources, if such measures are made effective in conjunction with restrictions on domestic consumption (g).

By virtue of the FTA's Article 1201, these provisions "are incorporated into and made part of this Part of the Agreement".

2. The Bilateral Dispute Settlement Mechanism
There are two branches to the bilateral dispute settlement mechanism (BDSM) under the FTA: the Chapter Eighteen panel and the Chapter Nineteen dispute settlement mechanism.[38] Resolution procedures under Chapter Eighteen are patterned, in large part, on the dispute settlement regime in the GATT, although some important differences will be noted.

It is likely that, if and when environmentalists' fears are realized, actual cases will be subjected to the BDSM set up under Chapter Eighteen of the FTA. The BDSM establishes a process for disputes arising from interpretation and application of the FTA and questions respecting a measure's consistency with the FTA. An examination of how these issues might be interpreted under the BDSM of the FTA provides some guidance as to how the FTA will affect the environment.[39]

Under the FTA's Chapter Eighteen dispute settlement mechanism, consultation is the first step in the formal process and cannot be avoided. If, after 30 days, consultation is not successful, either country may request that the Canada-U.S. Trade Commission (the Commission) consider the dispute.[40] The FTA is silent about the composition of the Commission, other than that the principal representative from each nation is of Cabinet level or is a Cabinet-level designee. At present, the Commission comprises Michael Wilson, representing

Canada, and Carla Hills, the US.

Once the Commission is asked to consider a matter, the BDSM is initiated and recourse to the GATT is foreclosed. (At any time prior to the request, the parties may choose whether to proceed under the GATT or the BDSM.)

If the Commission fails to resolve the dispute, the issue can be sent to arbitration or be put before a panel of experts. Arbitration is possible only if the Commission agrees to it, but it cannot deny a request by one party to have the matter considered by a panel of experts. The panel's role is to report its findings and recommendations to the Commission and it is a unique feature of the BDSM that one party can force the other to go before the panel.

(This is not the case in the GATT: a complaining country cannot force a reluctant one to agree to a panel, which leads to stalemates, such as occurred in the EC-U.S beef hormone case).

A BDSM panel consists of five members: each party being guaranteed two and the fifth being suggested by the Commission. If the Commission cannot agree on the fifth member, the panellists make the choice and, if they cannot agree, the fifth panellist is selected by lot from a list of potential panellists maintained by the Commission. The process, which has a great deal of flexibility to ensure that a panel is composed of trade and issue-specific experts, is considered one of the positive features of the BDSM. Of the 25 people named on the initial Chapter Eighteen roster, two were familiar with environmental issues and could be loosely termed "environmentalists". (Both were Canadians and one has since died.)[41]

The BDSM always returns the dispute to the representatives of both countries in the Commission to be settled; the Commission is directed to agree on a resolution of the dispute that "normally shall conform with the recommendation of the panel". However, there is no requirement for consensus, and even unanimous recommendations by the panel are not binding on the Commission or the parties. This is in keeping with the tradition of Canada-US dispute settlement by adjudication and to avoid the perceived difficulties encountered in the GATT's consensus approach. There, members must agree to the adoption of a report, while the losing party can delay or block the process and the GATT Council's or contracting parties' acceptance of the panel's recommendations.[42]

It was anticipated that the notification and consultation requirements in the BDSM would lead the parties to agreement, except in the most difficult cases, and that expectation appears to have been borne out. As of June 1992, three panels had been invoked under the Chapter Eighteen process, two of which considered the issue of "conservation" under Article XX(g) of the GATT.

3. BDSM Panel Interpretations of GATT Article XX(g)

The first and only FTA panel to actually work through an Article XX(g) analysis related to the *West Coast Salmon and Herring Case* (1989).[43] In it, the US invoked the BDSM on the grounds that Canada's 100% landing requirement of all salmon and herring caught in West Coast Canadian waters violated Article XI(1), of the GATT. Canada argued that the landing requirement was not a restraint on trade but an essential component of its resource conservation regime and, as such, was subject to exemption under Article XX(g).

The panel noted that it was not the purpose of Article XX(g) "to allow trade interests of one state to override the legitimate environmental concerns of another", but that the only measures protected by Article XX(g) are those that are part of a "genuine conservation program".[44] In a unanimous decision, it concluded that landing requirements could be considered "primarily aimed at" conservation, if provisions were made to exempt from landing that proportion of the catch which, when exported without landing, would not impede data collection. The panel was of the view that a 10-20% proportion would provide necessary information.

The Commission then negotiated for four months to

reach a consensus, allowing Canada to maintain its landing requirement regulations, but requiring it to exempt 25% of the salmon and herring quota from the landing condition in 1991-93. In 1993, the Commission will review the situation.[45]

The decision is important because the test applied by the FTA Panel for applying Article XX(g) is broader than the test previously applied by the GATT Panel. In 1987, the GATT had considered Canada's previous regulations, which imposed a 100% processing requirement on West Coast salmon and herring, and found that it was inconsistent with Article XI(1) and was not saved by Article XX(g). The test applied by the GATT panel was that Article XX(g) would save a restrictive trade measure only if it were taken "in conjunction with production restrictions", and if it were primarily aimed at rendering those restrictions effective. It is likely that, under the GATT test, the landing requirement subsequently imposed would have been found in violation of Article XI(1), and would not have been saved by Article XX(g).

The BDSM was invoked for a second time, by Canada, in the *Lobster Case* (1990),[46] at which the panel was asked to decide whether US legislation banning the sale of undersized lobster was inconsistent with the GATT Article XI(1).[47] The US argued that the measure should be evaluated under Article III of the GATT (national treatment) because it dealt with an internal measure that applied to both foreign and domestic products, and that, even if it fell under Article XI(1), it was saved by Article XX(g). The panel took the US view that the issue was governed by Article III and declined jurisdiction in the dispute.

If this decisions influences future cases, it has potentially far-reaching effects: It suggests that anything is permissible as long as it is applied equally to imports and domestic producers. However, the panel decision was three-to-two (it comprised three Americans and two Canadians) and may not be followed.

A dissenting opinion rejected the contention of the majority that a measure is covered by Article XI only if it applies exclusively to importation. The majority reasons seem inconsistent with the liberal interpretation of Article XI(1) in the *Salmon and Herring Case*. Moreover, it appears well-settled in the GATT that Article XI is about measures that block access to the market and Article III (national treatment) is not about access to the market but about treating goods once they have entered the market. [48] At the same time, the GATT makes it clear that internal measures enforced at the border still fall within Article III of the GATT.

Nevertheless, these two cases suggest that the FTA panels are departing from the GATT interpretations of Article XX(g). Thus far, it appears that the "conservation" test is less stringent under the FTA than under the GATT; this suggests that conservation arguments will be more successful in the future under the FTA dispute settlement mechanism. More cases are necessary before it becomes clear whether the "internal measure" argument that was successful before the Lobster Case Panel stands up in other circumstances. If it does, the door may be even more open to a wide array of legitimate "conservation" measures that are properly developed and implemented.

It is important to note that neither dispute was caused or raised by any issue unique to the FTA; both would have been challenged under the GATT, irrespective of the FTA. The current advantage of the FTA BDSM is not a substantive, but a procedural, one. Because of the imposition of strict time limits, it is a speedier process than that offered by the GATT.

4. *Other Provisions*

Article 1907 of the FTA established a Working Group to negotiate its subsidies code within seven years. It is likely that any such code will parallel that of the GATT and will not be forthcoming until the conclusion of the Uruguay Round. At one time, a draft GATT code included a category of non-actionable subsidies, but the recent Dunkel text did not include any reference to it.

In the FTA's Chapter Six, Canada and the US affirm their obligations under the GATT Agreement on Technical Barriers to Trade (the Standards Code). In so doing, they have agreed to avoid the use of standards-related measures as obstacles to trade. Chapter Six also provides a framework for the eventual elimination of technical standards as non-tariff barriers. Standards and regulations designed to protect health, safety, and the environment are acceptable only if they do not exclude goods that meet those objections. The harmonization of standards is not mandatory.

Although it appears that the FTA's framers may have missed an opportunity to improve on the GATT provisions as they apply to the environment, the FTA does not seem any worse for the environment than the GATT. Remedies available under the FTA are available under the GATT and the same principles apply. In fact, the two decisions of the BDSM panels of experts suggest that they may be inclined to give more weight to environmental arguments than have the GATT panels.

However, relying on the philosophy of individual panels of experts may not be satisfactory, particularly because the influence of environmental regulation on trade is likely to increase in the future. The essential questions are:

• What economic trade-offs must be made for adopting ever-higher levels of environmental protection?

• At what point is there sufficient environmental risk to warrant and legitimize a barrier to trade?

• Who decides?

As environmental issues become more important to the public and politicians, means must be found to strike the balance between minimum impediments to trade and protection of the domestic and global environments.

A North American Free Trade Agreement
The governments of Canada, Mexico, and United States

have recently announced the creation of the NAFTA, a regional trading bloc. It will link the three countries in one of the world's largest open markets, with 350 million people and more than $6 trillion in output.[49] However, a number of concerns have been expressed about the potential environmental consequences of a NAFTA, most notably that existing laws might be considered non-tariff barriers to trade, which, given lower environmental standards in Mexico, will effect the competitiveness of Canadian industry and/or force weaker environmental standards in both Canada and the United States.[50]

It is also argued that Canadian firms and foreign firms that would have invested in Canada will now invest in Mexico in order to take advantage of laxer pollution laws and cheap labour, which means the loss of investment and jobs in Canada. Ecologically, this would only displace the problem of polluting industries, without solving it.

Concerned environmentalists and others point to the Mexican "maquiladora" as an experiment in free trade that has borne out these concerns and has led to serious environmental degradation in the affected area of northern Mexico, just south of the US border.

The maquiladora program was established in 1965, by agreement between the US and Mexican Governments. Under it, firms in Mexico are able to import machinery, equipment, parts, raw material, and other components, duty-free on a temporary "in bond" basis from the US.[51] These components are used in the assembly or manufacture of semi-finished or finished products that can then re-enter the US market, with duty levied only on components not of US origin and on the "value added" during assembly or manufacture in Mexico. Industry is attracted to maquiladoras because of the Mexican government's hands-off attitude toward environmental protection and labour costs· and the fact that Mexico allows 100% foreign ownership of maquiladora plants.[52]

Over the last 24 years, the maquiladora industry has become the fastest-growing sector of the Mexican economy.

In 1965, the first year of operation, 12 plants, employing 3,000 people, were established. Five years later, 120 maquiladora plants were in operation and, by 1980, that number had reached 620. In 1989, 1,490 companies operated under the program, employing some 400,000 workers, or 1% of Mexico's total employment. The number of maquiladora-zone inhabitants, which was 2.6 million in 1989, is 3.3 million today, and is expected to surpass 5 million by the year 2000.[53] In 1989, the value added to material for export from the maquiladoras totalled $1.6 billion (US).[54] The maquiladora sector is Mexico's largest producer of foreign exchange, second only to the petroleum industry.[55]

The expanding manufacturing sector in the maquiladora has already overwhelmed the region's essential infrastructure and natural resources; the pace of waste generation exceeds Mexico's capacity to handle it. There is a very real fear that increasing trade liberalization through a NAFTA will increase the maquiladra problem. Moreover, a growing trend toward more sophisticated and complex production processes (as opposed to the light-industry, sub-assembly operations that dominated the maquiladora industry in the past), may result in more use of hazardous substances and the additional production of toxic waste.[56] The disposal of dangerous industrial waste is rigorously controlled in the US and Canada, but Mexico has only a handful of sites for dangerous wastes.

While the Mexican government may have strict environmental laws on its books, modelled largely after those in the US, there are inadequate enforcement resources. The current per-capita spending on environmental protection in Mexico is US $0.48, compared to $24.40 in the US.[57] At best, Mexican enforcement measures are spotty and the government will have to police its environmental regulations more vigorously if it is to achieve compliance with the standards it has set. However, it does appear to be putting aside more resources to this end.[58]

In light of the environmental degradation of the maquiladora, it is argued that the border areas' natural resources cannot handle the extra economic development free-trade advocates foresee. Under a NAFTA, further significant growth in the border regions of both countries could completely overwhelm efforts to develop and protect border resources properly, further endangering the environment and people in both countries.

At present, Canada's trading relations with Mexico are modest: in 1989, Mexico ranked seventeenth as a Canadian trading market, while our exports to Mexico were worth $603,000,000 - less than half of 1% of Canada's total exports;[59] Mexican imports into Canada in 1989 totalled $1.7 billion, or 1% of Canada's total imports.

The current average duty rate on dutiable imports from Mexico is 10.6%. However, most Mexican goods are eligible for preferential rates under Canada's Generalized System of Preferences (GSP) for developing countries, and many products enter duty free. This lowers the average rate of duty on all imports from Mexico to 2.4%. It is argued that there will be no significant environmental consequences of the agreement because 85% of the existing trade between Canada and Mexico is now duty free.

The environmental effect of a NAFTA was put on the agenda of some American decision-makers during the fast track debates in the spring of 1991. As late as April of that year, neither the Bush administration nor the Mexican administration had conceded that a direct link existed between trade and the environment.[60] The position of the Canadian government at that time was that a NAFTA would address trade-related environmental issues, while non-trade related environmental issues would be addressed in parallel agreements, separate from the trade agreement.[61]

A year later, the Canadian government's position had not changed and the general approach to the environment and the NAFTA remained on two parallel tracks. The trade-related environmental aspects of the NAFTA will be

315

included in the text, including standards related exclusively to products. The goal is to reduce any environmental impact and perhaps make environmental standards higher by facilitating new technology and investment. The term "environment" will be included in the preamble to the general part of the agreement, in the chapter dealing with investment, and in the dispute settlement mechanism. Non-trade related measures (such as harvesting practices, manufacturing processes, enforcement measures, etc.) will be dealt with in a parallel process.

The Mexican, American, and Canadian governments agreed to conduct environmental reviews of a NAFTA. However, the review undertaken by the Canadian government will not be released for public comment. Instead, Canada has chosen to conduct an environmental assessment of a NAFTA at the Cabinet level, based on terms of reference drawn up through a consultation process that includes some environmentalists.

During the spring of 1991, a strong US environmental and labour lobby, the Public Citizen Watch, made it clear that environmentalists would oppose any free trade agreement with Mexico that was not linked, directly or indirectly, to strong environmental accords. There was concern that if the fast-track process were approved without a commitment being made to the environment, the environment would not be considered, given that, under that process, Congress has only 60 days after a completed trade agreement to debate, approve or reject it without amendments. The environmental groups lobbied Congress to oppose any fast-track negotiating process until such a guarantee was secured.[62]

The lobbying efforts of Public Citizen Watch and other groups met with some success. In his letter to the congressional leadership on May 1, 1991, in which he sought an extension of the fast-track procedure, President Bush responded to concerns about the environmental effects of a NAFTA. In order to secure votes for his negotiating authority, the President released an Action

Plan to deal with environmental, labour, and health issues in the negotiations; it included a promise to conduct a detailed review of the US-Mexico environmental issues, to be coordinated by the United States Trade Representative (USTR), with the assistance of various other departments.

Some members of Congress made fast-track support conditional on the implementation of the Action Plan; however, dissatisfied with the Administration's response, the Sierra Club, Public Citizen Watch, and Friends of the Earth filed a law suit on August 1, 1991, against the Office of the US Trade Representative. This was an attempt to force that Office to prepare environmental impact statements on the Uruguay Round and the NAFTA negotiations, which would publicly examine their environmental implications.[63]

In October 1991, the US Administration completed the Review of US-Mexico Environmental Issues that had been announced in the letter to Congress, and released it for public comment. On February 25, 1992, Carla Hills and William Reilly announced the conclusions of the final Review in Los Angeles.

The Review begins by stressing the strong record of bilateral cooperation on the environment between the US and Mexico;[64] it argues generally a NAFTA would encourage industry to shift away from the maquiladora sector, which would reduce environmental stress on the border region.

The Review also argues that a NAFTA will not turn Mexico into a pollution haven for firms seeking to escape US environmental standards. It asserts that pollution abatement represents a small share of total costs for most industries and compliance costs tend to play a minimal role in decisions on plant locations.[65]

It also suggests that any decision to relocate, based on such costs, would involve a highly questionable assumption about the future of compliance costs in Mexico. This, combined with what the Review called "historic sensitivity of foreign investment in a developing country such as Mexico", led the authors to suggest that the public stance

317

of many large American companies may be to follow US pollution control practices and standards in their facilities outside of the US.[66] While that may be true of some large capital investors, the philosophy may be less prevalent among smaller firms with minimal capital to invest.

Congressional leaders were quick to respond to the Administration's Environmental Review. In a letter to President Bush signed by more than 70 Democrats, Representative Ron Wyden charged that the draft Review "relies on trickle-down environmentalism to make all the problems magically disappear".[67]

Opposition to the three-way trade deal exists in Canada as well. Groups, such as the Pro-Canada Network and the Council of Canadians, claim that a North American trade pact "would give multinationals Canada's resources, the US market, and Mexico's cheap labour".[68] The Canadian government seems to hold the view that Mexico already has stringent environmental regulations on the books.

In 1988, the Mexican government passed the *General Law on Ecological Equilibrium and Environmental Protection*, but there is widespread agreement that the lack of financial and human resources have made enforcement difficult.[69] It appears to be the Canadian Government's position that, with the improved economic growth trade will bring, Mexico will be able to address the issue of environmental protection in a more satisfactory way.[70] This is consistent with the fundamental premise of the World Commission on Environment and Development (WCED): a reduction in poverty itself is a precondition for environmentally sound development.

In its 1987 report, *Our Common Future*, the WCED illustrated clearly the links between patterns of economic development, including trade, and environmental stresses.[71] It thoroughly documented the manner in which poverty and rising populations make it enormously difficult for developing countries to pursue environmentally sound policies, even in the best of circumstances. The Commission based its conclusions, in large part, on the rationale that the poor cannot afford to protect the environment. Therefore, if developing countries are to achieve sustainable development, they must enjoy an increase in the standards of living and more efficient use of their resource base.

The Canadian government articulated its support for the developing world in it's 1991 *Green Plan,* which is intended to serve as a blueprint to guide Canadian environmental policy during the 1990s. Among the broad environmental policy objectives in the Plan, the government has committed itself to pursuing global solutions to global environmental problems.

Specifically, this involves persuading as many developed and developing nations as possible to agree to the international conventions on climate change and biodiversity. The Canadian government has also committed itself to helping developing countries achieve sustainable development by, among other things, increasing efforts aimed at helping them gain access to the latest skills and technology.[72]

It appears that the Canadian government's dedication to sustainable development supports a trilateral free trade deal insofar as one will lead to economic growth and prosperity in Mexico. As a major developing country, Mexico, for its part, will increase the levels of environmental protection its government can afford to offer.[73] Addressing Mexico's problems through freer trade may also increase the likelihood that it will agree to the global conventions discussed in the *Green Plan.*

However, while the WCED spoke of wealth being a *precondition* for environmental protection, there are no guarantees. Perhaps, according to Canadian values, a richer Mexico is likely to be a more environmentally conscious Mexico. As yet, however, it is unclear whether many of Mexico's present problems stem from its government's inability, or unwillingness, to finance basic public services, such as clean water and sewage disposal. The assumption that an increase in wealth *will* cause a corresponding increase in environmental protection leads to questions about the power structure and domestic priorities in Mexico.

A NAFTA represents a real challenge to those seeking to link trade and the environment in a single negotiated agreement: each country approaches the issue with different standards, a fact illustrated most clearly by the difference between the highly developed economy of the United States and the less developed Mexican economy. Canada is able to bring a unique perspective to the NAFTA bargaining table because, while it has a highly developed economy, Canada is able to empathize with developing countries heavily dependent on the exploitation of natural resources and because it has experienced "green protectionism" at first hand.

The failure of the US to convince a GATT panel that its domestic dolphin conservation measures were acceptable when applied extra-territorially (see page 335), has led environmental groups in the US to place even greater importance on the inclusion of environment issues in a NAFTA and has given environmentalists added ammunition in presenting their case to Congress.[74] It has been suggested that the environment may well be the swing issue in the congressional debate over whether the NAFTA should be adopted now that it has been negotiated.[75]

Whether the environment is included in the trade agreement or in parallel bilateral agreements, it is clear the pressure to improve the state of its environment will be brought to bear on Mexico. This might provide opportunities for Canadian exporters of environmental monitoring equipment, process control technology, consulting and engineering services, and (potentially) the chemical and the oil and gas industries.[76] As well, considerable expertise and technology will be needed to deal with problems of toxic waste disposal and gas and waste emissions.

The European Community

The European Community (EC) is Canada's second-largest

partner for trade, investment, technology, and tourism; its trade policies, therefore, have a significant impact on the Canadian economy. In 1988, Canadians bought more than $16 billion worth of EC goods and exported $11 billion worth to EC countries - 18% of all Canadian exports.[77] Most are resource commodities such as lumber, newsprint, grains, ores and metals, petroleum, natural gas, and fish. Few manufactured goods of Canadian origin are sold in Europe.

There are currently 12 member countries in the EC, whose population has recently been increased by the inclusion of the former East Germany.[78] As a trading bloc, the EC will probably expand further to include the six European Free Trade Association (EFTA) countries (Sweden, Norway, Iceland, Switzerland, Austria, and Finland) and perhaps, eventually, the remaining countries of Eastern Europe (including Poland, Hungary, Romania, Albania, Bulgaria, and the countries of the former Czechoslovakia and the former Yugoslavia).

In July 1987, amendments to the Treaty of Rome, known as the *Single European Act*, became effective. They set the course of the program known as "Europe 92", the object of which is to eliminate all internal barriers to trade among the members of the EC and to create a single European market. This will be achieved by harmonizing product standards, resolving differences in national trade laws, and liberalizing financial services, among other actions.

The Single Market Europe will create the world's largest economic bloc, with more than 340 million people, (even if the EFTA countries or Eastern Europe are not included), a common trading strategy, and a GDP equal to that of the US.

Among the effects of a Single Market Europe will be:
- consolidation of European companies;
- the reduction of production costs (thanks to economies of scale);
- the reduction of transportation costs; and
- the elimination of border measures within Europe.

There is no doubt that trade patterns between the EC and countries outside the Single Market will be affected over the next few years by these developments. It is important that Canada respond proactively, in order to maintain its present market in the EC and to capitalize on opportunities presented by the change.

A further effect of Europe '92 could be an increase in trade barriers with non-EC countries, because of increased environmental regulation in a Single Market Europe. As this new market unfolds, the extent to which a satisfactory balance is achieved between restrictive trade practices and environmental protection will become clearer. The creation of a balance, acceptable to interests on both sides, is a fundamental step in continued progress towards sustainable development.

The European Community's Environmental Program
In conjunction with the implementation of Europe '92, there appears to be a trend toward more extensive and more stringent environmental regulation in Europe. In July 1988, the Community issued an environmental impact assessment directive (integrating ecological awareness into the planning and decision-making process in all sectors) and ordered that certain categories of projects be subjected to impact assessments.

The Community claims that strict environmental standards are an economic, as well as an ecological, necessity - which probably means even stricter environmental controls in the future. The EC is currently creating a European Environment Agency (EEA) to act as the nerve centre for the existing national and regional agencies, thus enabling the EC to monitor environmental quality and developments on a European scale. The EEA will also provide objective and comparative data on the state of the environment in member states.

These measures were prompted, in part, by the deteriorating state of the environment in Europe, and by increasing concern among members of the European public

322

about environmental quality. Surveys show that, in recent years, public opinion has swung dramatically in favour of a more dynamic environmental policy. This was evident in June, 1989, when "green" parties won 30 seats in the European Parliament, making the greens the fifth-largest group in that body.[79] The increased environmental regulation and growing public support will affect already changing trade rules and consumption patterns in the EC.

1. Structure of the European Community

The *Single European Act* will have implications for further environmental regulation in Europe, both substantively, through concrete provisions, and procedurally, in changes to the decision-making process. Therefore, it is important to understand the role of the primary policy making and decision making bodies. A brief outline follows.

The European Commission is the executive arm of the Community; it proposes regulations and directives that, in addition to treaties, make up Community law. The Commission ensures that the common market is operating properly and enforces that law. The Commission is composed of 17 commissioners, two from each of the larger states (Germany, France, Britain, Italy, and Spain) and one each from the smaller member countries. The Commission has an administrative staff, based mainly in Brussels, consisting of some 14,000 officials working in approximately 20 Directorates-General (D-G). The environment falls under the jurisdiction of D-G XI.

The Council of Ministers comprises ministers from member state governments and makes the Community's major policy decisions. They participate, depending on the issues on the agenda: for example, agriculture ministers discuss farm prices while environmental ministers discuss environmental issues, and so on. The Council of Ministers, which meets in Brussels and, a few times a year, in Luxembourg, has a general secretariat of about 2,000 people; in 1988, it met 77 times.

The Council can deal only with proposals from the

Commission and can alter them only by unanimous agreement; unanimity is also required for certain important decisions. However, in order to strengthen the decision-making process, the *Single European Act* has extended the use of a qualified majority formula for voting on certain decisions, particularly in relation to the completion of the European internal market under Article 100A. In order to obtain a qualified majority, 54 votes, out of a total of 76, are needed to approve a Commission proposal.[80]

The European Court of Justice, which sits in Luxembourg, comprises 13 judges, appointed for six years by consent of the member states. The Court's role is to pass judgements, at the request of a national court, on the interpretation or validity of points of Community law, and, when asked by a Community institution, a government or an individual, to quash any measures adopted by the Commission, Council of Ministers or national governments that it finds are incompatible with the treaties of the Community. Judgments of the Court, in the field of Community law, overrule those of national courts.

Finally, the European Parliament, made up of 518 deputies elected for five years, sits in Strasbourg.[81] The Parliament serves as a legislature, participating in the formulation of directives, regulations, and Community decisions and commenting on Commission proposals; in addition, it is the EC's budgetary and supervisory body. The *Single Europe Act* provides for cooperation between the Council and the Parliament, thus strengthening the Parliament's legislative powers in such important areas as completion of the European internal market, among others. The effect of this change has already been felt in the Council's environment-related decisions.

2. The Single European Act and the Environment
Prior to 1987, there was no explicit legal provision for dealing with Community environmental concerns: Article 30 of the Treaty of Rome guaranteed the free movement of goods and services between member states, although certain

exceptions were permitted, such as measures that could be justified on environmental grounds. Environmental initiatives were traditionally pursued under Article 235, which allows the Community to take appropriate measures to attain Community objectives not expressly provided for by treaty power.

However, changing environmental attitudes in Europe are evident in the legal provisions of the *Single European Act* itself: these include articles that empower and encourage the EC to co-ordinate the objectives of free trade with a high level of environmental protection, and confirm the desirability of pursuing environmental objectives as a legitimate end.

There are now provisions in the *Single European Act* that require the EC Commission to establish and enforce a high level of protection for the environment and for human health. The environment is now a specific part of the Treaty of Rome; it is the underpinning of other legislation, a signal that environmental protection should be a component of the Community's other policies. Notably and for the first time, Articles 100A and 130R, S and T, acknowledge the need to combine free trade objectives with environmental protection. The philosophy of the Community's environmental program is stated in paragraph 2 of Article 130R:

"Action by the Community relating to the environment shall be based on the principles that preventative action should be taken, that environmental damage should, as a priority be rectified at source, and that the polluter should pay. Environmental protection requirements shall be a component of the Community's other policies."

Article 130R sets out the objectives of the EC, which are to direct environmental action as follows:
  i. to preserve, protect and improve the quality of the environment;
  ii. to contribute towards protecting human health; and

iii. to ensure a prudent and rational utilization of natural resources. (paragraph 1)

Currently, mixed signals are emanating from the European Court of Justice (ECJ) on how it will interpret the provisions of the *Single European Act* and the extent to which it will reinforce the general trend toward higher standards of environmental protection.[82] In the *Danish Bottle Case* of September 1988,[83] the Court considered whether the Danish system of requiring returnable containers for beer and soft drinks and requiring licenses for new types of containers was an unjustifiable restraint on trade, in light of Article 130R.

It applied a two-stage test:

First, the Court asked whether national measures taken to protect the environment could be considered to constitute a "mandatory requirement" limiting the application of Article 30 of the Treaty of Rome (which guarantees the free movement of goods and services between member states), in the absence of Community rules. It found, that by virtue of the provisions in the *Single European Act*, measures taken to protect the environment would constitute "mandatory requirements", which would limit the application of Article 30.[84]

Second, the ECJ asked whether the level of protection required was excessive or unreasonable and whether the measures taken were necessary and proportional; it found that the Danish legislation failed the test, that its measures were disproportionate to the objective pursued and that they could be pursued in a less discriminatory manner.

Notwithstanding the result in this case, it is significant that the ECJ accepted the principle that a measure taken to protect the environment could, in some circumstances, be a legitimate barrier to trade, as long as it was not so drastic that it had an effect on trade that was disproportionate to the legitimate environmental objective. Failing another test case, it is difficult to predict how this principle will be applied in the future.[85]

However, it was almost tested in 1989, in a case involving

catalytic converters, during the debate on EC car-exhaust standards. The Commission put forward a proposal on emission standards set at the level of the lowest common Community denominator. Some member states felt that they could not meet those standards and the Council of Ministers very nearly rejected the proposal. However, the Dutch wanted to move more rapidly with stricter standards and threatened to take the case to the Court, thus forcing the European Parliament to take the initiative and make some formal proposals itself in this area. The Council then had to decide whether to accept the Parliamentary proposals, knowing that, if the Dutch pressed their case in the Court based on the test in the *Danish Bottle Case*, they would likely have won.

Faced with the pending Court case, pressure from the European Parliament, and the possibility of European elections in 1989, the hitherto reluctant member states in the Council adopted the proposals much earlier than would otherwise have been the case and the issue did not come before the Court.

It is significant that the European Parliament took the initiative for the first time, as it is entitled to do under an amendment to the *Single European Act*, to make proposals to the Council. By virtue of this new role, the Parliament will increasingly be able to translate political pressure from its constituents into legislation.

In July 1990, the European Court ruled on a procedural point of interpretation that will affect the decision-making process in the Council on issues of waste management because it suggests that there is a high degree of environmental consideration in the Court. Articles 130R-T, which deal substantively with the environment, require unanimity in the decision making process. Article 100A is the basic Single Market Article which stipulates that, when legislation is being developed to ensure the circulation of *goods* within the Single Market, it can be based on a qualified majority in Council. Paragraph 3 of Article 100A sets out a fundamental requirement for stringent environmental regulation in this context:

> "The Commission, in its proposals, laid down in para 1, concerning health, safety, environmental protection and consumer protection, will take as a base a high level of protection."

Current legislative proposals on the environment that relate to product standards or their impact on competitiveness are subject to majority voting under Article 100A; the remainder will require unanimity under Article 130S. A test case on the Council's use of Article 130S, regarding a directive on waste from the titanium dioxide industry, has clarified the distinction between the use of the two articles and opened up the decision-making process in favour of increased environmental protection.

In the titanium dioxide case the Commission put forward legislation based on Article 100A, regulating trade in titanium dioxide and titanium dioxide waste, because the product would be circulated within the Community. Some member states disagreed that 100A should be the basis for the proposal, arguing that it was an environmental problem and should be dealt with under Article 130S. The Commission took the issue to the Court, which ruled that the proposal was properly made under Article 100A. By classifying the issue of the movement of waste as pertaining to the free movement of goods within the Single Market, the Court has effectively ruled that decisions of that kind can now be taken by a qualified majority; it will mean an easier decision-making process and will prevent a few "dirty" countries from blocking stricter environmental regulation in that area.

The debate between the use of 100A and 130S continues in the context of legislation being proposed to implement the Basel Convention on the Transboundary Movement of Hazardous Waste. However, in light of the decision in the titanium dioxide case, it appears that the legislation will be proposed under 100A and subject only to a qualified majority.

3. The Environmental Agenda

Regulations encouraging and enforcing higher levels of environmental protection already extend into much of the European economy. In a number of instances, the EC's environmental legislation sets standards that must be met by products offered for sale in the Community.

Eighty standards-related directives have been proposed by the EC Commission as part of the 1992 Single Market Program: maximum noise levels for such products as motorcycles, aircraft, and other types of machinery have been established and the EC is setting stricter standards for: automobile emissions; lead in gasoline; the importation of CFCs; air and water pollution; recycling; toxic waste; and, of particular importance to Canada, standards relating to forest products. The latter include: phytosanitary requirements; better control of imported lumber that has been treated with anti-stain chemicals; greater use of recycled fibres in newsprint and other paper products.

There is a real possibility that the EC will ban pulp produced by processes exceeding certain emission requirements; in addition, the EC's expected approach to testing and certification will be important to Canadian exporters. The EC Council will permit the EUROCOM to negotiate agreements recognizing third-party testing and certification; regimes are now being established for both mandatory and voluntary standards. A scheme of environmental labelling, which would enable consumers to make buying decisions that encourage higher standards, is also being considered.[86]

The Challenges and Opportunities for Canadian Industry

How should Canadian industries and governments respond to the trend toward higher levels of environmental protection in Europe? In particular, what challenges and what opportunities do environmental developments in the EC present to Canadian exporters?

1. Challenges for Canadian Industry

Canadian industry has a number of concerns about environmental legislation in the EC. Many small and medium-sized firms are worried that changes may occur so quickly that it will be difficult for them to obtain information, on a timely basis, about EC standards. Even when information on proposed changes is available, Canadian firms may be unable to influence their content. Canadian exporters will be forced to modify designs in order to meet new EC standards, often on very short lead times; moreover, differences between Canadian and EC standards will probably also increase their costs of doing business. Therefore, convenient procedures for mutual recognition of certification and testing of third-country products are important for Canadian exporters. The EC has indicated that, when there is a requirement for testing products of so-called third parties (for example, Canadian firms), it will accept results only from an EC-recognized testing facility unless a bilateral agreement has been reached with the third party. The Canadian government is currently negotiating such an agreement.

Some sectors of the Canadian economy face particular threats. For example, Canadian exporters of forest products may have to respond to EC regulations affecting the standards for structural timber, the importation of Canadian green softwood (which EC plant health authorities believe contains a microscopic organism that is perceived as a threat to European forests), and the previously mentioned importation of lumber treated with allegedly toxic anti-stain chemicals. As well, EC consumers are demanding greater use of recycled fibres in newsprint and other paper products. An EC ban on pulp produced by processes exceeding certain emission requirements is a possibility.

The importance of the EC as an export market for Canadian forest products should be noted: in 1989, it totalled $3.3 billion, making the EC Canada's second-largest market for forest products, after the United States.

Other Canadian industries may face threats as well: EC directives that set upper limits on noise emissions from such machines as lawn mowers mean that, if they are to continue to sell in the European market, North American producers will have to lower the operating speeds of their equipment or redesign engines to make them quieter. The occasional or low-volume exporter may find that it is no longer profitable to remain in the EC market.

2. Opportunities for Canadian Industry
Canadian exporters also stand to benefit from the developing EC framework for environmental protection: common European standards and testing procedures will enable them to develop and sell products more efficiently than ever before, on a Europe-wide basis. In general, Canadian firms (both exporters and manufacturers in the EC) will face a more coherent, open, and organized EC marketplace. The development of European standards will help open up the EC's government procurement market. Moreover, the principle of non-discrimination means that products originating in Canada must be granted access to certification systems on an equal footing with products originating in the EC, whether those systems are voluntary or mandatory. Canadian products can be refused only for the same reasons as products originating within the EC: non-conformance to standards or lack of safety.

Among the types of Canadian exporters that could benefit from higher levels of EC environmental protection are the automobile industry and suppliers of environmental equipment and services. By 1992, automobiles sold in Europe will, in large measure, have to conform to higher emissions standards, comparable to those already in place in North America. On the basis of current technology, these standards can be met only by catalytic converters, giving Canadian suppliers of catalytic converters and other emission control equipment the benefits of the EC's higher environmental standards and its Europe-wide approval processes.

Canadian suppliers of environmental equipment and services able to compete in the European marketplace could also profit from higher EC environmental protection standards. The West European market for pollution control equipment, such as waste disposal technology, is $40 billion annually. The EC chemical industry will be looking for expertise and technology to help it deal with toxic waste disposal and gas and waste emissions. These markets present opportunities for Canadian exporters of environmental monitoring equipment, process control technology, and consulting and engineering services.

However, Canadians will face well-established and technologically sophisticated European competitors. Nevertheless, the potential for all suppliers of environmental equipment and services is huge; it is estimated that more than one million people in the EC are employed in the pollution control industry and its related services.

The Major Multilateral Institutions

Within the global community, management of proliferating trade-environment relationships has been taken up by the three major international systems active in shaping global order:

First is the General Agreement on Tariffs and Trade (GATT), the de facto replacement for the intended International Trade Organization (ITO) designed as part of the UN galaxy of broadly multilateral institutions during and after the Second World War.[87]

Second is the more recent and more narrowly multilateral Organization for Economic Co-operation and Development (OECD), centred on the developed countries of the "Atlantic" region, but with Pacific countries included as well.

Third is the modern plurilateral Group of Seven, of the major industrial democracies and the European Community, founded in 1975.

All three have recently institutionalized trade and the

environment on their agendas.

The General Agreement on Tariffs and Trade (GATT)

The GATT, a multilateral treaty, is subscribed to by 108 countries, known as "Contracting Parties", which, together, account for nearly 90% of world trade. Established in 1947, the GATT lays down agreed-on rules for international trade and functions as the principal international body negotiating the reduction of trade barriers and other measures that distort trade.

In order to achieve sustainable development, it is important that the international trading system establish a mechanism that balances the economic trade-offs associated with legitimate domestic measures for environmental protection and the restrictions on free trade that often result.

Articles I-III of the GATT embody the fundamental rules of most favoured nation treatment and national treatment. Under the latter, domestic taxes and regulations can be extended to imports if they are applied equally to domestic and all sources of imported "like products", and do not provide protection to domestic industries. Most subsidies are tolerated under the GATT if they do not harm other export interests; however, production subsidies that injure domestic industry can be countervailed. With some exceptions, quantitative restrictions on exports or imports are prohibited in principle by Article XI.

Even the most conservative traders now accept that there is a link between international trade and environmental protection, a link which the GATT has recently acknowledged in a published report. While the report recognizes the relationship, it denounces unilateral acts purporting to protect the global commons at the expense of export partners.[88] At present, some perceive an apparent failure of the multilateral trading system to take the environment adequately into account, and see a contradiction between the principles of trade policy in the GATT and current requirements for protecting the environment.

The GATT has tangentially dealt with environment-related trade issues within the context of general provisions most applicable to environmental issues: Article XX, the Standards Code, and the Subsidies Code. As environmental issues become more important to the public and to politicians, it is vital that a means be devised to balance the fewest trade impediments with protection of the national and global environment.

1. Article XX

In the GATT, environmental measures that impinge on trade, in contravention of the GATT rules, may be justified as falling within the scope of Article XX. Although protection of the environment is not specifically mentioned in the objectives included in that Article, sub-paragraphs (b) and (g) permit countries to exempt measures from their GATT obligations if these measures meet the stated criteria (see top of page 307).

Such measures must not result in "arbitrary or unjustifiable discrimination between countries where the same conditions prevail" and they must not represent "a disguised restriction on international trade".

There are a number of problems associated with using Articles XX(b) and (g):

• Most fundamentally, there is no clear understanding concerning the application of Article XX to environmental measures. Where there is interpretation, it provides little guidance.[89]

• A second problem is that Article XX does not specify where the "protection" should occur, in the importing or exporting country. This blurs its application in regard to product and process-related measures and to transnational pollution.

A broad interpretation would extend the scope of Article XX to process-related pollution in other countries and allow importers to justify domestic protection, which would ultimately lead to the collapse of the GATT rules. That interpretation was rejected in the tuna/dolphin ruling.

Article XX(g) appears best-suited to embrace environmental issues generally and has been invoked twice in cases involving Canadian exports. In 1981, the American government invoked XX(g), in an attempt to justify an embargo on Canadian exports of tuna to the US. The Canadian government invoked it in 1987, in an attempt to exempt its processing requirements for all West Coast salmon and herring from the application of Article XI of the GATT. In both cases, GATT panels held that the prohibitions were not saved by Article XX(g).

In its most recent interpretation, a trade measure could be considered to be made effective only "in conjunction with" production restrictions (which had been the finding in the tuna case), if it was *primarily* aimed at making such restrictions effective.[90]

In the case of health and phytosanitary exceptions, there is no clear understanding of whether Article XX(b) (which may be used by contracting parties, in certain circumstances, to justify measures that would otherwise be contrary to their GATT obligations) applies to imports of products which, themselves, could pose a direct threat to human, animal or plant life in the importing country, or whether they can be applied to environmental control measures and to trade sanctions aimed at enforcing process standards.

Neither is there a definition in the GATT of the requirement that a measure be "necessary" to achieve a stated goal; interpretation by GATT panels has given this word a very restrictive meaning.[91] Article XX provides no guidance or interpretation for assessing the extent to which a restrictive trade practice is warranted by environmental objectives. Because the issue of proportionality has not been addressed, there is a question of how to establish an appropriate balance between environmental goals and trade barriers.

GATT, Tuna-Dolphin Panel Decision

The most recent commentary on Article XX (b) and (g) by a GATT Panel occurred in the Tuna-Dolphin decision of

September 1991. In February 1990, Mexico complained to the GATT that provisions under the US *Marine Mammals Protection Act*, compelling an embargo on tuna from Mexico because Mexican vessels caught too many dolphins in their nets while harvesting tuna, was inconsistent with the Article XI prohibitions on quantitative restrictions in the GATT. A panel considered the question and found in favour of the Mexicans. The panel held that the ban on imports of tuna from Mexico was inconsistent with Article XI. Dismissing the US argument that these were not "like products" because of the manner in which they were harvested, the panel held that the discrimination was not based on the *product* but on the *process* by which it was harvested, which is not allowed. The US sought to defend the embargo under the Article XX(b) and (g) exceptions.

Article XX(b)

The GATT panel found that the US direct import prohibition could not be justified under the exception in Article XX(b). In so doing, it ruled that Article XX(b) could not be applied to processing standards outside the jurisdiction of the country imposing the trade measure. The US had argued that the trade measures taken under the MMPA were "necessary" within the meaning of Article XX(b) because there were no alternatives reasonably available to the US to protect dolphin life and health outside its jurisdiction.

The panel examined the provision's legislative history and found indications that the drafters of Article XX focused on the use of sanitary measures to safeguard life or health of humans, animals or plants within the jurisdiction of the importing country. This supported the panel's conclusion that the provision was intended to apply only to measures within the jurisdiction of the contracting party applying them.

While Article XX(b) allows each contracting party to set human, animal, and plant standards, the *trade measure* requiring justification under Article XX, and not the standards itself, must be "necessary" and not "constitute a means of arbitrary or unjustifiable discrimination". Article XX was intended to allow contracting parties to impose trade restrictive measures inconsistent with the GATT to pursue overriding public policy goals to the extent that such inconsistencies were unavoidable. In this case, the panel held that the US had not exhausted all reasonably available options for protecting dolphins, using measures consistent with the GATT (in particular, by negotiating international co-operative arrangements). The panel further ruled that, even assuming an import prohibition was the only resort reasonably available to the US, the particular measure it had chosen could not be considered "necessary" within in the meaning of Article XX(b). This was based largely on the fact that the maximum rate of incidental dolphin-taking that Mexico had to meet was linked to the taking rate actually recorded for US fishermen during the same period; therefore, Mexican authorities could not know at any given time whether their policies conformed to the US dolphin-protection standards.

Article XX(g)

The US also argued that measures taken under the MMPA are "primarily aimed at" protecting an exhaustible natural resource - dolphins. It argued that the import restrictions on certain tuna and tuna products under MMPA were "primarily aimed at rendering effective restrictions on domestic production or consumption of dolphins". Mexico argued that US measures were not justified because the provision could not be applied extra-jurisdictionally.

The panel noted that XX(g) requires that the measure relating to the conservation of exhaustible natural resources be taken "in conjunction with restrictions on domestic production or consumption". It found that a country can effectively control the production or consumption of an exhaustible natural resource only to the extent that the production or consumption is under its jurisdiction.

This suggests that Article XX(g) was intended to permit contracting parties to take trade measures primarily aimed at effectively restricting production or consumption within their jurisdiction. The panel also pointed out that, while Article XX(g) allows each contracting party to adopt its own conservation policies, the trade measure involved (not the conservation regime) must be related to conserving an exhaustible natural resource and not constitute a "means of arbitrary or unjustifiable discrimination...or a disguised restriction on international trade".

The panel decided that, in this case, the restriction was based on uncertain conditions and could not be regarded as aimed primarily at the conservation of dolphins.

In rejecting an extra-jurisdictional application of Article XX(g), the panel said that, if it accepted the US argument, each contracting party could unilaterally decide the conservation policies from which others could not deviate without jeopardizing their rights under the GATT.

The ruling suggests that the extent of exceptions to Article XX allows a contracting party to tax or regulate imported products and similar domestic products, as long as taxes or regulations do not discriminate against imported products or afford protection to domestic producers. It also suggests that a contracting party is free to tax or regulate domestic production for environmental purposes. However, a party may not restrict imports of a product merely because it originates in a country with environmental policies different from its own. If the product is not dangerous to either a consumer or the environment, the GATT would consider the import ban an illegal non-tariff barrier. Import restrictions "must concern the characteristics of the product itself" and cannot reflect the processes by which the product is made or caught, as the case may be. Clearly, taxes could apply only to the product, as such, once it arrived at a nation's border, and could not be attached to the method by which it was produced.

The panel rejected the argument that Article XX(b) can be extended to cover process standards, citing as its reason that "a contracting party cannot unilaterally decide what is best for the international community". The panel interpreted the GATT's language narrowly but in a way consistent with prior decisions and with the legislative history of the GATT provisions.

Nevertheless, in acknowledging the ability of countries to set internal standards aimed at environmental protection and to tax and regulate for that purpose, the GATT went further in recognizing legitimate environmental concerns of the contracting parties than it had in the past.

2. The Agreement on Technical Barriers to Trade (Standards Code)

The Agreement on Technical Barriers to Trade (Standards Code) provides a framework for dealing, at the multilateral level, with trade-related issues arising from technical regulations and standards. The Code was concluded in 1979 during the Tokyo Round of trade negotiations within the GATT. It includes a provision that mirrors the language of GATT Article XX, but speaks explicitly to the environment. The Preamble recognizes that:

> "no country should be prevented from taking measures necessary ... for protection of human, animal, or plant life or health, or the environment."

However, these provisions are subject to a requirement that the standards not be applied in an arbitrary or unjustifiable manner that would allow discrimination between countries in which the same conditions prevail. They prohibit technical environmental measures in agreements and standards that create unnecessary obstacles to international trade. This implies that countries are not required to dilute their environmental standards vis-à-vis imports if such standards are higher than those of other countries, provided the measures are necessary to meet a valid environmental objective.

However, the Code provides no more clarification than does Article XX concerning the meaning of "necessary" or "justifiable" measures. Moreover, in principle, a country can set any standards for processes or production of goods, but it is unclear under the Code whether it can require similar treatment from countries from which it imports.

This issue was explored, but not resolved, in the US-EC hormone beef case, which could not be settled in the dispute settlement mechanism of the Code. The case was further complicated by the role of scientific evidence in the Code's dispute settlement mechanism; it provides for the establishment of a technical expert group to make findings on the detailed scientific judgments involved, and to rule on the legitimacy of the judgment. However, there is neither guidance on how to assess conflicting evidence nor an interpretation of risk acceptability.

Both the substantive and procedural shortcomings of the Code have been exposed by the hormone beef controversy, in which the EC refused to acknowledge the United States' use of the dispute settlement procedures for creating a technical expert group. The debate over the hormone level necessary or unnecessary to protect human health is, ultimately, a question of whether there is, in fact, a level of acceptable risk - a question that straddles the ground between science and public policy.

Similar environmental concerns will arise as environmental standards are challenged under the Code, given the undefined level of environmental risk that parties must demonstrate if they want to determine or challenge technical specifications - the existing Code machinery appears unsuited to dealing with such issues. The hormone beef case has resulted in a stalemate and, since 1989, formal dispute settlement talks have gone on, while proper application of the dispute settlement procedures of the Code to the EC ban remain in dispute.[92]

3. GATT Subsidies Code
The cost of compliance with new environmental standards and regulations involves problems, particularly for countries or industries that find it difficult to finance necessary technology. Currently, some government

subsidies to domestic industry might be considered as "unfair trading practise" under the GATT. This is because the Subsidies Code includes no definition of subsidies, and because its rules are based on the concept that government support to reduce industrial costs give domestic firms an unfair advantage in international trade and are subject to trade actions by other countries.

The vulnerability of environmental subsidies to countervail generally depends on whether they are linked to specific industries and cause injury to foreign producers of similar products.

Under a draft subsidies code that was being negotiated at the Uruguay Round, there would have been three tiers of subsidies: "red", "amber", and "green". Red subsidies would be banned as constituting unfair trading practices; amber-category subsidies would be permitted, subject to a countervailing duty; while green subsidies would be non-actionable. The draft code would consider a subsidy to be green and non-actionable if it constituted assistance to promote the "adaption of existing facilities to new environmental requirements imposed by law and/or regulations which result in greater constraints and financial burden on firms"; however, among other things, the subsidy would have to be a one-time, non-recurring measure, limited to 20% of the cost of compliance.[93]

In the latest version of the draft subsidies code, non-actionable environmental subsidies have been omitted, perhaps because of some opposition to a non-actionable category of subsidy.[94]

4. The GATT's Environmental Agenda
These are just some problems in the GATT that may leave it ill-equipped, in its present form, to deal with the growing number of environmentally related trade issues. The environment has not been on the table during the Uruguay Round negotiations and little work has been done within the GATT to strengthen certain aspects of the rules in Article XX and the Standards Code.

Among the issues at the Uruguay Round that would have environmental implications is that of reducing tariff and non-tariff barriers to tropical products. Environmentalists are concerned that this would reduce the cost of raw timber products and the revenue of the producer countries, thus increasing the exploitive pressures on tropical forests, and present GATT rules prohibit the use of import restrictions levied on the grounds of quantity.

Environmentalists are also concerned that the Round's stated goal of working toward harmonization of phytosanitary regulations will lead to an overall weakening of standards. Further discussion of the Standards Code revolves around a draft of a "proportionality principle", to test the validity of standards: trade-restrictive effects should be proportional to the legitimate objectives of the proposed regulation (protection of the environment, etc.). The need to base standards on scientific evidence is also more explicitly recognized.[95]

In July 1989, the GATT Council agreed to establish a Working Group on the Exports of Domestically Prohibited Goods and Other Hazardous Substances. This was largely in response to concern expressed by some developing countries at what they perceive as an increasing trend by industries and firms to export to Third World countries products that have been banned or restricted in domestic sale for reasons of health, safety or environmental protection.

Countries would be required to participate in a notification system for such products and the Group is working to complete a draft agreement which, when ready, will be presented to the GATT Council. While the Group's mandate was extended in December 1990, there had been no decision, as of March 1992, on the export of domestically prohibited goods. Any agreement that is finally reached will undoubtedly have trade implications.

At the December 1990 contracting parties' session, Switzerland made a statement on behalf of the EFTA member countries, suggesting that the GATT should begin studying the inter-relationship of trade and environmental policy. A proposal for the reactivation of the 1971 Group on Environmental Measures and International Trade was offered by Austria (again on behalf of the EFTA countries) at the GATT Council meeting in February 1991. This Group met for the first time in November, 1991 and has agreed to focus on three issues: package labelling; transparency; and the relationship between the GATT and existing international environmental agreements.

5. *The GATT Under Attack*

Recently, the ruling of the GATT Panel in the tuna/dolphin dispute led some to label the GATT as being "anti" the environment. The preliminary ruling provoked swift and hostile reactions in the United States over such questions as US.sovereignty in enforcing its environmental laws and maintaining its self-defined role as a leader in international environmental stewardship.[96]

This backlash has led to proposals that the US change international trading rules unilaterally to protect its ability to enforce its environmental laws, regardless of their effects on trade. The idea threatens to undermine multilateral trading rules generally.

On October 30, 1991, Senator Max Baucus, chair of the trade subcommittee, introduced his "New Trade Initiative".[97] It calls for creation of an *Environmental Code* in the GATT, modelled on the current Subsidies Code. He suggests that, under it, each nation should be allowed to set its own environmental standards; be permitted to ban or curb imports of goods produced in a manner that violates internationally recognized norms "such as tuna taken by drift net fishing"; and should be able to impose trade sanctions to enforce international environmental agreements.[98]

Senator Baucus also proposed imposition of *offset duties*. If imported products (or the processes used to produce those products) do not meet the importing nation's environmental standards, duties could be applied to the imported product, provided the following criteria are met: that the environmental protection standards being applied have a sound scientific basis; and that the same standards be applied to all competitive domestic production. The offsetting duties would be set at a level sufficient to offset any economic advantage gained by producing the product under less stringent environmental production regulations.[99]

Widespread support for similar protection for US industry has led to introduction of the *International Pollution Deterrence Act of 1991*, sponsored by Senator David Boren.[100] The Boren bill cites the burden on US industries posed by US environmental laws, and the resulting competitive disadvantage they suffer.[101] It seeks to capture environmental degradation as a cost in the production process by allowing the imposition of countervailing duties on imports from countries that do not impose strict environmental standards. The bill would use the proceeds of the countervailing duties to finance transfer or sale of pollution and control equipment to developing countries, and create a fund to help US companies develop new environmental technologies.[102]

While this legislation has been praised in the US as an innovative approach for dealing with environmental issues, it is important to note that the level playing field is a double-edged sword: lax environmental standards may give less developed countries an unfair trade advantage but this kind of proposal shows clearly why third-world nations fear that the industrial world will use its tougher health, safety, and environmental standards to erect non-tariff barriers to trade.

It is not surprising that the GATT approaches such proposals with cautious disapproval. Under existing GATT rules, it is very difficult to increase a country's tariffs on products originating in countries with less strict environmental polices. First, many tariffs are "bound" under the GATT and cannot be raised, except through an elaborate re-negotiation process. More important, however, such a tariff would violate the GATT's "most favoured nation" (MFN) principle.[103] Even those who would dismiss the relevance of current GATT rules in this debate might have reservations about opening the floodgates to any number of barriers to trade.

Meanwhile, the European Community asked the GATT to put the tuna dispute on the agenda of the meeting of the GATT Council on February 18, 1991. The US Commerce Secretary had convinced the Mexican government not to press the panel decision at the GATT General Council meeting on October 8, 1991.[104] Mexico agreed to defer pursuit of its GATT victory indefinitely while the parties worked out a plan that would make Mexico's tuna harvesting less dangerous to dolphins. The GATT Council must formally adopt the report before the decision has legal force.

In January 1992, a US Federal Court decision extended the tuna ban to 20 other nations suspected of trans-shipping Mexican tuna.[105] The EC has the support of a number of non-European countries that asked the Council to adopt the panel report opposing the embargo.[106] The EC claims that the secondary embargo imposed by the US on so-called "dirty tuna" affected some 4 million ECUs in Community exports of tuna to the US.[107] Seventeen nations (the EC counted as one) spoke in the tuna debate, and all but the US and Mexico called for adoption of the report.

American and Mexican representatives at the Council meeting were convinced that their ongoing bilateral talks were the best way of resolving the dispute and said they were not ready to accept the GATT panel's preliminary finding. Recently, the two parties came to an agreement by which the Mexicans will amend their fishing laws to ensure that dolphins are protected; Mexico is committed to making the changes within two years. By 1994, there should be a total moratorium on fishing for yellow-fin tuna using the current nets.

However, the debate brought the issue of unilateralism to a head in the GATT. A spokesman for the European

Community issued a statement insisting that the panel report be adopted and threatening to launch its own complaint on the issue in the GATT. Moreover, the statement noted that, while the Community does not contest the validity of the US objective to protect dolphins, it did "oppose all unilateral action to impose US standards on third countries". The Commission said that "measures for the conservation of living resources including dolphins, should be agreed through multilateral work rather than through the unilateral setting of trade-restrictive conservation/ecological rules".

This viewpoint is consistent with the position of the GATT, set out in its Report of February 12, 1992, "Trade and Environment", which defended the panel's ruling and condemned the use of unilateral action. It argued that trade measures are, at best, inefficient ways to reach environmental goals and, at worst, are seen as the powerful rich countries forcing their values on small ones. It criticized the efforts of some countries to influence the environmental policies of others by taking unilateral trade measures, such as import bans, and also criticized countries that, in attempting to enable "clean" companies to compete, advocate duties on imports of products made in countries with lax, less costly environmental standards.

The GATT Report warned against "environmental imperialism",[108] and Arthur Dunkel, in promoting the report, expressed concern about "the risk of the issues of the environment being kidnapped by trade protectionist interests" through the unilateral imposition of special environmental duties.[109]

The report concluded that the GATT rules and dispute settlement procedures will not frustrate any country's efforts to improve *domestic* environmental standards, although they might frustrate unilateral "vigilante action" by one country against another. These comments and conclusions appear to be directed in support of the panel decision in the tuna/dolphin case.

6. A World Trade Organization (WTO)

In April 1990, Canada's International Trade Minister, John Crosbie, presented his counterparts in the GATT with a proposal to strengthen the global trading system by establishing a world trading organization. The WTO would provide an institutional framework to govern world trade after the Uruguay Round was successfully completed; it would manage the post-Round trade policy agenda and provide a formal structure for the GATT to administer all the agreements, especially because the Uruguay Round anticipated that the GATT would extend into new areas, such as investment and intellectual property.

The WTO would not change any of the GATT's substantive obligations, other existing agreements, or the Uruguay Round agreements. It would centre on reform of the GATT's dispute settlement system, including procedures for adopting and implementing the GATT panel findings and for establishing an appeal process. It is proposed that the WTO would also provide the institutional capacity and credibility for the new GATT trading system to engage in more sustained and effective co-operation with the International Monetary Fund and the International Bank for Reconstruction and Development.

Over time, the WTO might be granted the power to look at new issues, revise agreements, provide a forum for negotiating new rounds, and be an ongoing policy-making body with representatives from the contracting parties. This would provide the GATT with a way of dealing with new issues that have an impact on the environment, as they arise.

At present, the idea of establishing a WTO is in abeyance, pending the outcome of the Uruguay Round.

The Organization for Economic Cooperation and Development (OECD)

The OECD has a long history of dealing seriously with environmental concerns, notably during the early 1970s, when it pioneered the "polluter pays principle". Because

347

of its interdisciplinary character, the OECD is well placed to explore the various facets of the relationship between trade and the environment. Moreover, unlike the GATT, the OECD comprises 24 "like-minded" (industrialized) members. While it is very difficult to achieve consensus in the GATT, the OECD feels that it can provide the leadership necessary to have these issues considered at the highest levels.

The trade and environment program at the OECD started in 1988, based on a Swedish initiative supported by the EFTA countries and Canada. It was first discussed by the trade committee and focused on the impact of environmental policies on trade. Following the OECD Ministerial meeting of May 1990, the trade committee began a detailed study of issues that relate trade to the environment.[110] This initiative was taken, in large part, because of an increased fear that countries would use environmental measures unilaterally, as a means of protecting domestic markets. It also recognized that the basic GATT articles were drafted at a time when environmental concerns were virtually non-existent and, as a result, that the articles might not be adequate to deal with new developments.

In the autumn of 1990, at the suggestion of Canada and with the consensus of its members, the OECD's trade and environment committee began to work on these issues. Its aim was to produce a common analysis, requiring immediate attention, to be presented to ministers at the January 1991 OECD Environmental Ministerial meeting.

The agenda was expanded to include a detailed examination of the effects of trade on the environment, including the environmental effects of free trade agreements. The issue was taken up in the Communiqué that followed the January meeting. The two committees were given directions to examine all the elements in the relationship between trade and the environment, with a view to presenting an analysis to the OECD ministers at the time of the OECD Ministerial Meeting in June 1991, at which time the joint work was endorsed and suggestions were made for further areas of analysis. The aim was to draw up guidelines on protecting the environment while preserving the open multilateral trading system.

During the summer of 1991, the Trade Committee focused on the trade ramifications of environmental policies in those few areas where those effects were likely to be most severe. Included were environmental policies (such as environmental standards not covered by the Standards Code) which, because of the use or misuse of trade instruments, re-introduce a certain degree of protectionist discrimination against foreign products - discrimination that, in principle, had been eliminated in earlier liberalization processes. Another area on which the Trade Committee has focused its analysis is in the attempt, by some countries, to influence environmental policies in third countries, through the manipulation of import or export measures. There is a general sense in the Committee that unilateral measures that impede trade are far more dangerous than those that result from international agreements, whether or not restrictive trade measures in such agreements would violate the GATT.

Meanwhile, the Environment Committee examined a number of issues, including the environmental effects of free trade agreements. Its aim is to develop criteria to decide when environmental measures are protectionist and when they serve legitimate environmental purposes. Studies under way in the summer of 1991 included the effects of trade on the environment in sectors such as forestry, agriculture, energy, transportation, fisheries, endangered species, and hazardous materials.

In the fall of 1991, the OECD created a group made up of joint experts on trade and the environment. As of March 1992, there had been five joint sessions of these experts. In order to participate effectively in this process, the US added two observers to its delegation, one from business and one from environmental non-governmental organizations (ENGOs). While this move has not been wholeheartedly supported by all members, to date, there have been no reported instances of environmental observers abusing their positions by misusing information.

The OECD is using its Guiding Principles Concerning the International Economic Aspects of Environmental Policies of 1972 as a base for developing its new set of principles. However, they must be reviewed and updated, if they are to be relevant to the current trade and environment debate. By the time of the May 1992 ministerial meeting, work had progressed to the point where the OECD was able to declare that:

"...trade and environmental policies can be mutually supportive in the pursuit of sustainable development, particularly if those policy interventions which have negative trade and environmental impacts are removed and if environmental benefits and costs are internalised into national and international prices. OECD governments will give priority to pursuing further analytical work and discussion with a view to developing appropriate guidelines for submission to Ministers, as soon as possible, for the improvement of the compatibility of environment and trade policies, and to ensuring that environmental regulations and environment-related trade measures do not operate as disguised barriers to trade."[111]

The G-7 Summit Process

A further international institutional network relevant to managing the current array of trade-environment issues is the Group of Seven major industrial democracies and the European Community.[112] Although the G-7 system is centred on the annual summit of the heads of state and government of the eight members, its work is supported by institutionalized meetings of the members' ministers responsible for trade, foreign policy, finance, and, possibly, the environment.

Although the seven-power summit was conceived and

launched in 1975 as an economic institution, the summit system has readily taken up and highlighted the modern challenges to the global environment.[113] The summit first dealt with the trade-environment issue directly at the 1989 Paris summit. There the heads noted in their concluding Declaration that:

> "Environmental protection is integral to issues such as trade...Therefore, environmental considerations must be taken into account in economic decision-making."[114]

At Houston the following year they called for the OECD to accelerate the work they had assigned previously on integrating the economy and the environment.

At their London summit in July 1991, the leaders of the G-7 provided direction on where (and, thus, implicitly how) they wanted the definition of a new trade-environment regime to proceed. In an unprecedented inclusion of the environment as part of their review of the global trade system, the heads devoted an entire paragraph to trade and the environment. In it, they commended the OECD's "pioneering work in ensuring that trade and environment policies are mutually supporting." They also instructed the GATT "to define how trade measures can properly be used for environmental purposes".[115]

The work on trade-environment links was taken up by the summit's trade ministers at their quadrilateral meetings in September 1991 and April 1992.[116] Despite the lack of environmental representation on the "quad", its make-up - four principals sharing fundamentally similar conditions (and, therefore, interests) - make it an appropriate institutional setting for considering the complex relationship between trade and the environment.

Moreover, its small size, major power structure, and the politico-economic similarities between quad members enable it to reach effective consensus with relative ease; its critical contribution comes from its ability to energize and establish the direction for the OECD and the GATT. If the quad reaches consensus on an issue, the consensus can be taken to the OECD and transformed into an acceptable OECD consensus; in light of the importance of an OECD consensus in the GATT, the quad can thereby provide important input into the GATT process.

The trade-environment relationship was addressed by the quad for the first time in 1991. At the September 1991 meeting in Angers, the EC produced a paper on trade and the environment, and asked that it be put on the agenda for discussion. Canada and the US agreed, on condition that it not distract attention from their priority subject of the badly overdue completion of a successful Uruguay Round. In fact, the latter left little time for the ministers to deal with the trade-environment question.

At the next quad meeting, in April 1992, the Japanese hosts returned to the issue with an agenda item, a paper, and a desire to have the group endorse a set of principles for defining the trade-environment relationship. The ministers took up the issue in a discussion centred on the acceptability of unilateralism and various forms of multilateralism to shape the trade-environment relationship.

While the Japanese did not secure a formal endorsement of their principles, the meeting succeeded in lessening tensions that has arisen among the G-7 members as a result of unilateral action by some of them, and helped define a cooperative approach they would utilize as the foundation for work in the OECD and the GATT. It is possible that further progress of a similar sort could be made at the next quad meeting, to be hosted by Canada, probably in the autumn of 1992.

Most recently, the environment ministers of the G-7 joined their trade colleagues in collectively addressing the trade-environment issue. The G-7 environment ministers met for the first time in Bonn, on May 16-17 1992, primarily to review their approach to issues at the United Nations Conference on Environment and Development in June 1992.

During the course of their deliberations, they dealt with several trade-environment issues, within a broader context than the heads and trade ministers had employed. The environment ministers dealt with the role of trade and investment as a supplement to Official Development Assistance in financing sustainable development in the developing countries; the advantages of a concerted, rather than differential, adoption of carbon taxes among G-7 countries; the need for integration between the trade and environment communities after the Uruguay Round; the value of integrating environmental concerns in NAFTA; the need to preserve trade in the products of sustainably managed forests; and the inclusion of trade-related measures in any convention on forests.

Conclusion

The United Nations Conference on the Environment and Development, held in Brazil in June 1992, signalled a global recognition of the truism that "pollution knows no borders" and that some environmental issues must be dealt with on the global stage. Therefore, the frustration of some countries with the historical failure of the multilateral trading regime to embrace environmental imperatives is understandable. While the environment is likely to be on the agenda at the next round of Gatt negotiations, it could be years before there are any substantive changes that incorporate environmental considerations into the international trading rules. Moreover, international agreements, endorsed by the GATT tuna-dolphin panel as the appropriate means of addressing common environmental problems, also takes years to negotiate.

Many domestic constituencies understand the urgency of the modern environmental agenda and want to do the right thing, now. However, countries should avoid the temptation to impose environmentally-motivated tariffs and other restrictions in a trading context that is moving towards open markets - they must be careful not to build new barriers when it has taken so long to dismantle old ones. Certainly less developed countries would have legitimate concerns if the industrialized world could impose strict production standards on its trading partners. The environmental threats and the allocation of resources to promote individual agendas for economic growth are very different in the developing world. Nevertheless, there appears to be a growing understanding of the issue and a growing consensus that a solution must be found to the problems that arise when international trade policy and antional environmental policies collide. In the meantime, it is clear that those countries with a history of high standrds at home are best equipped to avoid the threat of green protectionism and to open up new markets abroad.

The Canadian government's policy of moving towards regional free-trade blocs is established. Given Canada's historic reliance on exports for its economic well-being, maintaining existing markets and taking full advantage of increasingly liberal trade rules is critical to sustaining and increasing Canadian prosperity.

One area where economic opportunities clearly exist is in the development, manufacturing and marketing of technologies that foster environmental responsibility. The theme of the environmentally-sensitive marketplace as a cornerstone of future competitiveness has been ambraced by Canada's G-7 partners, Germany and Japan, and is gaining an audience in some circles in the US. Canadian policy makers now, and in the future, would be well advised to act upon this reality.

References

1. In 1973-74 the Canadian asbestos industry produced 1.7 million tons of asbestos and exported 800,000 tons to the US. In 1990 it produced 665,000 tons, of which only 60,000 tons were exported to the US.

2. GENERAL AGREEMENT ON TARIFFS AND TRADE (1992) *International Trade 90-91* Vol 1, p.25 (Geneva).

3. REINSTEIN, R A (1991) "Trade and Environment" draft paper, p.20 (Washington, DC).

4. GATT *supra* note 2, pp.19-20.

5. See MACNEILL, JIM (1991) "The Growth Imperative, Sustainable Development, Environment and Trade: Issues for IPC's Consideration" paper presented at the IIASA Program on Trade and Environment, April 24-25, pp.7-11.

6. *ibid* p.8.

7. *ibid* p.7.

8. SENATE OF CANADA (1984) *Soil and Risk: Canada's Eroding Future* (Ottawa: Government of Canada).

9. THE WORLD COMMISSION ON ENVIRONMENT AND DEVELOPMENT (1987) *Our Common Future* (Oxford: Oxford University Press). It is important to note, however, that resources that are considered to be "renewable" (such as forests and agricultural lands) are only renewable in theory. That is, countries must make the effort (and incur the cost) to renew (e.g. reforestation). This does not always happen.

10. For example, throughout the 1980s the world's forests were being harvested at the rate of 17 million hectares per

year. The most striking reduction of forest area occurred in the tropical and equatorial regions. Such rapid deforestation has both ecological and economic consequences. Ecologically, it is widely believed that the "greenhouse effect" (global warming) springs from the release of elevated levels of CO_2 into the atmosphere as a result of the burning of fossil fuels, and the cutting and burning of large areas of forest. Moreover, the loss of forests, particularly tropical forests, reduces the genetic diversity of the world's ecosystems. In economic terms, it is estimated that the export value of forestry exports to the developing world is $7 billion per year to the 33 countries that currently export tropical timber. It is estimated that by the year 2000, at the current rate of deforestation, only 10 countries will remain net exporters of tropical timber and the total value of these exports will have declined to $2 billion per annum. See INSTITUTE FOR RESEARCH ON PUBLIC POLICY (1991) "UNCED and North/South Issues: The Role for the national Round Table" January 28, pp.7-8.

11. For example, in 1983-4 in the Sahel regions of Africa there was widespread drought and hunger. However, the area produced record amounts of cotton, harvesting 154 million tons at a time when world cotton prices were falling (this was up from 22.7 million tons in 1961-2). During the same period it reported a record 1.77 million tons of cereals. The fact that farmers who can grow cotton cannot grow enough food to feed themselves suggests that cash crops are getting too much attention and food crops too little. (*supra* note 9, p.68).

12. In 1980 only 39% of all Third World exports of manufactured goods were ready for final use, while 43% of total exports were unprocessed. *ibid* p.214.

13. *ibid* p.80.

14. *ibid* p.29.

15. On April 30, 1992, the Ontario budget implemented a tax of 10 cents per can, to be levied on aluminium beer cans. While the government of Ontario has introduced the tax as an "environmental tax" in order to encourage people to drink beer out of bottles, which are re-usable, rather than cans, which are only recyclable, the tax has generated heated opposition from Canadian aluminium and can producers, American beer producers and unions. Opponents of the tax claim that it is, in fact, a barrier to trade cloaked as an environmental initiative, because the majority of US beer imported into Canada is sold in cans, whereas most domestic beer in Ontario is sold in bottles. This new tax would increase the cost of a case of 24 cans of beer by $2.40 and, according to the director of human resources and communication for Ball Packaging Products, a Burlington-based can producer, would bring about a 50% drop in canned beer consumption. See STRAUSS, MARINA (1992) "Industry foaming over beer can tax" *Globe and Mail* May 22.

16. Some contend that one example of such behaviour is the James Bay Hydro Electric Project (Phase I) and the proposed Phase II. Under Phase I, large tracts of land around James Bay were flooded in order to provide hydro-electric power - some for export and some for domestic use such as aluminium smelters on the North Shore of the St Lawrence. The social, economic and environmental degradation associated with the flooding affected the fish, the wildlife, the climate, and the socio-economic conditions of the indigenous native population of the region. Thus the economic benefits for the North Shore came with environmental costs. The St Lawrence River has been affected by increased levels of toxins, such as PCBs, and the aluminium is exported in a semi-processed state to the US and Europe. Critics argue that Phase II of the James Bay project involves new smelters built at a subsidized rate, further flooding in northern Québec and attendant environmental problems, both in the flooded region and at

the site of the smelters.

17. STATISTICS CANADA (1990) *Canada 1990 An International Business Comparison* (Ottawa).

18. GOVERNMENT OF CANADA "North American Free Trade: Securing Canada's Growth Through Trade" (Ottawa: External Affairs and International Trade Canada).

19. All tables taken from STATISTICS CANADA *supra* note 17.

20. Within the industry the breakdown is as follows: Motor Vehicle Assembly = 53,000; Truck Bodies = 20,900; Parts = 73,000; Fabrics = 8,900.

21. GOVERNMENT OF CANADA (1990) "Forests of Canada: The Federal Role" Report of the Standing Committee on Forestry and Fisheries (Ottawa) November, p.2.

22. *ibid* p.10.

23. SHRYBMAN, STEVEN (1990) "Selling the Environment Short: An environmental assessment of the first two years of free trade between Canada and the United States" p.7 (Toronto: Canadian Environmental Law Association).

24. The following is transcribed from a BCTV News Hour Broadcast, September 28, 1990:
"And there is another threat to the BC forest industry: environmentalists in Europe are threatening a boycott of BC lumber because of logging practices here. The provincial government has sent top forestry officials to Europe to try to head off the movement which views BC clear-cut logging policies as worse than methods employed in the rainforests of Brazil. It's feared that such a boycott could have the same effect as the one that devastated the sealskin industry in eastern Canada."
The following appeared on page B1 of the *Globe and Mail*

on April 8, 1991 in an article entitled "Forest industry fearful of boycott, critical film stirs flap in Europe":

"Fears of a boycott are growing since last month's airing on German prime time television of a Vancouver-made film that called British Columbia the 'Brazil of the North' ... Federal Forests Minister Frank Oberle ... has seen the film called 'A Paradise Despoiled'. He said that, in effect, it told viewers that by buying Canadian forest products, they are helping to destroy the planet."

25. British Columbia possesses 38% of the 24 billion cubic metres of standing timber in Canada *supra* note 21, p.9.

26. "Forestry industry fearful of boycott" *supra* note 25, p.B2.

27. Figures taken from THE MINING ASSOCIATION OF CANADA (1990) "Mining in Canada: Facts and Figures".

28. Goods and services suppliers in Ontario's EPI report average annual growth rates of 17% and currently provide over $2 billion output annually. The BC EPI has annual sales exceeding $100 million. See also GOVERNMENT OF ONTARIO (1990/91) "Europe 1992 and the Ontario Environmental Protection Industry" A Report prepared for the Ontario Ministry of Industry, Trade and Technology. (Toronto).

29. In export earnings, tourism was behind only motor vehicles ($24 billion) and automobile parts ($10.8 billion).

30. TOURISM CANADA (1991) *Canadian Tourism Facts* (Ottawa: Industry, Science and Technology Canada, Research Directorate) February, p.2.

31. TOURISM CANADA (1986) *US Pleasure Travel Market - Canadian Potential: Highlights Report* (Ottawa) January.

32. D'AMORE, L J (1978) "The Significance of Tourism to Canada" *Business Quarterly* (London, Ontario: The School of Business Administration, University of Western Ontario) Autumn, p.1.

33. WORLD WILDLIFE FUND (1990) *Ecotourism: The Potentials and Pitfalls* in TIOSAVIJEVIC, NATASHA "Ecotourism: Travel plus Ecology" *Financial Post* November 8, p.14.

34. PATTERSON, BRUCE (1991) "Ecotourism" *Environment* April, pp.37-38.

35. See, for example, STEVEN SHRYBMAN (1988) "Selling Canada's Environment Short" (Toronto: Canadian Environmental Law Association) August. This analysis was endorsed by over 90 Canadian environmental groups.

36. *ibid* p.19.

37. From an environmental perspective, see STEVEN SHRYBMAN (1988) *supra* note 24.

38. The Chapter 19 BDSM affects anti-dumping and countervailing duty laws and cases. Its provisions are temporary (5 years) pending the development of a substitute system of rules in both countries for anti-dumping and countervailing duties as applied to their bilateral trade. The FTA does not alter the substance of existing anti-dumping and countervailing duty laws. A Binational Panel Review will only be invoked if a Party proposes to amend an anti-dumping or countervailing duty "statute" or to resolve disputes involving final anti-dumping and countervailing duty determinations as a substitute for judicial review. As of the summer of 1991, there had been nine (9) cases that invoked the Chapter 19 process, none of which dealt with the environment.

39. For a complete examination of the Free Trade Dispute

Settlement Mechanism see McDorman, Ted (1989) "The Dispute Settlement Regime of the Free Trade Agreement" *Review of International Business Law* Vol 2.

40. The Commission is established by Article 1802 and is charged with the responsibility to supervise the implementation of the Agreement, to oversee its further elaboration, to resolve disputes over its interpretation and application, to review its functioning at least once a year, and to consider any other matter that may affect its operation.

41. Armand de Mestral was involved with the Third UN Conference on the Law of the Sea. He was a consultant to UNEP in 1977-78 and has written extensively on international law, including pollution of the marine environment. Frank Stone (deceased) was the Economic Minister and Deputy Head of the Canadian Permanent Mission to the UN in Geneva (1973-77), responsible for Canadian interests in international organizations concerned with trade, economic and environmental issues. In the early 1970s he was seconded to Environment Canada where he coordinated the Canadian side of the negotiations, which led to the 1972 Canada-US Agreement on Great Lakes Water Quality.

42. This rarely occurs because diplomatic pressure usually prevails to ensure that a panel's report is adopted but, in some cases, this has not happened and, in many cases, adoption is delayed by excuses, such as a need to study the ruling or that the party still wants to find a negotiated settlement.

43. *In the Matter of Canada's Landing Requirement for Pacific Coast Salmon and Herring* Final Report of the Panel, October 16, 1989.

44. *ibid* p.30.

45. Under the negotiated settlement, Canada allowed up to 25% of salmon and herring caught in BC to be transported directly to the US in return for the remainder of British Columbia salmon and herring remaining subject to verification and sampling at sea, aboard Canadian tender vessels licensed and equipped for direct exports.

46. *Lobsters from Canada* USA 89-1807-01, Final Report of the Panel, May 25, 1990.

47. One of the arguments of the Canadian government was that mature Canadian lobsters are inherently smaller than those caught in the US because of the lower water temperatures.

48. McDORMAN, TED (1990) "Dissecting the Free Trade Agreement Lobster Panel Decision" August, p.12.

49. BUSH, GEORGE (1992) Remarks at US-Mexico Environmental Border Plan Meeting, Los Angeles, February 25, in "The Environment and Free Trade with Mexico" US Dept of State Dispatch, March 2.

50. See, for example, Mr Barrett (Esquimault-Juan de Fuca) before the House of Commons Committee, March 19, 1991:
"Now that raises the question about domestic pressure to lower our standards so we can keep our jobs here in Canada. If I am a politician, I represent British Columbia and Mexico is producing pulp and paper [that] we are buying and they are producing it at much lower costs because they have lower environmental standards [] what do we do with the clamour here at home to lower our environmental standards so we can compete with that product?... Are we prepared to file petitions ... ensuring that any competitive product coming in from Mexico at least meets our minimum standards so that

we are playing on a level playing field? Are we prepared
to do that to protect Canadian industries who must meet
Canadian laws? ... what is the government's position on
maintaining Canadian standards, and at the same time,
putting ourselves at risk because of someone else's lower
standards; for example, the State of California said no
automobiles come into California without proper emission
control standards so everyone had to conform to sell in
that market; now if the State of California can do it, can
we do it here?"

51. Countries other than the US, including Canada, are
now participating in the program.

52. For example, as emission standards have become
more stringent in the southern US states, industry from
California is relocating to the maquiladora. Specifically,
furniture and woodworking manufacturers who use
solvent-based stains and lacquers are relocating as the Los
Angeles district aims to virtually eliminate the substances
altogether by 1996. The solvent-based coatings produce
ozone smog through photosynthesis and were responsible
for 3% of all hydrocarbons sent into the air above the Los
Angeles basin before 1988. See KRAUL, CHRIS (1990) "A
Warmer Climate for Furniture Makers" *Los Angeles Times*
May 14, p.D1.
Salaries range from $2.90 per day - see KOCHAN, LESLIE
"The Maquiladoras and Toxics: The Hidden Costs of
Production South of the Border" - to $6.50 per day - see
NAZARIO, SONIA (1989) "Boom and Despair" *Wall Street
Journal* Sept 22 p.B26 - for workers in the Maquiladoras
compared with the average hourly wage for a skilled
Mexican worker of approximately $3.20 per hour and
nearly $19 per hour for a skilled worker in Ontario -
MORTON, PETER (1991) "Enviro-talks begun: Mexico"
Financial Post March 25, p.10.

53. NATIONAL WILDLIFE FEDERATION (1990) "Environmental Concerns Related to a US-Mexico-Canada Free Trade Agreement" (Washington, DC: National Wildlife Federation) Nov 27, p.5.

54. INVESTMENT CANADA (1990) "Canada-US-Mexico Free Trade Negotiations: The Rationale and the Investment Dimension" (Ottawa) Dec, pp.15-16.

55. Among the industrial sectors that have experienced particularly strong expansion in the number of maquiladora factories are automotive accessories (+290%), electrical and electronics industries (+51%), and metal products (+44%). It is estimated that approximately 200 auto parts manufacturers have established maquiladora facilities, which produce mostly labour-intensive, low technology components. GM, Ford and Chrysler have established approximately 42 plants in the maquiladora region. See DEPARTMENT OF FINANCE, CANADA (1990) "Canada and a Mexico-United States Trade Agreement" Working Paper, July, p.10.

56. For example, the border town of Juarez, with over 300 maquiladora plants and a population that has increased from 700,000 in 1980 to 1.2 million in 1988 has no sewage treatment system and no near-by, state-of-the-art hazardous waste disposal facilities - KOCHAN, LESLIE *supra* note 53, p.12.

57. Per capita spending on environmental protection in $US between Mexico (SEDUE) and the US (EPA):

1989	EPA budget per person	$20.80
	SEDUE budget per person	$00.08
1990	EPA budget per person	$21.60
	SEDUE budget per person	$00.20
1991	EPA budget per person	$24.40
	SEDUE budget per person	$00.48

Source: Congressional Research Service, based on

information obtained from the EPA - in DARLING, JUANITA ET AL (1991) "Can Mexico Clean up its Act?" *Los Angeles Times* Nov 17, p.1.

58. For example, in 1991 Mexico hired 100 inspectors to help enforce environmental rules, posting 50 in Mexico City and 50 at the border. That brought the number available to monitor the entire nation's factories to 255 - i.e. roughly the same number fielded by the South Coast Air Quality Management District, which regulates air quality in four counties in the Los Angeles area. In 1992 Mexico expects to hire another 100 inspectors, bringing the total along the border to 200. *ibid*

59. DEPARTMENT OF FINANCE, CANADA *supra* note 58, p.7

60. "The administration has turned a blind eye to issues raised by a NAFTA contending that international trade and the environment are not related" in BURROWS, BETH AND DURBIN, ANDREA (1991) "Fast Track: Trading Away Food-Safety and Environmental Rules" *The Seattle Times* April 24, p.A7. In March 1991, the Mexican Minister of Commerce, Jaime Serra Puche, responded to the question of whether his government thinks issues such as "fair" wages and pollution control should be a part of the trade negotiations, as follows:
"What we'll have in the negotiation is trade issues; that is, flows of goods and services, investment issues and intellectual property. That will be the scope of the agreement"
see "Mexicans discover politics of trade" *The Globe and Mail* March 26, 1991, p.B8.

61. CHAREST, JEAN (1991) - the Minister of the Environment was speaking at the Plenary Session of the National Round Table on the Environment and the Economy, May 25, in Banff. Although "trade-related environmental concerns" were not defined, it is likely that this refers to

the inclusion of provisions such as the exceptions contained in the Gatt Article XX in the agreement.

62. This included sending them documents with the following:
   "Every US environmental law, including standards for pesticides, could be challenged as a non-tariff trade barrier if Congress fails to revoke the fast-track process for the North American Free Trade agreement sought by the Bush Administration."
Press Conference, "Fast Track Process for Trade Agreement Threatens Environmental Laws, Groups Warn" reported in *International Trade Reporter* Vol 8/19, May 2, 1991, p.698.

63. The complaint charged that USTR is a federal agency subject to the *National Environmental Policy Act*, which requires Environmental Impact Statements on major federal actions that significantly affect the quality of the human environment. On Jan 7, 1992, the US District Court for the District of Columbia (*Public Citizen v USTR* No 91-1916) dismissed the complaint for lack of standing. An appeal is expected.

64. Measures announced at the same time included a Draft Integrated Environmental Plan, aimed at cleaning up pollution along the US-Mexico border.

65. 86% of US industries have abatement costs of 2% or less. USTR (1991) "Review of US-Mexico Environment Issues" prepared by an inter-agency task force coordinated by the Office of the USTR (Washington DC) Oct, p.136.

66. For example, Ford has made the following announcement:
   "Though not required by Mexican law or regulation, Ford's policy is that Ford environmental practices in the US also be applied at our Mexican maquiladora facilities."

in FORD MOTOR COMPANY (1991) "Environmental Practices, Health and Safety Standards and Employee Welfare at Ford Motor Company's Maquiladora Facilities in Mexico" (Detroit) March 19, p.4.

67. "Special Report: NAFTA" *International Trade Reporter* Vol 9/2, Jan 8, p.82.

68. Maude Barlow of the Council of Canadians in HART, MICHAEL (1990) *A North American Free Trade Agreement, The Strategic Implications for Canada* (Centre for Trade Policy and Law/Institute for Research on Public Policy) p.9.

69. Among other things, this new law requires all toxic wastes from the 1,400 or so maquiladoras to be returned to their country of origin for disposal. EPA records on wastes shipped back from Mexico, however, account for only a fraction of the chemical debris of the border plants. In November 1988, for example, the Mexican Environmental Protection Agency (SEDUE) issued a regulation requiring all industries, including maquiladoras, using toxic chemicals, to register with the government and submit monthly reports on waste production. See TOMASO, BRUCE AND ALM, RICHARD (1990) "Economy vs Ecology: Mexico's Drive for Growth Eclipses Concerns about Toxic Waste from Border Plants" *Transboundary Resources Report* Vol 4/1 (University of New Mexico. School of Law) Spring, p.3.

70. DON CAMPBELL, Deputy Minister for International Trade and Associate Under Secretary of State for External Affairs, to the House of Commons Committee in response to questions from Mr Barrett (Esquimault-Juan de Fuca) March 1991.

71. THE WORLD COMMISSION ON ENVIRONMENT AND DEVELOPMENT *supra* note 9.

72. GOVERNMENT OF CANADA (1990) *Canada's Green Plan* (Ottawa: Minister of Supply and services) pp.123-129.

73. See, for example, DON CAMPBELL *supra* note 71.

74. See KATZ, ABRAHAM (1992) *New York Times* Jan 19, Section 4, p.5.

75. "Special Report: NAFTA *International Trade Reporter* Jan 8, 1992, Vol 9/2 p.82.

76. For example, TransAlta Utilities is currently testing a low NOX and CO_2 burner that produces reduced quantities of sulphur and would allow for the "clean" burning of coal.

77. EXTERNAL AFFAIRS AND INTERNATIONAL TRADE CANADA (1989) "The European Community: A Canadian Perspective" *Canadian Foreign Policy Series* Sept.

78. The 12 EC member states are Belgium, Denmark, France, Germany, Greece, Ireland, Italy, Luxembourg, The Netherlands, Portugal, Spain and the UK.

79. European deputies take their parliamentary seats on the basis of political groups rather than nationality. Following the election in June 1989, there were 3 members of the Green Party from Belgium, 8 from Germany, i from Spain, 8 from France, 7 from Italy, 2 from The Netherlands and 1 from Portugal.

80. Each country's voting rights are weighted according to their size. Germany, France, Italy and the UK have 10 votes each, Spain has 8, Belgium, Greece, The Netherlands and Portugal have 5 each, Denmark and Ireland 3 each and Luxembourg has 2.

81. 81 each from Germany, France, Italy and the UK, 60 from Spain, 25 from The Netherlands, 24 each from

Belgium, Greece and Portugal, 16 from Denmark, 15 from Ireland and 6 from Luxembourg.

82. It should be noted that trade disputes within the EC go to the EJC, while trade disputes with nations outside the EC go to the GATT.

83. *EC Commission v Denmark* (Case 302/86, (1989) 2 CEC 167.

84. As recognised by the EJC in *Cassis de Dijon* (1979) ECR 649, p.662 para8.

85. Currently, there is legislation pending in Germany that will create an almost identical problem and will likely end up at the European Court. If the legislation is applied it will require that packaging be returned to the manufacturer. This will inevitably act as a barrier to trade as it will serve to complicate the chain of transmission of goods and increase the cost to the exporter/manufacturer. Using the test set out in the *Danish Bottle Case*, that it is permitted to introduce environmental laws that effectively constrain free trade as long as the level of environmental protection is reasonable, it is likely that the Court would rule in favour of the Germans.

86. Information for this section was taken primarily from GOVERNMENT OF ONTARIO (1990/91) "Europe 1992 and the Ontario Environmental Protection Industry".

87. Environmental issues were absent from the concerns of the UN system at its birth and were taken up in a serious way only a quarter of a century later with the creation of the UN Environmental Program (UNEP). Although UNEP, The UN Conference on Trade and development (UNCTAD) and, most recently, the UN Conference on Environment and Development (UNCED) have moved to address trade-environment issues, their contribution to the debate has

thus far been limited. They are therefore dealt with only in passing in this paper.

88. GATT *supra* note 2.

89. Article XX(b) was intended to protect "quarantine and other sanitary regulations" in 1947. The environment was not an issue, and the basic tenet of legal interpretation dictates that the meaning and application of a provision is to be determined by the intent of the parties at the time the agreement was concluded. There is no precise explanation of the original intention of the Contracting Parties with regard to the meaning of Article XX(g) in the negotiating history.

90. See *United States - Prohibition of Imports of Tuna Products from Canada* Report of the Panel, Dec 22, 19981, L/5198 and *Canada - Measures Affecting Exports of Unprocessed Herring and Salmon* Report of the Panel, Nov 20, 19987, L/6268.

91. Defined by the GATT Panel in a recent case as "no alternative measure less inconsistent with the GATT which [a country] could reasonably be expected to employ to achieve its health and policy objectives. " *Thailand - Restrictions on Importation of and Internal Taxes on Cigarettes* (1990).

92. For a detailed discussion of this case see HALPERN, ADRIAN RAFAEL (1989) "The US-EC Hormone Beef Controversy and the Standards Code: Implications for the Application of Health Regulations to Agricultural Trade" *North Carolina Journal of International Law & Commercial Regulation* * Vol 14, pp.135-155.

93. Text of Revised Subsidies Negotiating Draft *Inside US Trade* Special Report Sept 28, 1990, p.S-3.

94. CHARNOVITZ, STEVE (1992) "Trade Negotiations and the Environment" *Bureau of National Affairs Environmental Daily* (Washington DC) March 27.

95. SORSA, P (1991) "GATT and the Environment" Paper presented at a IISA Workshop on Trade and the Environment (Luxembourg) April 25-26.

96. WAXMAN (1991) "TV Monitor: Free Trade and the Environment" *Greenwire* Nov 22:
"... the tuna-dolphin decision is a worst case scenario come true. There will be pressures to repeal vital environmental laws if it's found to be in conflict with this little-known trade agreement...We are losing too much sovereignty, giving up too much control over things that are important to Americans, all in the name of free trade."

97.   Luncheon Address by Senator Max Baucus to the Institute for International Economics, Washington DC, October 30, 1991.

98.   *ibid*

99.   As part of his plan to penalize environmentally lax countries with tariffs that counter "ecological dumping" Senator Baucus used the example that "clear-cut timber from Canada, where laws are looser, would carry an import duty to offset the cost advantage that Canadian loggers enjoy." *ibid*

100. S.984, 102nd Congress, 1st Session, 1991.

101. *ibid* S.2, Section 2(5):
"moreover, US industry cannot reasonable be expected to incur increasing capital costs of compliance with environmental controls while its foreign competitors enjoy a substantial and widening competitive advantage as a

result of remaining unfettered by pollution obligations."
102. S.984, S.4, 16 USC s.1671e would be amended by adding new paragraphs (c), (d) and (e) directed at the use of proceeds from "Countervailing Duties Attributable to Lack of Effective Pollution Controls."

103. GATT (1992) "Trade and Environment" Draft Report (Geneva) Feb 12, p.17 fn.19.

104. This is ironic in light of the rumour circulating in some circles in Washington that: "... the Bush administration, which has long been a keen opponent and indifferent imposer of tuna-importing restrictions, first suggested to the Mexicans that they take America's dolphin provisions before the GATT. Embarrassing rumours for George Bush who, as the price for congressional support for a 'fast-track' bill this summer, has sworn that a North American free-trade agreement would not undermine American environmental standards" *The Economist* Oct 5, 1991, p.31.

105. On January 9,1992, a San Francisco Federal Court ruled that despite the GATT ruling, there should be strict rules against tuna imports caught under methods that also net dolphins. The Court ruled that the US government must bar roughly half of the 266,000 metric tons of tuna imported in the US and that Mexico and other countries were in violation of US laws. Mexico has said that its fishing regulations have been amended to make sure that dolphins are not swept up on fishing operations aimed at tuna.

106. These include: Argentina, India, Canada, Peru, Japan, Columbia, South Korea, New Zealand, Pakistan, EC and Hong Kong. *International Trade Reporter* Vol 9/13, March 25, 1992 p.524.

107. *International Trade Reporter* Vol 9/9, Feb 26,1992.

108. GATT Report *supra* note 2.

109. "GATT: Gains for the Environment come with Trade" *European Report* Feb 15, 1992 p.1

110. OECD Ministers Meeting Communiqué, May 13, 1990:
"Ministers welcome the progress made by the organization in the analysis of environmental issues, and call for a further broadening and deepening of its work in this area. This includes in particular... analysing the interlinkages between environmental and trade policies."

111. OECD (1992) Communiqué (Paris) May 19, para. 18.

112. The 7 country members are the US, Japan, Germany, France, Italy, Canada and the UK.

113. HESKINS, VALERIE (1990) "The Greening of the Summit: The Group of Seven Industrialized Democracies and the Environment Issue" (Toronto: Centre for International Studies, University of Toronto); KIRTON, JOHN (1990) "Sustainable Development at the Houston Economic Summit" Paper for NRTEE Foreign Policy Committee, Sept; MACNEILL, JIM, WINSEMIUS, PIETER AND YAKUSHIJI, TAIZO (1991) *Beyond Interdependence: The Meshing of the World's Economy and Earth's Ecology* (New York: Oxford University Press).

114. HAJNAL, PETER (1989) *The Seven Power Summit, Documents from the Summits of Industrialized Countries 1975-1989* (New York: Kraus International Publications) p.400.

115. LONDON ECONOMIC SUMMIT (1991) *Economic Declaration* para 15.

116. The Trade Ministers' Quadrilateral includes the Ministers of Japan, Canada, the US and the EC.

Bibliography

ARDEN-CLARKE, CHARLES (1991) "The General Agreement on Tariffs and Trade, Environmental Protection and Sustainable Development" World Wildlife Fund. Discussion Paper, June.

AUERBACH, STUART (1991) "Raising a Roar over a Ruling: Trade Pact Imperils Environmental Laws" *The Washington Post* October 1, p.D1.

BENEDICT, RICHARD ELLIOT (1991 "Ozone Diplomacy: New Directions" in *Safeguarding the Planet* (Cambridge Massachusetts: Harvard University Press).

BENNETT, TIMOTHY "Lessons for Mexico of the Canada-US Free Trade Agreement" Paper prepared for the International Forum: "Mexico's Trade Options in the Changing International Economy".

BERGEIJK, PETER A G (1991) "International Trade and the Environmental Challenge" *Journal of World Trade* Vol 25/6 December.

BOWES, ROBERT (1990) "Heritage and Economy at the Local Level: Building Public Participation in Sustainable Development" A Presentation to the Conference on Heritage Conservation and Sustainable Development (Ottawa: Heritage Canada) May 15.

BRINKHORST, LAURENS JAN (1989) "Environmental Policy in the European Communities" (Brussels: Commission of the European Communities, Directorate General XI) Summer.

BROCKWAY, R A (1990) "Testing and Certification in the New Europe" (Brussels: Commission of the European Communities, Directorate General for Internal Market and Industrial Affairs) November.

BURROWS, BETH AND ANDREA DURBIN (1991) "Fast Track: Trading Away Food-Safety and Environmental Rules" *The Seattle Times* April 24, p.A7.

BUSINESS COUNCIL ON NATIONAL ISSUES (1992) "Business Principles for a Sustainable and Competitve Future" (Ottawa) May.

BUSINESS COUNCIL ON NATIONAL ISSUES (1992) "Towards a Sustainable and Competitive Future" (Ottawa) May.

CANADA-US FREE TRADE PANEL DECISION (1989) *In the Matter of Canada's Landing Requirement for Pacific Coast Salmon and Herring* Final Report of the Panel, October 16.

CANADA-US FREE TRADE PANEL DECISION (1990) *Lobsters from Canada* Final Report of the Panel, May 25.

CARRILLO, JORGE (1989) "Tranformaciones en la Industria Maquiladora de Exportacion", in BERNANRDO GONZALEZ-ARECHIGA AND ROCIO BARAJAS ESCAMILLA (Eds), *Las Maquiladoras: Ajuste Estructural y Desarrollo Regional* (Tijuana, Mexico: El Colegio de la Frontera Norte - Funcacion Friedreich Ebert).

CHARNOVITZ, STEVE (1991) "Exploring the Environmental Exceptions in GATT Article XX" *Journal of World Trade* Vol.25/5, October.

CHARNOVITZ, STEVE (1992) "Trade Negotiations and the Environment" *Bureau of National Affairs Environmental Daily* Washington, March 27.

COMMISSION OF THE EUROPEAN COMMUNITIES (1990) "Environmental Policy in the European Community", *European Documentation* (Luxembourg: Office for Official Publications of the European Communities).

COMMISSION OF THE EUROPEAN COMMUNITIES (1990) "The European Community   and Environmental Protection", *European File* April.

COMMISSION OF THE EUROPEAN COMMUNITIES (1990)   "The Institutions of the European Community" *European File*.

COMMISSION OF THE EUROPEAN COMMUNITIES (1988)   "The Removal of Technical Barriers to Trade" *European File* November.

CURZON PRICE, VICTORIA (1987)   *Free Trade Areas, The European Experience. What Lessons for Canadian-US Trade Liberalization* (Scarborough Ontario: C D Howe Institute).

D'AMORE, L J (1978) "The Significance of Tourism to Canada", *Business Quarterly* Canada's Management Journal (London: School of Business Administration of the University of Western Ontario) Autumn.

DARLING, JUANITA (1991) "Tuna Turnabout: Mexico Announces a Dolphin Protection Plan" *Los Angeles Times* September 25, p.D6.

DARLING, JUANITA, LARRY STAMMER AND JUDY PASTERNAK (1991) "Can Mexico Clean up its Act?" *Los Angeles Times* November 17, p.1.

DEL MATEO, FERNANDO Y FRANCOISE CARNER (1989) "Mexico frente a las negociaciones de serviceios en la Ronda Uruguay" in BLANCE TORRES (ET AL) *La Adhesion de Mexico al GATT. Repercusiones Internas e Impacto sobre las Relaciones Mexico-Estados Unidos* (Mexico: El Colegio de Mexico).

DUNNE, NANCY (1991) "US Call for a GATT Code on Environment" *Financial Times* September 18, p.6.

DUNNE, NANCY (1991) "Environment rules set stage for GATT conflicts" *Financial Times* December 5, p.6.

DUNNE, NANCY (1992) "Fears over "Gattzilla" the trade monster" *Financial Times* January 30, p.3.

EC Commission v. Denmark (Case 302/86), [1989] 2 CEC, 167.

The Economist (1991) "Divine Porpoise" October 5, p.31.

The Economist (1992) "GATT and Greenery: Environmental Imperialism" February 15.

The Economist (1991) "Should Trade go Green?", January 26, p.13.

EISLER, H H (1989) "Canadian Steel Industry and Sustainable Development", Canadian Steel Producers Association, A National Steel Conference, October 20.

ELWELL, CHRISTINE (1992) "On the Use of the Trade System to Deliver Environmental Objectives" Speaking notes for the Centre for Trade Policy and Law and the Faculty of Law at the University of Ottawa, Seventh Annual Conference on Canada and International Trade, "International Trade and Sustainable Development", Ottawa, May 14, 1992. This piece is to be published as part of the conference proceedings.

ESKELUND G AND E JIMENEZ (1991) "Choosing Policy Instruments for Pollution Control", A Review, PRE Working Paper No.624, World Bank.

FEDERAL NEWS SERVICE (1991) *News Conference on Potential Environmental Effects of the GATT and NAFTA* (Washington) August 1.

FEDERAL NEWS SERVICE (1991) "New Trade Initiative Linking Environmental Issues to Trade Negotiations" Luncheon Address by Senator Max Baucus to the Institute for International Economics (Wasington) October.

FEDERAL NEWS SERVICE (1991) *Press Conference with Representative Henry Waxman* (Washington) November 21.

FEDERAL NEWS SERVICE (1991) *Hearing of the International Economic Policy and Trade and Western Hemisphere Affairs Subcommittees of the House Foreign Affairs Committee* [Subject: US-Mexico Free Trade] (Washington) December 9.

FEDERAL NEWS SERVICE (1992) *Hearing of the Trade Subcommittee of the House Ways and Means Committee* [Witness: Ambassador Carla Hills, US Trade Representative] (Washington) March 11.

Financial Post (1991) "Green Trade" Editorial, November 18.

GENERAL AGREEMENTS ON TARIFF AND TRADE (1992) *International Trade, 90-91* Vol 1 (Geneva).

GENERAL AGREEMENT ON TARIFFS AND TRADE (1991) *United States - Prohibition of Imports on Tuna and Tuna Products from Canada* Report of the Panel, December 22.

GENERAL AGREEMENT ON TARIFFS AND TRADE (1991) *United States - Restrictions on Imports of Tuna* Report of the Panel, September.

GENARAL AGREEMENT ON TARIFFS AND TRADE (1987) *Canada-Measures Affecting Exports of Unprocessed Herring and Salmon* Report of the Panel, November 20.

GOVERNMENT OF CANADA   "Canada...A World Leader in Environmental Products and Services" (Ottawa: Department of External Affairs and International Trade Canada).

GOVERNMENT OF CANADA (1992) "North American Free Trade: Securing Canada's Growth through Trade" (Ottawa: External Affairs and International Trade Canada).

GOVERNMENT OF CANADA (1992) "Notes for an Address by Prime Minister Brian Mulroney, Environment Week, Canadian Museum of Civilization, Hull Quebec" (Ottawa: Office of the Prime Minister) June 1.

GOVERNMENT OF CANADA (1991) *Canadian Tourism Facts* (Ottawa: Tourism Canada, Industry, Science and Technology Canada, Research Directorate) February.

GOVERNMENT OF CANADA (1991) "Europe 1992, Report of the Working Group on Standards, Testing and Certification" (Ottawa: Department of External Affairs and International Trade) January.

GOVERNMENT OF CANADA (1990) "Canada and a Mexico-US Trade Agreement" Working Paper (Ottawa: Department of Finance) July.

GOVERNMENT OF CANADA (1990) *Canada's Green Plan* (Ottawa: Minister of Supply and Services).

GOVERNMENT OF CANADA (1990) "Canada-US-Mexico Free Trade Negotiations: The Rationale and the Investment Dimension" (Ottawa: Investment Canada) December.

GOVERNMENT OF CANADA (1990) "Forests of Canada: The Federal Role" Report of the Standing Committee on Forestay and Fisheries (Ottawa) November.

GOVERNMENT OF CANADA (1989) "The European Community: A Canadian Perspective" *Canadian Foreign Policy Series* (Ottawa: Department of External Affairs and International Trade) September.

GOVERNMENT OF CANADA (1986) *US Pleasure Travel Market - Canadian Potential: Highlights Report* (Ottawa: Tourism Canada) January.

HAJNAL, PETER I (1989) *The Seven Power Summit, Documents from the Summits of Industrialized Countries, 1975-1989* (New York: Kraus International Publications).

HALPERN, ADRIAN RAFAEL (1989) "The US-EC Hormone Beef Controversyand the Standards Code: Implications for the Application of Health Regulations to Agricultural Trade" *N C J International & Commercial Law Review* Vol. 14.

HART, MICHAEL "The Elements of a North American Free Trade Agreement", Paper prepared for the International Forum, "Mexico's Trade Options for the Changing International Economy".

HART, MICHAEL (1990) *A North American Free-Trade Agreement: The Strategic Implications for Canada* (Centre for Trade Policy and Law/The Institute for Research on Public Policy).

HART, MICHAEL AND SUSHMA GERA (1992) "Trade and the Environment: Dialogue of the Deaf or Scope for Cooperation?" Paper prepared for the Canada-United States Law Institute Conference on the Law and Economics of Environmental Regulation in the Canada/US Context (Cleveland, Ohio) April 24-26.

381

HESKINS, VALERIE E D (1990) "The Greening of the Summit: The Group of Seven Industrialized Democracies and the Environment Issue" (Seven Power Summit Project, Centre for International Studies, University of Toronto).

HILZ, CHRISTOPH (1992) *The International Toxic Waste Trade* (New York: Van Nostrand Reinhold).

HOLMES, JOHN AND JOHN KIRTON (Eds) (1988) *Canada and the New Internationalism* (Toronto: Canadian Institute of International Affairs).

HUFBAUER, GARY C AND JEFFREY SCHOTT (1992) *North American Free Trade: Issues and Recommendations* (Wahington D C: Institute for International Economics).

HURTADO, MARIA ELENA (1991) "The Threat of Environmental Protection" *Crosscurrents* No. 4, April 3.

INSTITUTE FOR RESEARCH ON PUBLIC POLICY (1991) "UNCED and North/South Issues: The Role of the National Round Table" (Ottawa: IRPP Sustainable Development Program) January 28.

Inter Press Service (1992) "GATT: Tuna fish row Highlights Growing Concern for Environment" February 20.

Inter Press Service (1992) "Trade: GATT Keeps Tuna Fish Dispute Alive" March 19.

International Environmental Daily (1992) "GATT Environmental Committee of the GATT seeks to mesh trade, environmental issues" March 12.

International Environmental Daily (1992) "EC, Others Pressure US, Mexico to accept Yellofin Tuna Report" March 20.

International Environmental Daily (1992) "Trade Negotiations and the Environment" March 27.

International Environmental Daily (1991) "Baucus Calls for GATT Environmental Code modelled after Subsidies Code" October 28.

International Trade Reporter (1992) "Special Report: NAFTA" Vol 9/2, p.82, January 8.

International Trade Reporter (1992) "General Developments: Agriculture" Vol 9/8, February 19.

International Trade Reporter (1992) "GATT Council refuses EC Request to adopt Panel Report on US Tuna Embargo" Vol 9/9, February 26.

International Trade Reporter (1992) "EC Urges Adoption of Tuna Report but US, Mexico Claim Accord is Near" Vol 9/13, March 25.

International Trade Reporter (1991) "Fast Track Process for Trade Agreement Threatens Environmental Laws, Group Warns" (Press Conference, May 2) Vol 8/19, p.698.

International Trade Reporter (1991) "NAFTA Should Include Provisions Making Labour Violations Actionable, Panel Told" Vol 8/36, September 11.

International Trade Reporter (1991) "Waxman Measures Urges Administration to Safeguard US Laws in GATT, FTA", Vol 8/47, November 27.

JOGEN, E (1990) "The Creation of an Internal Market for Industrial Goods in Europe through Technical Harmonization, Standardization, Certification and Mutual Recognition" (Brussels: Commission of the European Communities Directorate General for Internal Market and Industrial Affairs) September.

KINDRED, HUGH M (ED) (1987) *International Law: Chiefly as Interpreted and Applied in Canada* (4th ed) (Canada: Emond Montgomery Publications Ltd).

KIRGIS, F (1972) "Effective Pollution Control in Industrialized Countries: Internatioal Economic Disincentives, Policy Responses and the GATT" *Michigan Law Review* Vol 70/5 April.

KIRTON, JOHN J (1990) "Sustainable Development at the Houston Economic Summit" Paper prepared for the National Round Table on the Environment and the Economy, Foreign Policy Committee, September.

KRAUL, CHRIS (1990) "A warmer Climate for Furniture Makers" *Los Angeles Times* May 14, p.D1.

LIPSEY, RICHARD AND MURRAY SMITH (1989) "The Canada-US Free Trade Agreement: Special Case or Wave of the Future?" in JEFFREY SCHOOT (ED) *Free Trade and US Trade Policy* (Washington, D C: Institutute for International Economics).

MACNEILL, JIM, PIETER WINSEMIUS AND TAIZO YAKUSHIJI (1991) *Beyond Interdependence: The Meshing of the World's Economy and the Earth's Ecology* (New York: Oxford University Press).

MACNEILL, JIM (1991) "The Growth Imperative, Sustainable Development, Environment and Trade: Issues for IPC's Consideration" Paper presented at the IIASA Program of Trade and Environment, April 24-25.

MAGNUSSON, PETER, PETER HONG AND PATRICK OSTER (1992) "Save the Dolphins - or Free Trade?" *Business Week* February 17, p.130D.

McDORMAN, TED L (1989) "The Dispute Settlement Regime of the Free Trade Agreement" *Review of International Business Law* Vol 2, pp.303-330.

McDORMAN, TED L (1990) "Dissecting the Free Trade Agreement Lobster Panel Decision" Draft Paper August.

McLEOD, ALEXANDER (1992) "GATT Report Draws Fire from Environmentalists in Runup to Key Summits" *The Christian Science Monitor* February 18, p.4.

McSLARROW, KYLE E (1992) "GATT and the Politics of Environment in Trade" (Washington D C) February.

MINING ASSOCIATION OF CANADA (1990) "Mining in Canada: Facts & Figures" (Ottawa).

MORICI, PETER (1992) "Free Trade with Mexico" *Foreign Policy* 87 (Summer).

MORRISON, DONNA (1991) "Plugging into Europe 1992" *Business Insights* January/February.

MORTON, PETER (1991) "Enviro-talks begun: Mexico" *Financial Post* March 25, p.10.

MUNTON, DON AND JOHN KIRTON (1987) "The Manhattan Voyages and their Aftermath" in FRANKLYN GRIFFITHS (ED) *Politics of the Northwest Passage* (Montreal: McGill-Queen's University Press).

MUZANDO, T R , K M MIRANDA AND A L BOVENBERG (1990) "Public Policy and the Environment: A Survey of the Literature" IMF Fiscal Affairs Department: Working Paper 56.

NATIONAL WILDLIFE FEDERATION (1990) "Environmental Concerns Related to a United States-Mexico-Canada Free Trade Agreement" (Washington D C: National Wildlife Federation) November 27.

NAZARIO, SONIA (1989) "Boom and Despair" *Wall Street Journal* September 22, p.B26.

NECTOUX, FRANCOIS AND YOICHI KURODA (1989) "Timber from the South Seas: An Analysis of Japan's Tropical Timber Trade and its Environmental Impact" (Switzerland: World Wildlife Fund International) April.

NICOLAISEN, J AND P HEOLLER (1990) "Economics and the Environment: A Survey of the Issues and Policy Options" OECD, Economics and Statistics Department Working Paper No 82.

ONTARIO MINISTRY OF INDUSTRY, TRADE AND TECHNOLOGY (1990) "Europe 1992 & The Ontario Environmental Protection Industry" (Toronto: Ministry of Industry, Trade and Technology).

ONTARIO MINISTRY OF INDUSTRY, TRADE AND TECHNOLOGY (1990) "Harmonization of Technical Standards in the European Community: Implications for Ontario and Canada" (Toronto: Ministry of Industry, Trade and Technology).

ORGANIZATION FOR ECONOMIC COOPERATION AND DEVELOPMENT (1992) "Sustainable Development: Policy Statement" *Environmental Policy and Law* 22/1 pp.56-57 (Paris:OECD).

ORGANIZATION FOR ECONOMIC COOPERATION AND DEVELOPMENT (1991) "Executive Summary. Trade and Environment" C/Min (91) (Paris: OECD).

ORGANIZATION FOR ECONOMIC COOPERATION AND DEVELOPMENT (1991) *The State of the Environment* Annual Report (Paris:OECD).

ORGANIZATION FOR ECONOMIC COOPERATION AND DEVELOPMENT (1991) *Trade and the Environment: A Discussion of Some Current Views* Working Party of the Trade Committee (Paris:OECD).

ORGANIZATION FOR ECONOMIC COOPERATION AND DEVELOPMENT (1991) *Environment and Trade: Major Environmental Issues* Environment Directorate, Environment Committee (note by the Secretariat) ENV/EC(91)4 March (Paris:OECD).

ORGANIZATION FOR ECONOMIC COOPERATION AND DEVELOPMENT (1991) *Joint Report on Trade and Environment* Environment Directorate, Trade Directorate COM/ENV/EC/TD(91)14/REV2 May 14 (Paris:OECD).

ORGANIZATION FOR ECONOMIC COOPERATION AND DEVELOPMENT (1991) *International Trade in Clean Technology, Preliminary Assessment and Draft Project Proposal* May 23 (Paris:OECD).

ORGANIZATION FOR ECONOMIC COOPERATION AND DEVELOPMENT (1991) *The Activities of Multinational Enterprises and Their Effects on International Trade* Trade Directorate, Trade Committee, Working Party of the Trade Committee TD/TC/WP(91)43 July 9 (Paris:OECD).

ORGANIZATION FOR ECONOMIC COOPERATION AND DEVELOPMENT (1990) *Economics and the Environment: A Survey of Issues and Policy Options* Working Papers No 82 July (Paris:OECD).

PALMETER, DAVID (1992) "Environment and Trade: Who will be Heard? What Law is Relevant?" *Journal of World Trade* Vol 26/2, April.

PATTERSON, BRUCE (1991) "ECOtourism" *Environment* April.

PEARCE, DAVID (1991) "Trade and the Environment: A Discussion Paper" (London: UK Department of the Environment) 1st draft, May.

POFE, GERALD V AND DANIEL M HOROWITZ (1990) "Phantom Reductions: Tracking Toxic Trends" (Washington D C: National Wildlife Federation).

PORTER, MICHAEL (1992) "Canada at the Crossroads; The Reality of a New Competitive Environment" (Ottawa: Gilmore Reproductions) January.

The Recorder (1992) "International Environment", (American Lawyer Media) January 23, p.8.

REILLEY, WILLIAM (1991) Letter to Senator Tim Wirth - in National Wildlife Federation, Trade and the Environment Information Package, May 17.

REINSTEIN, R A (1991) "Trade and Environment" Draft Paper for IIASA Conference on Trade and the Environment(Laxenburg, Austria).

RICHARDSON, SARAH (1990) *Sustainable Development and Canada's Bilateral Treaties* Background Document prepared for the National Round Table on the Environment and the Economy's Foreign Policy Committee (Ottawa).

SAND, PETER H (1990) "Innovations in International Environmental Governance" *Environment* Vol 3/9 November.

SANKEY, JOHN (1989) "Domestically Prohibited Goods and Hazardous Substances - A New GATT Working Group is Established" *Journal of World Trade* No 6, December.

SENATE OF CANADA (1984) *Soil and Risk: Canada's Eroding Future* (Ottawa: Government of Canada).

SCHNEIDER, KEITH (1992) "Balancing Nature's Claims and International Free Trade" *New York Times* January 19, Section 4, p.5.

SCOTT, DAVID CLARK (1991) "Mexico Wins Battle over US Tuna Bank, But Backs off to Save Image, Trade Talks" *The Christian Science Monitor* September 27, p.8.

SHAIKEN, HARLEY (1990) *Mexico in the Global Economy: High Technology and Work Organization in Export Industries* Monograph Series 33 (La Jolla, CA: Center for US-Mexican Studies, University of California, San Diego).

SHRYBMAN, STEVEN (1991) "Selling the Environment Short: An Environmental Assessment of the first two years of free trade between Canada and the United States" (Toronto: Canadian Environmental Law Association) January.

SHRYBMAN, STEVEN (1990) "International Trade and the Environment: An Environmental Assessment of the present GATT Negotiations" *Alternatives* Vol 17/2, July/August.

SHRYBMAN, STEVEN (1988) "Selling Canada's Environment Short" (Toronto: Canadian Environmental Law Association) August.

SMITH, MURRAY (1990) "A North American Free Trade Agreement: Agenda and Modalities for the Negotiations", Paper prepared for discussion at a Meeting at the Council of Foreign Relations, New York City, November 5.

SORSA, P (1991) "GATT and the Environment", Paper presented at an IISA Workshop on Trade and the Environment, Luxembourg, Austria, April 25-26 (Geneva: World Bank).

SPELLMAN, JAMES DAVID (1991) "Environmental Needs Challenge the Global Marketplace" *Europe* September.

SPENCER, ROBERT, JOHN KIRTON AND KIM NOSSAL, (EDS) (1982) *The International Joint Commission Seventy Years On* (Toronto: University of Toronto Centre for International Studies).

ST PIERRE, ANTOINE (1991) *Impact of Environmental Measures on International Trade* Report 76-91-E (Ottawa: Conference Boards of Canada).

STEVENS, CANDICE (1991) "Industrial Internationalisation and Trade Friction" *OECD Observer* (Paris: Organization for Economic Co-operation and Development) December.

STRAUSS, MARINA (1992) "Industry foaming over beer can tax" *Globe and Mail* Friday May 22.

SWENARCHUK, MICHELLE (1988) "Environmental Impacts of the Canada-US F ree Trade Agreement" Paper prepared for the Standing Committee on Finance and Economic Affairs: Free Trade Review (Toronto: Canadian Environmental Law Association) February 29.

UNITED STATES DEPARTMENT OF STATE (1992) "The Environment and Free Trade with Mexico" President Bush Fact Sheets, (Department of State Dispatch) February 25 - Remarks at US Mexico Environmental Border Plan Meeting, Los Angeles, March 2, 1992.

UNITED STATES GENERAL ACCOUNTING OFFICE (1990) *US Mexico Trade: Trends and Impediments in Agricultural Trade* (Washington) January.

UNITED STATES INTERNATIONAL TRADE COMMISSION (1990) *Review of Trade and Liberalization Measures by Mexico and Prospects for Future United States Mexican Relations* (Washington D C: USITC) Publication 2275, April.

UNITED STATES TRADE REPRESENTATIVE (1991)"Review of US-Mexico Environmental Issues" Prepared by an Interagency Task Force Coordinated by the Office of the USTR, (Washington D C) Draft, October.

WORLD COMMISSION ON ENVIRONMENT AND DEVELOPMENT (1987) *Our Common Future* (Oxford: Oxford University Press).

Notes

Notes

Notes